NORTH
VIETNAM

LAOS

Da Nang

THAILAND

Pleiku
Qui Nhon

Cheo Reo

Tuy Hoa

CAMBODIA

SOUTH
VIETNAM

Saigon

South China Sea

▨ Central Highlands

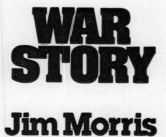

WAR STORY

Jim Morris

Jim Morris

Sycamore Islands Books

Boulder

First Edition.
Published by Sycamore Island Books,
A Division of Paladin Enterprises, Inc.
Post Office Box 1307, Boulder, Colorado 80306

ISBN 0-87364-147-7
Printed in the United States of America.

This book is dedicated to anybody
who ever died for something he
believed in, whether he was right
or not.

The difference between a fairy tale and a war story is that a fairy tale starts out "Once upon a time," and a war story starts out "This is no shit . . ."

Book One

"We are men and our lot is to be hurled into inconceivable new worlds."

— Don Juan
A Separate Reality
by Carlos Castaneda

1

I was running up the steps, the rough wooden steps carved out of the mountain. I started to top the military crest of the hill and jumped to the left as a slug tore through my right shoulder. I squeezed the trigger on my rifle and heard it go *kschlugg*. There was a terrible feeling of desperation as I went to the ground behind a tree stump.

I called for an M-79, but there was no M-79. I said, "Awright, goddammit, gimme a fucking carbine!"

Some fellow I hadn't seen before threw one from behind a little clump of bushes. I grasped it and put the switch on full auto. The guy who was firing at me was ahead about twenty meters, down behind a tree trunk. I squeezed a three round burst off at him. I counted ten seconds and he came back up again. I squeezed off another burst. In ten seconds I could get up there and kill that son of a bitch. I went down and I got up and some guy I hadn't seen shot my left nut off.

I rolled over, feeling cold fear crawling in my guts. It was dark and moonlight sprawled over the covers. My wife slept beside me and the baby was in the next room. I was safe.

I turned over irritably. This dream was a nuisance. Had I been asleep, or just thinking about it? I had thought about it a lot. In the time since then I had learned fear. I had never been afraid before, and now I was. It was most unpleasant. I shut my eyes to go back to sleep.

I was running up the steps . . . bounding, bounding, heroic, oh, Jesus, was I ever heroic, leading the charge. Shot in the shoulder but undaunted, getting another weapon, firing, waiting, firing again, then up on my feet. This time I made it up a little farther and was shot in the chest. I expired there on the jungle floor, alone, red froth coming through my charred and torn tiger suit, wheezing, bubbling. Dead.

The dream was becoming more stylized. It was like a movie with me as hero. I would get weird close-up shots of jungle boots charging up the hill, close-up cuts of the rifle jamming, then stills from my own eyes as I went down behind the stump. But it always ended the same way. Me dead.

Night after night. I was working on some free lance writing during the day, and doing insurance investigations. Quarreling miserably with my wife during the rest of my waking hours and then dreaming this wretched dream at night; four, five, fifteen, twenty times every night, slick with sweat, sick with fear, I charged that goddamned hill over and over again.

I had run out every possible outcome of that dream but one. I had been shot in the groin, and lost all my equipment. I had been shot in the head and died before I hit the ground, like Herb Hardy. I had been shot in the chest, in the gut, in the heart, in the brain, in the nose, in the left nostril, in the eye. You name it, I dreamed I had been shot there.

I had almost relaxed to it. I knew I would get killed a certain number of times and then I would sink into a deeper sleep and get some rest.

Then one night I made it.

I started the dream just like always—firing the familiar three round burst. He went down and I counted. He came back up and I fired again. He went down. I was on my feet, sprinting through a hail of hot lead to the stump. I fired down into it and the NVA died miserably, a frightened look on his face. I charged on, but the dream faded. I suppose it was over and the mission was accomplished, and I probably won a medal, although it never got that specific. Anyway, the fear was gone.

I could go home.

2

"You are very fat." The Vietnamese lieutenant driving the jeep said this, not as a gibe, but a simple statement of fact. The Vietnamese respect fat people on the grounds that they have to be rich to get that way. Anyway, my feelings weren't hurt. But he was right, by Vietnamese standards I was very fat. By American standards I was "husky." While on convalescent leave from when my nut got shot off, I had gained weight. I didn't like it much, but I couldn't seem to lose it. Still, I wasn't insulted. He was nice enough to drive me all over Kontum, looking for Phillip.

Someone had told me Phillip Drouin, the Cowboy, was an aspirant, which is a kind of third lieutenant in the Vietnamese army, there. But the Vietnamese sector command had him listed as a deserter, and I couldn't find anyone who knew where he was.

None of the Vietnamese I had talked to seemed to be particularly offended that he had deserted their army. In fact, they all seemed to hold him in high regard. This lieutenant, who was with me now, gave no evidence of using me to trace him so that he could be prosecuted. He was just trying to help out a fellow who was trying to find an old friend.

I had been quite surprised to find that Phillip was in the ARVN. Sympathy for the Vietnamese had never been one of his strong points.

The story of how he came to be commissioned was rather complicated. It seems as though the Montagnards, the mountain tribesmen of Vietnam, had revolted, right on schedule, just as my commanding officer had predicted in his report, but nobody had been ready for it. At some places,

3

such as Buon Brieng, the situation had been handled with tact and precision. Vern Gillespie, the American Commander there, had simply talked his Yards out of it and they'd had a ceremony making their Vietnamese Special Forces honorary Montagnards and that had been pretty much the end of it. This situation had been helped by the fact that the Vietnamese there were not actively hostile to the Yards.

At Buon Sar Pa, however, the situation did not go so well. The Viets there were shoved down the holes in the outhouse and machinegunned to death. A little social criticism mixed with the revolution.

At my old camp, Buon Beng, a misguided psychopath named Nay Re had been given the mission of taking the Phu Thien district headquarters. He apparently decided not to do that, however, but settled for mortaring the place, killing about twenty-five people, most of them women and kids. For some reason after that he just took his company back to camp and put their weapons in the arms room. After the revolt had cooled down the Viets came out and arrested, tried, and convicted him and five of his assistants. They were dead within the hour.

When I heard about that I remembered my earlier desire to assassinate the little bastard and regretted I hadn't. Blood on my hands for sure, but it would have been worth it to eliminate one psychopathic killer and save the lives of twenty-five more or less innocent people.

When the revolt was finally stopped a settlement was negotiated which stipulated, among other things, that some of the young Montagnard leaders would be given a chance to go to OCS and become officers in the Vietnamese army. Phillip was one of those. The name of the Montagnard separatist organization was FULRO, Fronte Unite de Lutte des Races Opprimes, the United Fighting Front of the Oppressed Races.

We pulled to a stop in front of a Montagnard longhouse on the outskirts of Kontum and I swung out of the jeep. A few moments later I was choking down a drink of *numpai*, the wretched Montagnard rice wine, and listening to a wizened elder of the tribe tell me, "Phillippe go long time now."

4

"Where he go?" I asked, sipping as little as I could.

He shrugged.

The lieutenant and I stayed a moment longer and then went back out in the road.

As I got in the jeep two North Vietnamese soldiers rode by and gave us hard looks. Since we were only running around town I had left my rifle back at the "B" team compound. The NVA, apparently, were just coming into town on pass, or maybe they were intelligence agents for a day. But I was pretty sure they were North Vietnamese. They were each riding a bike and wore Ho Chi Minh sandals and black shorty pajama bottoms. That wasn't unusual for Vietnamese, and they wore sport shirts instead of black shirts. The clincher for me was the haircut, a sort of high topped crewcut that I've never seen on anyone other than a North Vietnamese soldier.

But since they had no weapons, and I had no weapons, and I couldn't prove they were North Viets anyway, and the lieutenant either didn't notice, or didn't care, I ignored the whole thing.

We drove back to Kontum, and he let me off at the "B" team. I wasn't going back to Pleiku until the next day so I wandered next door to the MACV compound for a drink. They had a concrete patio with tables and chairs. I got a beer and sat down. There were several troopers from the 1st Cav there, grimy from the field. They didn't look like SF troops in from the field, not as professional, not as casual. Also they were made to shave on patrol for some reason I was never able to fathom, and wore far too much gear.

I sat down with a bunch of them, and once they got over the idea that I wouldn't bite, captain or no captain, we had a pleasant chat.

The kid I was talking to wore grubby U.S. jungle fatigues and had dirt-rimmed eyes and a dirty face.

His hair was very short but shaggy, as though he were overdue for a haircut and was trying to keep it that way.

"You guys been in the woods?" I asked. It was a dumb question, since he obviously had, but served as a conversation opener. I was mildly interested in the activities of the conventional units in Vietnam. I had been amazed, the

5

day I got back, to see churning down the road huge dirt movers and all the other paraphernalia of the U.S. Army. I wasn't particularly pleased to see it, since I joined the Forces in the first place out of a distaste for all that. While I had been gone some moron had let all this dullness in. In 1964 the war had a nice "Terry and the Pirates" ambiance to it. Now it was full of psychotic commanders who thought they were refighting World War II with robots. The kids were generally all right, just trapped unwillingly in a stupid system.

This one nodded and kind of deliberately smoked his cigarette overhand, playing the role. I was obviously a headquarters trooper, my jungle fatigues were pressed, I was clean shaven *that very morning* and my white sidewall crewcut made me look like a pinheaded lance corporal in the Bavarian Balloon Corps. I have never understood why a professional soldier is required to make himself as physically unattractive as possible. Probably because the army is run by people who like to make other people miserable.

Me, I soldiered because I loved the Montagnards, the jungle and parachuting. In my present job I was getting damned little of any of those things.

"What outfit you guys with?" I asked the kid. It was the standard number two remark.

"Fifth of the seventh," he replied.

"Did you know Captain Swain?" I asked.

He shook his head. "I think maybe that guy over there used to talk about him." He indicated another kid at another table in the same grubby fatigues and the same shaggy haircut.

"I'd like to talk to him," I said.

He took me over to where the kid was seated and I stuck out my hand.

He gave me a suspicious glance.

"I understand you knew Captain Swain."

He nodded.

"How'd he get it?" I asked. "I heard several different versions and I'd like to know." I'd heard that he had been shelled by our own artillery, and that he stepped on a mine. Lots of different stories.

"I didn't know him too long," the kid said. "It happened right after I got into the Company. We were out on a heliborne assault. He checked the perimeter the first night and stepped on a mine made of a 105 shell."

I nodded solemnly. The stories were each half right.

"They tried to save him," the kid said. "But he died on the operating table, a couple of hours after it happened."

"Yeah!" I stayed a minute longer, then went back to the "B" team.

It's a very funny profession we're in. We're always being transferred around at odd times to odd places and you'll make friends with someone and then never see him again, or maybe you'll go to some new place and walk into the club and there's some guy you saw last maybe three or four years before and you've both been promoted, and maybe you didn't know him too well then, but this time you wind up on the same team or live next door to each other or something like that and he stops being a face and becomes a person. And then you leave again and maybe you see him again and maybe you don't. And maybe you never see him because you just never run into each other and maybe it's because one of you is dead.

For a while there was a rumor out that I was dead and I've walked into places and seen people go white.

And every so often I'll see a tall skinny guy in a Special Forces uniform with blond hair, and a longlegged confident stride, but just a little stifflegged, going along and I'll start to call out "Walt!" and strangle on it, because I know where Walt Swain is. He's at Arlington. Hilda saw them put him there.

I didn't hear about his death until my wife and I went to visit the Drurys at Fort Bragg. It was after I had gone back on active duty and was taking a course at Fort Gordon, Georgia. Art Drury was a Lieutenant Colonel, who had been my commanding officer, and Walt's at different times. While we were there Skip, Mrs. Drury, took me aside and told me gently about Walt's death. She told me the first of the many tales I was to hear about how it happened.

It didn't soak through at first. I accepted the knowledge, the intellectual knowledge, of Walt's death and went ahead

7

and we had a nice weekend. Then on the drive back to Fort Gordon I began to think about it. It finally came through that the bastards had got Walt Swain. I had never figured them to do it. Walt was the perfect soldier. I have never seen anyone before or since as good in the woods as he was. I just never thought they could get him.

But I received my orientation in war in a guerrilla war, where there were elements of skill involved. In the kind of war waged by the conventional units like the 1st Cav it was largely a matter of bucking the law of averages. Some got it and some didn't, and knowing what you were doing didn't help that much. For surer'n hell if you knew what you were doing, either your commanding officer, or his commanding officer didn't.

So they got Walt Swain. It was the first time I cried in four years. I cried, I believe, for better than an hour. I didn't want to, of course, but it was simply insupportable. Walt Swain was not supposed to die, and somehow someone had slipped up and it had happened and nothing could undo it.

So we called Hilda on the phone and asked if there was anything we could do and of course there wasn't. She was living with his folks in Miami, but eventually she moved back to Columbus, Georgia, near Fort Benning, with her daughters, Kim and Susie. Hilda was German, and her home in the U.S. was still the Army.

It was funny, what she said on the phone. She said Walt told her before he left that he wouldn't be coming back. She said when he got command of the company she spent the next two months waiting for the staff car with the officer and the sergeant to come and tell her the news. And then finally they did come.

She said in that two months he was company commander Walt spent exactly two nights in base camp and that he made seventeen heliborne assaults. His commanding officer wrote her, which is the custom, and told her that he had been the happiest man in the Cav. I can believe it. Walt would have loved the Cav.

It's funny. I still think about him a lot. I see him on that one patrol we went on together, and I see him bouncing along stifflegged, his fair-haired handsome face grinning, the

8

perfect movie star hero, except maybe really too handsome
to be cast as the kind of person he was. He'd be cast in
drawing room comedies or something like that. I think of all
my friends who are dead, for among them are the best men I
have ever known. Sometimes I wonder why I, of all of them,
should have been picked to survive. Sometimes I feel guilty
about it. I sought service in an elite force and sometimes the
battalion of the dead seems the most elite of all. When I get
to thinking like that I try to think about something else.
Perhaps I was just left alive to tell the tale.

The next day in Pleiku I checked into my office, then went
over to look through the intelligence files to see what
FULRO was up to. Having been in on the formation of that
organization, I took a thoroughly non-regulation paternal
pride in their activities.

I skipped down a couple of steps into the Tactical
Operations Center (TOC) which was half tin roof shack and
half bunker, walked past a couple of doors of offices on
either side and into the big room full of maps and radio
equipment. Several sergeants were rummaging through
reports back there and others were posting changed
positions on the map.

I turned the corner and came to the Dutch doored
classified control room. It smelled musty in there. My friend,
Bill, a tall skinny warrant officer in Intelligence, was inside,
reading. He looked up and smiled.

"Hello, Bill. Anything new on FULRO?"

He nodded and threw me a stack of Intelligence Reports
(IR's) on a clipboard. I sat down and started reading them.

"There's one in there you might find real interesting,"
he said.

I nodded. I liked Bill a lot. He was a thorough intelligence
professional with a lot of years experience for a man of his
age, which was about twenty-six. He was a college graduate,
had an outrageous I.Q. and a sort of good natured disdain
for his present assignment. He was trained for a civilian
cover in Europe, spoke German like a German, and had no
Vietnamese at all. He had no particular interest in Vietnam,
but enjoyed the fact that I did, and was very cooperative in
everything I tried to do.

It took only a few moments to find the document I was looking for.

It said in effect that a group of Montagnards had presented themselves, in uniform, at the airport in Ban Me Thuot and requested transportation to Nha Trang. The following letter was their authorization.

FULRO

TO WHOM IT MAY CONCERN:
The bearer of the documet [sic], 3d Lt Y Guk Nie, is an officer of this organization, detached to Nha Trang on military duties. He is authorized to travel on U.S. military aircraft, and any assistance you may furnish any member of this command is duly appreciated.

Sincerely:

Col. Phillip Drouin
Commanding
Dam-Yi Mobile Division of Commando Paratrooper

I straightened up in my chair and grinned at Bill.

"You think that's your boy?" he asked.

I laughed. "No question about it. No one else in the world could think up an organization called the Dam-Yi Mobile Division of Commando Paratrooper. That's my friend the Cowboy all right. The next question is how the hell do I find him?"

Bill laughed. "That's a question a lot of people are asking."

The poor little third lieutenant who was "authorized travel on U.S. military aircraft" had immediately been clapped into jail by the Vietnamese authorities.

Vietnamese relations with FULRO were most peculiar. FULRO was considered an outlaw organization. Its president and commanding general, Y Bham Enoul, was in exile in Cambodia where he had a headquarters set up, thought to be in Mondul Kiri. But nonetheless, even though illegal, FULRO had been assigned a Tactical Area of Responsibility (TAOR) somewhere south of Ban Me Thuot, where they could go forth and fight the Cong and North Vietnamese. FULRO, you see, was not particularly picky. Their quarrel was with all Vietnamese, not just the South Viets, and they were perfectly happy to fight the Cong if they could get the South Vietnamese to leave them alone to do it.

I scraped my chair back from the desk in the classified documents room and went back to my office. It was set up in a little shack next door to the headquarters building. I opened the door and went inside. I had two American sergeants, a Montagnard interpreter, a Vietnamese interpreter and a Vietnamese girl typist.

I nodded to the typist. She was a pretty young lady, bright, and very pleasant, although marred slightly by some acne scars, or maybe smallpox. I didn't want to ask her. She looked up as I walked in the door.

"Chao, Co Tien," I nodded and smiled at her. Everybody in the office was Co Tien's big brother, Co being Vietnamese for Miss. She was that kind of girl. Everybody except Tony, my Montagnard interpreter. He had eyes for Co Tien, and I think she did for him, but both had enough sense not to let it show very much. Her father would have hired him shot for a stray thought.

"Chao, Dai Uy," she replied. *"Manh Yoi Khanh?"*

"Toi Manh Yoi," I said and went to my desk.

Master Sergeant Bennett looked up and nodded.

"Mornin', Top!" I said. In the old army Top was a nickname reserved for a company first sergeant, but Bennett was the top soldier in my shop and no master sergeant has ever been insulted by being called that.

He looked up from his papers, a chubby, amiable, paper-shuffling soldier, and wished me a good morning.

I sat down and started shuffling my own stack of papers. When I looked up again it was noon and the shop was cleared except for Tony and me. I smiled at him. His name was Ksor Tanh, but they called him Tony. He was a good-looking man, tall for a Yard, quite slender with dark wavy hair and thin full-lipped features. He had been an interpreter at Plei Ta Nangle during the great ambush there. I had met him when I flew up to get the bodies. He was brother to my old interpreter Kpa Doh. He looked around stealthily and walked to my desk. "I see Kpa Doh this weekend," he said, looking around from the corners of his eyes.

I looked up immediately. Kpa Doh was a Major in FULRO, a wanted man, and Tony had reason to believe he was being watched too. But next to Phillip, Kpa Doh was my best friend in Vietnam. I wanted to see him too. "Where?" I asked anxiously. There was nothing to worry about in my office, but if Tony wanted to play spy there was no reason not to go along with it.

"Ban Me Thuot," he murmured almost inaudibly.

I nodded eagerly. "Can I see him there?"

He smiled. "I will give you name of man to look up in 'B' team there."

3

It didn't take me long to manufacture some urgent business in Ban Me Thuot and the next morning at seven I was on a helicopter going that way. The ground looked so much different than it had in '64, so many villages were at least half roofed in USAID tin. And there were bomb craters in some places. There had been no bomb craters before. They were appallingly ugly. So were the orange swatches that had been defoliated. There weren't too many of these in the highlands, but any at all were too many for my taste. I couldn't see how turning the vegetation orange made the Cong under it any easier to see. Aside from which if one wants to kill off the Cong the way to do it is to go into the village and ask someone where the trails are, then go out and ambush them.

That was my dream, to get out of the headquarters, get an "A" team, set up an intelligence net and clean the area of Cong so efficiently that it would be plain to anyone with any brains at all that this was the way to do it. I lay awake nights dreaming that dream. The dream was to train my companies in ambushes so well that we could ambush and annihilate an entire NVA company. I knew if we did it I would probably be sick at the sight of so many bodies, but God, it was a lot better than destroying Vietnam to save it.

The thing I didn't realize was that nothing could dissuade America from her cost-effective gadgetry-ridden anti-human course. Nothing I could do anyway.

Wars are never really won or lost. There is only a process of cross-culturalization. The side which succeeds in imposing the most of its culture on the other is declared the winner, but a hell of a lot of the loser's culture is soaked up by the winners. I think that America conquered Germany in World War II, but in the process some of the more loathsome aspects of the German character were absorbed by our professional military—except for outfits like the Forces. We had assimilated the British Commando-Jedburg team style. The American uniform of 1967 looked more like a Wehrmacht uniform than it did like the old cunt cap and Ike jacket of World War II. But with jump boots and a green beret it looked British.

I kept mulling this stuff over in the chopper on the way down. I don't much care to ride in choppers. They shake. We flew with both doors wide open, unless we got up out of the range of rifle fire, where it was very cold. It was like sitting next to a picture window two thousand feet up. Very beautiful where the long winding rivers flowed sluggishly through the jungle and the paddies. Very beautiful, and, as always, I loved Vietnam more than any other place, for the beauty and the strangeness of it. I always had a weird feeling in Vietnam, as though I were in the presence of exotic, mystical happenings. As though I had arrived in a place where spirits prowled and sorcerers plucked at strings that controlled natural laws. I felt valid there, as though this was my place and my time and was where I counted. I was happy.

The thought of returning to America was almost enough to make me physically ill. America was dullness and death of the spirit. America was bouffant hairdos and gleaming chrome and Robert Strange McNamara's curious belief in statistics.

And the U.S. Army had invaded Vietnam while my back was turned. It was enough to make a man walk into the jungle and join the Cong. If they had not been agents of the idea of the human anthill I would have done it.

I always get a little queasy in helicopters. They bring back a fantasy nightmare of suddenly being two feet to the right of where I was, in which case I would be falling straight down. There was a story of a captain who either forgot to strap his belt, or it had come loose. They hit some rough air and his last recorded remark on the face of the earth was "Oh, shit!"

The chopper set down at the Ban Me Thuot airstrip and the other passengers and I were met by a jeep from the "B"

14

team. The ride through town convinced me that Ban Me Thuot was going to be my favorite town in Vietnam. It wasn't a large place, but most of the buildings had the graceful flavor of French construction in the Tropics. Nha Trang had been my favorite town before it became infested with Americans, but now it was going to be Ban Me Thuot. The place was like Vietnam back in the "Terry and the Pirates" days.

It was graceful and slowpaced. The French buildings were of a kind of yellow stucco construction with latticed windows. Since the French departed, the Viets hadn't taken much interest in lawn mowing and the town had a seediness that makes most of Mississippi look bustling by comparison. The Americans there were all either advisors, administrators or aviators. They hadn't been harrassed like troops in the units, or become shufflers of paper in big headquarters. The place was small and personal.

It was about lunch time when I got there and I went over to the mess hall to eat.

It took about fifteen minutes after lunch to satisfy the business that had brought me to Ban Me Thuot. After that I wandered over to their TOC and hung out for awhile. Then I asked if they had a driver around named Y Blik. Sure enough they did. He drove a three-quarter ton truck attached to the S-3 section. Nobody asked me why I wanted to talk to him, although I had a story all prepared. Fortunately the sergeant who introduced us lost interest immediately after the introduction and went back to his typewriter.

Y Blik was quiet, but not deferential and he shook hands in the American manner. I suggested we go outside. He declined a cigarette and I asked, "Have you heard of a camp called Buon Beng?"

He gave me a questioning look and nodded affirmatively. He didn't seem especially eager to talk.

"I used to be XO there," I said. He nodded and I went on. "I had a good friend there named Kpa Doh."

His face registered no recognition.

"His brother Tony works for me now," I went on, "and he says you can take me to Kpa Doh. I would like to see him

15

again. We are good friends."

Carefully keeping his face neutral, he asked, "Can we talk this afternoon? Maybe four o'clock?"

I said sure and went back to the club for a beer. A few minutes later he drove out of the compound in a jeep.

That afternoon, I followed his instructions and casually walked down the street outside the compound.

It's hard to imagine anything more conspicuous than the sight of a Special Forces captain walking down that road at that hour, without a vehicle but in full uniform. I doubt it had ever happened before. But I wasn't worried about the cloak and dagger aspects of it. Anybody who has ever studied intelligence work as it is conducted in Europe is aware of how unsophisticated this Vietnamese operation was. But it was more effective for the environment than the European number would have been. James Bond would have gone bananas in Vietnam.

I heard the sound of a medium-sized motorcycle behind me, but carefully avoided looking around. The bike drove by and stopped a little down the road. The driver, a husky, dark fellow with longish wavy hair, got off. One of the things I noticed about him even from that distance was the casual air of authority he carried, as though he were bloody well in charge of himself and his situation. In Vietnam you usually see that only on high ranking military officers. Correction. You don't usually see it on anybody. People there are usually either obsequious or overbearing. This guy was neither. I got closer and he looked up.

"Kpa Doh. . ." I all but gasped. He grinned and a strange voice rasped out, "Captain Morris!" We grabbed and hugged each other in the middle of the street, amazed at the changes in each other. He had filled out and gained that casual air of command. Before, he had a sort of functionary chief clerk's attitude, jealous of his borrowed authority. Now he was quite sure of himself. He wore Levis, white socks, loafers and a plaid sport shirt, all spotlessly clean and ironed. His hair was longer and his smile bigger. He also had that big Honda, which was the most expensive personal vehicle I had ever seen a Montagnard ride.

We looked at each other fondly for a long time, then

16

grinned while almost dancing in the street. We had both gained weight, but he had gained assurance, and acquired that curious rasp in his voice. "What happened to your voice?" I asked.

He pointed to his neck. "I was Chief Interpreter, Mike Force," he said. "I get shot on long range patrol. Cut vocal chords."

I nodded. "I got shot up too," I said.

He grinned. "I hear. You give left nut for thirty days leave."

I laughed. "How's your wife?"

Kpa Doh was married to the most beautiful Montagnard woman I had ever seen, very nearly the most beautiful woman, period. She had a pretty rough time giving birth to their first child while we were at Buon Beng. "How's the baby?"

"Two babies now," he said, grinning and holding up two fingers. We went on chatting like that for about ten minutes in the middle of the road. Finally I pointed out that we couldn't keep that up all day and could I come to his place some time.

"Sure, you get jeep. Y Blik will drive you out."

"You need anything? Maybe I can get you some stuff."

An hour later Y Blik and I loaded four fifty-kilo bags of rice, two cases of carbine ammunition and all the medical supplies I could scrounge from Dr. Howie Cohen, the mad physician of Ban Me Thuot, into the back of a jeep and took off for Buon Ale A, the village where Kpa Doh lived.

It turned out that the village was the Montagnard suburb of Ban Me Thuot, contiguous with the larger city. It was the most peculiar village I ever saw, built on a steep hill, with ugly ruts for roads, and Rhade longhouses side by side with Vietnamese stucco houses down on the ground. The Vietnamese houses were owned by rich Montagnards, a couple of missionary families and some International Volunteer Service people, IVS being a sort of private Peace Corps that operated in Vietnam.

It made for an interesting atmosphere, normal Montagnards, members of the FULRO revolutionary party, the usual quotient of GVN and Viet Cong spies, two families of

17

Americans, normal in every way except that they were practicing Christians, a Canadian kid who was an IVS volunteer and two IVS girls, one of whom was the first freak I'd ever seen, outside of Haight Ashbury.

We pulled up outside of Kpa Doh's place which was one of the Vietnamese style houses, he having achieved considerable status. There were a lot of young Montagnards of military age wearing jungle fatigues and close haircuts lounging around in the barren living room, barefoot. They grinned a lot but said little. Kpa Doh's wife came out smiling her terrific smile. She wore a blouse and a black Montagnard sarong type skirt. She had a good figure, a great smile and long, sleek black hair.

I sat down and had tea while the soldiers lounging around the house dragged in the rice, the carbine ammo and the medical supplies. I had debated for a moment about bringing the ammo. FULRO was more or less at war with the South Vietnamese, and I was in the U.S. Army and we were sort of allied with the South Vietnamese, I supposed, although I thought about that as seldom as possible. Had my Colonel found out I was giving ammo to the enemies of our friends it might have got a little sticky. I brought the ammo anyway.

We chatted for a while. Kpa Doh had been at Pleiku, first as Company Commander, then as chief interpreter with the Mike Force, which was a battalion of Montagnard paratroopers. Then he had been caught collecting taxes from his troops for FULRO and was fired.

It turned out that virtually every Montagnard trooper working for Special Forces in the Second Corps was a member of FULRO, and they were all turning ten percent of their wages over to the organization. That amounted to about fifty thousand troops, all armed and trained by the U.S. and fighting to get rid of the North Vietnamese and Cong so they could start in on the South Vietnamese.

That didn't bother me any. I doubt if it bothered any of the rest of Special Forces. I was pretty sure that I wasn't the only American running ammo and other supplies to FULRO.

Kpa Doh told me about FULRO and his adventures with the Mike Force and I told him all my Kham Duc stories. But after awhile we started to run down. I love the man like a brother and the feeling is mutual, but there is simply not sufficient overlap in our cultures to afford continuous smooth flowing conversation. The only Yard I have ever felt completely at ease with was Cowboy. Kpa Doh and I were as brothers, but Cowboy and I were just mislaid parts of the same person. If we had nothing to say to each other we didn't feel it necessary to say anything, but we almost always had something to say.

So when other topics started to pall I asked, "Do you know where Cowboy is?"

Kpa Doh smiled and nodded. "Oh sure! He live one block over."

I half lurched out of my chair. After three months of looking hard for him, to find he was in Ban Me Thuot, living in a house in a village on a public street. Jesus!

Kpa Doh appraised my mood correctly. "You want to go see him?"

"Yes!"

We bounced over the rutted road in my jeep, drawing stares as we drove around town. Probably the GVN and VC spies looking out the windows were taking furious notes at the American SF man riding in the street with the FULRO major. But then maybe not. Spies in Vietnam have the same marvelous nonchalance that the rest of the Vietnamese have, and since they invent most of the intelligence they turn in, they are freed from the more onerous aspects of intelligence work and can devote their time and effort to more interesting labors; sleeping, getting laid and hanging out.

We went down one street, across one and up one. Cowboy's place was a snazzy deteriorating villa with an old American jeep parked outside and a couple of Hondas scattered about. Two Yards in Mike Force tiger suits with American jump wings on them, also barefoot, lounged around on the front porch. For a clandestine organization this FULRO didn't seem to be hiding out too hard.

Kpa Doh and Y Blik and I dismounted from the jeep. The two barefoot paratroopers on the porch got up and sort of idly stationed themselves in front of the door, so we couldn't get past without either asking our way in or shoving them aside. Kpa Doh coughed out something in Rhade, the only word of which I caught was "Phillippe."

One of the Yard jumpers went inside, giving us hard looks as he went. The other stayed on the porch, also oozing hostile vibes. We waited. I stood in my usual unmilitary posture, shoulders hunched, shifting my weight from one foot to the other. Finally the first Yard jumper came back out, still shooting me these hard looks. He was followed by a trim figure that I didn't recognize. He had a regular U.S. Army crew cut, slacks and a green pullover sweater with a little alligator on it. He also gave me a very concerned long look.

I didn't blame him. I had changed just as much as he had, put on thirty pounds and aged more than the three years that had passed. The last time I had seen Cowboy, he had on a cowboy suit and an Elvis Presley haircut. I had never seen him with a worried look before. He really looked me up and down hard.

Then came the flash grin, that same hard delighted "we're all bad motherfuckers together in this bad motherfucker game" grin and I felt my answering one curling across my face. This was my man.

"Captain Morris!"

"Cowboy!"

His little thirty-two Berretta slid from the hand I hadn't noticed, being more or less tucked behind his right hip, and went into his pocket.

While shaking hands my mind reeled back three and a half years to the first time I had ever seen him, and the first time I'd seen Vietnam. It was December 17, 1963.

"There she is. First look at Vietnam," someone said. I got back up and went to look again. The clouds swirled below, then there was a break and a glimpse of hilly coastline. The clouds closed over again. Excitement burst into fear. For the first time in our long campaign to get to Vietnam I really understood there were people down there who would actively try to kill me. Fear was a cold feeling, centered in the belly.

The aircraft was down to about fifteen hundred feet and

fear was forgotten in the beauty of it. Below was rice field after rice field, an endless patchwork of varishaded green, and behind that the mountains rising green and jungly into clouds. Square tile roofs, and dirt roads, banana trees and palm trees. Even from that height there was a sense of the smell of things growing and things rotting; of life and death moving in continuous flux, fecundity and desolation.

We landed and offloaded our stuff. A Special Forces Captain drove my commanding officer, Crews McCulloch, and me to the headquarters to be briefed on our mission.

As we drove along the beach he pointed out an American LST, beached and unloading supplies. Naturally an American flag flew from the mast of this American ship.

"Look at the flag," the captain declared.

I looked. Sure enough there was a standard American flag flying from the mast. "What about it?" I said.

You don't hardly ever see one in Vietnam," he replied. "We're not allowed to fly them, since we're supposed to be advisors. All these installations are supposed to be Vietnamese installations and we can't fly the American flag."

He said it simply as a statement of fact, not bitterly or anything, but as though if the choice was left up to him he'd prefer to fly it.

I shrugged. "So?" I'd made the normal obeisances to the flag all my life, without thinking a great deal about it.

At least not since the fifth grade. That was the first time I ever spent a full year in one school, and I don't think I knew anybody. Having moved around that much I had long since given up trying to make friends. I'd just done my new-kid shuck and jive and tried to survive. But I remember once during assembly I'd had this really strange fantasy about some sort of evil person. As I recall he had a slouch hat and wore a cloak and carried some sort of pistol. Don't ask me why. It made perfect sense when I was ten.

Anyway in my fantasy I threw myself in front of the flag to protect it from the communist spy or whatever in hell he was, saving the flag from defilement, and dying a hero's death esteemed, even fawned over in my last gasping breaths by all the other kids, none of whom had previously known I was alive.

21

I had forgotten the incident since then, and having been through two military schools, where we stood reveille and retreat every day, and ROTC and the Civil Air Patrol Cadets, not to mention having been in the Army for almost four years, and the Army Reserve in college, I kind of took the flag for granted.

"There's one guy in the headquarters who drives by here at least once every day when there's an American ship in the harbor, just to see the flag," he went on.

I nodded. "How about that?"

I suppose this would be an appropriate place to pause and give some justification for the American presence, but I can't. At that time I was a twenty-six year old journalist who had stayed in the army because he wanted to become a paratrooper and prove he was hot shit. I didn't plan to stay in as a career, but I was in a professional outfit and I tried to act like a professional. I didn't know any more about international politics than a pig knows about geometry.

I knew a lot of technical stuff about revolutionary warfare, and I knew from that we were fighting the Vietnam war all wrong, totally assbackwards. But I never questioned that we should be there. If we shouldn't be there then they wouldn't have sent us.

I could, of course, question it now, but I don't. Now I am as much Montagnard as American anyway because I have staked my life for their cause. It was my life and I identified with it totally. If my life was not right then it was up to me to make it right. To end it was to end me, and that I would not do voluntarily.

That's the only kind of attitude you can take in a war. You have to be ready to shove in your whole stack and leave it in. If you aren't ready to do that, then you shouldn't play.

The captain's jeep braked to a stop in front of the head-quarters. We filed into the conference room and sat down. It had obviously been fitted out for VIP briefings. In the front was a little proscenium painted blue, with sliding doors for a wide variety of maps. The map of South Vietnam was scaled at one over two-hundred-fifty-thousands and the maps of the Corps Tactical Zones were scaled at one over one hundred thousands. Still, they weren't very accurate. On one a river jumped an entire kilometer moving from one map sheet to the next. The maps were covered with acetate and each was filled with multi-colored symbols to make it look like the guy giving the briefing knew what he was talking about.

The briefing proved little more informative than the maps. We caught a shower, a night's sleep and diarrhea at Nha Trang, and the next day deployed to our camp.

Green mountains, green mountains. They passed beneath in endless procession as the old C-47 droned on toward Cheo Reo. We were flying about eight thousand feet above the mountains, out of range of small arms fire. I stood in the door, covered by a frail H-shaped harness of nylon webbing. The wind blast came through icy cold, but I was unable to tear myself from the sight of Vietnam. We had flown down the coast until we picked up the Song Ba river winding its way down from somewhere north above AnKhe. Cheo Reo, the capital of PhuBon province, lay on the Song Ba south of Pleiku, at the intersection of Highways seven and fourteen.

Now the Song Ba wound its way beneath us, snaky, sluggish, the wide valley crisscrossed by lush green rice paddies stretching across the width of it. On either side of the valley mountains rose, green jungled, with wide areas cleared out for dry rice farming. Past the Chu Dle Ya mountains the Cheo Reo airstrip lay, a straight black, still growing ribbon stretched over the red scar of earth that had been prepared as a bed for it. A cluster of bulldozers, earth movers, graders and rollers lay at the construction end of the runway and beyond that lay Cheo Reo, indolent in the sun.

The aircraft made three quick turns and slowly lowered onto the asphalt. It ran the length of the runway, turned around, came back and parked on the hardstand.

We jumped out onto the pierced steel planking hardstand to face nothing.

We were all alone except for the somnolent guard beside the gas drums and pump. Beyond the runway, forest stretched off into the mountains.

From the far end of the runway we could see a tall column of red dust plowing toward us at breakneck speed. A black dot at the front of the column grew into an old World War II two and a half ton truck, slightly lopsided like the Toonerville Trolley, moving like an entry in the National Drags.

It squealed to a stop on the hardstand and a tall skinny young Special Forces sergeant with slightly protuberant teeth and a Smith and Wesson .38 on his hip exploded out of the cab and ran over saying "Jesus Christ, we thought you'd never get here. Let's get out to the camp. A big sacrifice's been going on all day and everybody's drunk out of their minds. Boy, am I glad to see you guys. Jesus Christ!"

Short brown men in camouflage fatigues hopped out of the back end of the deuce and a half. The skinny sergeant jumped back on it and backed up to the C-47. The short brown men swarmed aboard like gnomes, throwing our boxes on the truck.

I stood there nervously fondling my carbine, mouth open.

On the way to camp the town lay supine in the heat, red dust puffing up from our wheels as we drove through. Fish were rotting in bushel baskets in front of the grocery stores; and in back of the store fronts stood the owners, in the shade. Some wore slacks and white shirts. Some wore boxer shorts and undershirts, their skinny brown arms and legs protruding. Behind them the women moved quietly arranging things while the men scanned the street outside. Little half-naked kids ran out into the street and waved and yelled, "Hello! Hello! Hello! Okay! Okay! Okay!" as we passed.

The last of the Vietnamese shacks petered out at the end of town and we were in Montagnard country. They strolled along the roads in little clumps of little people, plain people, simple and straightforward. Most of the men wore loincloths, legs dusty to the knees, a few with old shirts, washed but never ironed and permanently stained with sweat. The women wore long tubular wrap-around skirts, always black, shiny black. Some wore blouses, but many wore nothing above the waist but a light coat of sweat.

Their skin was the color of good mahogany. Many of the young waved and smiled. The older ones stepped off to the side of the road and doffed their hats, if they had any, as the French had taught them.

Beyond the dirt highway and the single telephone line that

leaned and sagged and zigzagged from thin crooked poles stretched rice paddies, dry now, rice gone and stubble sticking up like an old man's one day growth of beard. The little rice storage huts, on stilts, were full and the fields were empty squares, separated one from another by low earthen dikes bordering each paddy square, worn flat and hard-topped by the padding of years of small brown feet.

I was enchanted, in love with the place immediately. But I could tell at this glance that nothing in our many briefings, nothing in all our orientations or our study or anything else we did could have prepared us for the total reality of this place. It was too alien, too different from anything any American had encountered before. It was some sort of fantasy land, like Oz, and I half expected that the physical laws would be different.

The totality of it began to affect me with a feeling of peace and happiness such as I'd never known before. It all looked very right to me somehow, and I was beginning to get the feeling that I always had while in Vietnam, that this was my place and my time and this was where I was going to be as one with myself and my environment. It was a nice feeling.

Out further we hit a row of villages next to the road, all surrounded by high bamboo stake fences and sharpened bamboo stakes and another outer sharpened stake fence. Behind the fences we could see the long bamboo houses of the Montagnards, on stilts thick as telephone poles, with thatch roofs. Naked children in the shade under the houses looked at us with big eyes. Some waved and others were solemn with the solemnity of little kids.

We turned off onto a road that ran through the center of the camp, under an aging yellow sign with black letters that said Buon Beng Strike Force Training Center, and under that in smaller letters the same thing in the language of our tribe of Montagnards, the Jarai.

An hour later at the sacrificial ceremony honoring our arrival, the old Witch Doctor sounded like he was having a bad coughing fit. He was chanting in Jarai. He entreated the god of the east wind, god of the west wind, the god of fire and all the other gods to come from their spiritual dwelling and make me a good Jarai.

Unlike tribal witch doctors in the *National Geographic* he was wearing camouflage fatigues and OD tennis shoes, called bata boots. I guess a more correct term would be Witch Chaplain.

All the members of our team were sitting on a bench in full uniform, except that we each had one bare foot. And in front of each of us was a large earthen crock of numpai, their rice wine. A big crowd of Strike Force soldiers, their wives and little kids were gathered around pointing and laughing, joking. The kids ran in and out of the crowd, chasing each other. There were also mangy goats and sad, saggy, grey prehistoric-looking pigs in attendance.

When my turn came, the Witch Doctor called on the gods and hosed down my foot with a long hollow reed using rice wine from my crock. The rice wine represented the spirit of the gods. My bare foot was resting on a flat of a rusty old knife blade, representing strength of something or other, and between my toes was a little piece of cotton, like Humbert Humbert doing Lolita's toenails. That represented the softness of something else. Somewhere along there I lost track of the symbolism.

A tall, quite handsome Yard in slacks and a sport shirt, who had been introduced as the interpreter, came up and said, "Now sir, you must drink the numpai through the straw. Then you will be Jarai." He was grinning, his teeth very white in his mahogany face.

"You must drink four canteen cups full, sir. As the numpai goes down in the jug we will pour water in on top to measure."

"Man," I said, looking up, strained. "That's two quarts."

"Yes sir," he said, "two quarts."

I decided I'd better get to drinking. At first it didn't taste so bad. Sort of sweetish. But the more I got down the worse it was, until it finally tasted like a combination of sugar, water and vomit. I got down a half a quart when the Witch Doctor came along and put a bracelet on my left arm signifying that I was a member of the Jarai in good standing. It was seven inches of quarter inch brass welding rod bent in a circle.

A little less than half through I began to feel a little bit drunk and a little bit queasy and had to urinate badly.

26

Excusing myself I wandered out to the urinal, a section of bamboo hollowed out and shoved into the ground at an angle with a waist high split bamboo partition around it.

The crying needs of my bladder taken care of I wandered around to the back of the urinal and stuck a finger down my throat, bent over and retched until I had thrown everything up. Then, throat raw and sour, but belly better I went back to the numpai jug. It wasn't too bad. I only had to puke one more time to get through it.

Two weeks later I was working on the Buon Beng camp fund, or trying to. My mind rejecting the numbers, I kept daydreaming. I started running down the column again, only slowly becoming aware that someone was standing over me.

When I looked up there was a three-fifth scale model of a Choctaw Indian standing there. That's what he looked like with that brown skin and those high cheekbones. An infectious grin spread all over his little Montagnard face. Size five cowboy boots, Sears Roebuck jeans and a jean jacket over an immaculate white shirt. He was standing with all his weight on one hip. One hand was in his hip pocket and with the other he dragged a Salem cigarette. He was two months overdue for a haircut and both his eyes were cupped by wraparound shades. Goddamnedest thing I ever saw, a Montagnard drugstore cowboy. I wondered what he wanted.

"I," he said, "am the Cowboy."

"You," I replied, "are something else. What can I do for you?"

"I work before this camp as interpreter. Then Captain Wesley, he fire me. Then I work for Captain Corn at Chu Dron Camp. He give me this paper." He handed me a piece of government bond. On it had been typed:

To Whom It May Concern:
This letter is to introduce Mister Phillip Drouin. He has worked for me at Camp Chu Dron for the past six months. During this time his work has been exemplary. Mister Drouin has displayed an excellent grasp of the English language. In

27

addition he speaks and writes French, Jarai, and Rhade. He has a small understanding of Thai, Cambodian and Cantonese. He has an excellent grasp of tactics.

His three-quarter ton truck is a salvage vehicle from this camp. The vehicle has been released from the books of the United States Government and was given by me to Mister Drouin only after he had repaired it himself.

Any assistance you may give in the registration of this vehicle will be appreciated.

I recommend him to the employ of anyone requiring the services of a superior interpreter-translator with a thorough knowledge of tactics.

> Sincerely,
> (Signed)
> Johnnie A. Corn
> Captain, Armor

I took a close look at him. "We can't start you off at top salary," I said. "We need an interpreter, but Kpa Doh's the head interpreter here and you'll have to start off under him. What'd you leave Chu Dron for anyway?"

"I only stay for Captain Corn. The Vietnamese Interpreter hate me because I like to go patrol and it makes them look bad. Besides my wife, her father live here. He is Nay Mul, the Jarai Chief."

"Okay, you're hired. Kpa Doh will fill out the employment contract, 6500 p's a month to start."

"How about jump pay?"

"You a jumper?"

"Yes sir. At Chu Dron we draw extra 1400 p's for to jump. I jump before with the French."

"Cowboy," I said, liking him immediately, "you have found the way to touch my heart. Paratrooping is my religion. What's yours?"

"VC," he replied. "My religion is to kill VC."

4

One night shortly after he came to **Buon** Beng, Cowboy came to me and said, "Sir, tonight you must come to Wally's. He was before Sergeant Major this camp, when I command Battalion. Captain Wesley fire him same time he fire me."

"What's he doing here now?" I asked.

"His family live here in village. He now Sergeant Major Plei Ta Nangle. He home to see family. All Americans in camp must come for beer."

It was easy to see why they called him Wally. He looked like Wallace Beery. He was very big for a Yard, maybe six feet and one hundred eighty pounds. He had a little store in camp and four of us squeezed into the back of the store where he had a table set up for us. Only Ken, Augie, Hank Johnson and I could make it. Everybody else was out on patrol.

Wally met us at the door, his face spread into a big toothless grin. He led us into the dark rattan interior. We sat at a big circular table. Each of us was given a private bottle of *Biere La Rue*. A bowl of water buffalo shish kabob on bamboo sticks was set up in the middle of the table. The buffalo was tough and the beer was warm but still it was damned nice of Wally to go to the trouble.

We made a few listless tries at conversation, but Wally's English was no better than my French and finally we got to where we just grinned at each other and said, "Bon! Bon!" every time we tasted something.

Mrs. Wally bustled around the table. She was tall too and a stately woman, even though she was barefoot and wore the standard wraparound skirt and an old blue blouse. Her face reflected great character. Wally's girls, four, eight and

29

thirteen, stood watching us out of great black eyes, saying nothing.

"Fine family," I said to Wally, *"uh-bon famille."*

"Oui, oui," he said. "Soon all come Plei Ta Nangle."

"How go Plei Ta Nangle?" I asked. The others let me carry the conversation ball.

"Bus," he replied, "bus to Ankhe; to Plei Ta Nangle, uh, *en camion.*"

Down the only road from Ankhe to Plei Ta Nangle, a hazardous procedure.

"Oui, many Buon Beng soldier must go to Plei Ta Nangle. All family go together."

Two of the three Strike Force companies at Plei Ta Nangle, the next camp north, were trained at Buon Beng. Their families were still in the camp.

"Good," I said, "all families go to Plei Ta Nangle, be together and we have more room in camp."

"Oui," he said grinning, "bon, bon."

"Wally," I said, "tonight we have good movie with Elvis Presley. It have color and beautiful women. You come?"

"Oui, Monsieur, maybe we come."

"Good," I said, "now we must go. Much work to do." I had to get out of there. The smoke in that cramped little room was stifling and it was torture trying to make conversation like that. I was glad we had come and I liked Wally fine, but enough was enough and now we would leave. I think he felt the same way. At least he made no objection.

As soon as it started to get dark that night, Minh, the cook's son, made a big bowl of popcorn and we got our chairs and went down to the formation area where the screen was stretched over the front of a longhouse.

All the Yards were there already, seated crosslegged in front of the screen. Vietnamese music played from many transistor radios, very sad and sing-song with all the phrases ending in a long haunting drawn-out minor note. Children ran, screaming and bubbling in and out, and a low level buzz of coughing Jarai conversation ran through the crowd.

The lights from Cowboy's old three-quarter cut through the murk, with Yards in the street stepping casually in front of the slow moving headlights and passing into darkness again. He drove down to where we were sitting and stopped. His wife and baby daughter were beside him in the front seat, and a half dozen in-laws were in back. One of them was rocking in a high-back rocking chair.

"Hey," I said, as he drove up beside us. "Your truck gives the place a lot of class."

"How class?" he said.

"We got the only drive-in in Vietnam."

"Captain Morris," he said, "this is my wife, and my daughter, Marina."

"Howdy Ma'am," I said. She didn't answer, just nodded. Cowboy's wife didn't like Americans. I heard that one of Wesley's men made a pass at her, but I didn't know for sure. It was easy to see how it could have happened. Both of her parents were half French and she was a good looking girl. Her complexion was a pale tawny color and her hair was shot through with red. Cowboy's little girl was about two years old, and had blonde hair, although she had her mother's pale tawny complexion. As soon as he had the truck stopped Cowboy reached out, picked her up and set her on his lap. She gurgled appreciatively and he clucked and tickled her.

The projectionist, a Montagnard with a self-important expression, came out carrying the projector protectively in his arms. Four sycophants followed along carrying the projection table and the film reels. The last one was carrying the running end of the long extension cord that ran off the generator.

Dramatically, like a team of magicians, they began to set the projector up. All eyes were on them.

"What flick tonight?" Cowboy asked.

"Dunno," I replied, "some Elvis Presley film, I think."

"No war?" he asked. "Just love song? Shit."

"It'll be okay," I said.

"Like John Wayne better." Cowboy got out of the truck and took a couple of lawn chairs down from the bed for himself and his wife. He set them up beside the truck. The relatives in back sat on the truck bed.

Hank Johnson, bulky and blond, came through the night with a couple of bottles of cold beer. We ignored our chairs and sat on the fender of the three-quarter for a better view. Old Hank looked like a college football player, which he had been. He had played Guard for the Citadel. An unfortunate collision with academics truncated his college career. Damn good weapons man.

A sudden expectant hush fell over the audience. Dramatically the projectionist reached down in the film box and picked up a reel at random. Quickly he threaded it through the projector, working in the light of a flashlight held by one of the sycophants. He started the machine and there was a hum of the projector and the numbers went by upside down from nine to zero on the screen. Then, there it was, in glowing color and garbled sound. Apparently he had grabbed the last reel first because Elvis was doing one of his big production numbers, and there were occasional cuts to the girl waiting in the wings to forgive him for whatever he had done or was supposed to have done. They were both eight feet tall and six inches thick because we had no cinemascope lens.

Also the five kilowatt generator we were running didn't pull enough juice to run the camp electricity and the movie both. All the lights in the camp were dim and the movie was running in slow motion.

On the screen the long skinny Elvis floated through the final bump and grind of his number, his voice singing low and deep, like gravel echoing in a rain barrel. Slowly he bowed to his imaginary audience.

The Yards were all watching, rapt; not an eye wavered from the screen. Even Cowboy's and Mrs. Cowboy's eyes didn't waver.

Elvis floated off the stage in slow and easy steps, the hands of the celluloid audience beating clap . . . clap . . . clap . . . clap. The girl waited in the wings of the theater. She flapped her arms around him and said, "UUUUUUUUIIIIIIII LLLLLLLLUUUUUUUUVVVVVVVV YYYYYYYEEE-EEEEWWWW EEELLLLLLLLLVVVVIIIIIIIISSSSSS!" and Elvis answered in a tone like God delivering the ten commandments. "AAHHHHH LLLLLUUUUUUVVVV EEEEEWWWWWWWW TTTTTEEEEEWWWWWW, BBBBAAAAAAAABBBBBYYYYYYY."

My face was all screwed up with the torture of it.

"Man," I said to Hank sitting beside me there on the three-quarter, "I hope we get that new generator soon. This is driving me nuts."

"Let's go get another beer, sir," he said.

"I'm with you." Wally hadn't shown up for the flick. I guess he was getting reacquainted with Mrs. Wally. Hank and I slid down off the fender and wandered up the street to the Mess Hall.

"You got the first guard tonight?" Hank asked, as we shuffled through the dust to the Mess Hall.

"Uh huh."

"I got the second guard."

"Okay, I'll wake you up at midnight."

Ken Miller and Augie Delucia, the Commo man and the medic, were playing a game of chess in the Mess Hall when we pushed through the screen door. The popcorn was about three-quarters gone. They were both drinking Budweiser.

"We got any of that San Miguel left?" I asked.

"I think there's one or two bottles left, sir," Ken replied.

"Good," I said, "that's all I want. One or two bottles." I opened up the kerosene refrigerator and got a beer.

I strolled back to the rear table, the dim lights casting long shadows in the Mess Hall. It did not seem very warlike except for the submachine guns hung on nails on the walls, kept clean and loaded in case the Cong dropped by. I scooped up a handful of popcorn and asked, "Who's winning?"

"Augie always wins," Ken said, shaking his head. "This is just an exercise in futility for me."

"How come you're such a good chess player, Aug?" I asked, propping one foot up on a chair.

"I study it," he replied with a silly grin. "I study lots of stuff. Ask me anything you want to know about John Paul Jones." Augie was a young guy with a kind of corn-fed innocence about him.

Hank went over to the radio and started fiddling with the knobs. It creaked and sputtered. I let another long swallow of San Miguel trickle down my throat. "Ahhh!" I said, "the beer that made Milwaukee jealous . . ."

33

"Augie is the idiot savant of the team," Ken said. He moved a knight. Ken himself was very bright, Navy from WW II, on his third Nam tour.

"Checkmate," Augie said, moving a pawn one space. Ken started looking the board over to see if there was any way out of it.

"Okay," I said, "John Paul Jones, what was his real name?"

"John Paul."

"What was the name of the ship he commanded during the Revolution?"

"The most famous was the *Bonhomme Richard*."

"What was the British ship he opposed?"

"You're probably thinking of the *Serapis*."

"I got to admit it," I nodded, "you got the widest range of completely useless information of anyone I ever saw."

"Listen," Hank said, "what freq is Radio Malaysia? I'm trying to get that Chinese disc jockey with the English accent."

Ken got up to help him.

"It's always been that way," Augie said, "even when I was a little kid. We was watching that Sixty-four Thousand Dollar Question one night when I was only nine years old and they asked a question which was when and where was the treaty signed that ended World War One.

"While that there expert was hemming and hawing around trying to answer it I said, 'In the Hall of Mirrors in the Palace of *Ver*-sails on June 28, 1919.' And all my folks was saying, 'Shut up, kid. We want to hear the answer.'

"That expert missed it, but I was right. They was all amazed."

"Terrific," I said. "I didn't know the answer either, but I do know it's pronounced Vair-sai, not *Ver*-sails."

"Well," he said, "I never did profound in English."

Ken finished tuning in Radio Malaysia. "And now," said the Chinese disc jockey with the British accent, "for Charlie Woo, Estelle Ling, Jackie and Shirley Wong and all the gang down at Hung Fat's Pizza Paradise, here's numbah four on the Kuala Lumpur top forty, the Beatles and 'I Want to Hold Your Hand.'"

34

The last of the San Miguel gurgled down my throat. I went to the refrigerator for the last bottle. When I got it opened and turned to come back Ken and Augie were going out the door. "Where you going?" I asked.

"Downtown," Ken said. "They've got a better flick at the MAAG compound. Then we may go to Cookie's."

They squeaked through the screen door. I could still hear Elvis droning from the flick over the Beatles from Radio Malaysia. Ken started the three-quarter and the lights came on as he and Augie lurched off to town.

Hank was hunched over the table reading a paperback. I went over to the bookcase and got out a paperback copy of Fanny Hill. I was going to torture myself with some of the choicer passages. "Whatcha reading?" I asked Hank.

He held the book up and I read the title, "Ambush at Rustler's Wells."

I switched to Coke. A couple of beers are okay, but it wouldn't do to be drunk on guard. At ten o'clock I said, "You'd better hit the pad. I'm about to turn the generator off."

He left. I read for another fifteen minutes to give him time to get undressed and then walked outside with my flashlight and went behind the sandbagged walls that shielded the generator shed and turned it off.

Then I got my patrol harness on, slung the carbine over my shoulder and went up to the Guard House. The night breeze was cool, the air clear. There was no moon.

On the way I passed the Vietnamese Team house. Somewhere from inside I could hear a late night radio station playing the House of Blue Lights. It made me think of my stepfather's collection of 78 s and how he hadn't got them all on tape before they were passed on or worn out. It seemed such an awful shame. Inside by the light of a Coleman lantern the Viets were playing some sort of card game. They didn't mount guard and they didn't get up until noon. They were all from Saigon and felt that merely by being stuck out here in the wilderness they were making a sufficient contribution to the war effort. At that, they were better than most Vietnamese teams. They stayed out of the way.

I walked up to the old ramshackle guard house and went

inside. Some of the off duty guard were sitting around a candle, talking in their coughing, hacking language. The rest were flaked out on bamboo sleeping platforms. I shined the flashlight on my face to show who I was and said, *"Ou est le chef du garde?"* A few moments later one of the guard emerged with a carbine slung on his back. He was rubbing his eyes. *"Je suis le chef,"* he said.

"Nous avon fait inspection du garde," I said. Don't laugh, damn it. He understood it.

"Oui, oui," he said and got his flashlight. We stumbled off in the night. I made him douse his light as we went around the zigzag trench that circled the camp, checking to see that one man at each post was awake. As we came up on a post the chef coughed out something in Jarai and I shined the light on my face to show who I was, keeping the eyes tight shut so as not to lose night vision.

We moved through the night like wraiths, jumping back and forth across the trench when trees got in the way, rats scurrying out of our path in the night. We came upon one post where the guard did not issue a challenge. I shushed the *Chef du Garde* and tiptoed up to the sentry who was flat on his back asleep. I took out my Kaybar, laid the dull edge up against his throat and put my mouth up close to his ear. "If I was a Cong," I murmured, "you'd be a dead mother-fucker." Slowly, slowly his head swiveled to face me, his eyes wide and shining. Slowly he got up and feigned alertness while the chef took his name.

As I escorted the chef back to the guard house we passed a Yard moving down the main street with a miner's lamp on his hat and a charged crossbow in his hands. A rat hunter, out looking for meat for breakfast.

I tapped the chef on the shoulder and we exchanged salutes. Then I went back to the Ops shack and got the M-79.

The M-79 is a forty millimeter grenade launcher that breaks down like a shotgun. It is one of the very best weapons in the new U.S. small arms inventory. I slung a bandolier of six grenades over my shoulder and pushed the lever that broke the M-79 open. I took out one round. It looked like a fat rifle bullet with a copper tip. The tip breaks into thousands of tiny fragments with a very good bursting radius of fifteen yards. The damned thing is incredibly accurate. I put the round into the M-79 and closed it up. Then I went back outside and across the street to the motor pool.

Right at twelve o'clock the three-quarter would come back. The Americans would dismount and go over to the urinal for one last call before going to bed. If I knew that the Cong must know it too. It would be a simple matter for them to sneak in close to the perimeter through the jungle and kill two or three Americans real fast. If they tried it I wanted to make sure they paid for it.

I walked softly through the motor pool and went around to the other side of the homemade grease rack, sitting down with my back braced against the grease rack's huge timber support. Slowly my eyes sorted out the foliage across the trench line and past the concertina. If I were doing it, I thought, I would be *there*.

It was a cramped position, crosslegged on the ground with the weapon in my hands. There was still an hour or more to wait. I threw my mind out of gear, and the imagination wandered off on its own course.

At precisely twelve o'clock the twin beams of three-quarter's headlights passed through the front gate and the boxy machine thrummed to its place in the motor pool. Augie and Ken went through their ritual at the urinal and scuffed off into the dark.

Nothing happened.

When they were gone I got up and went inside to wake up Hank. Then I went to bed.

5

At Buon Beng it took us two months to reach a plateau where the VC were so scared of us they would do anything to keep out of our way. And another two after that to reach the point where they weren't able to keep out of our way no matter how hard they tried. In the meantime we covered the northern end of the province like a blanket. We burned over fifty tons of rice and slaughtered over two hundred water buffalo, to deny them to the VC. Our campaign made Sherman's march to the sea look like some kind of Sunday School picnic.

We knew if we kept pushing sooner or later something had to break loose. Still we had no intelligence. Slowly the breaks came, though, a lot of small ones that added up.

Another project was to help build a leper colony, a cooperative effort with the local missionary and the Agency for International Development.

Getting the money for that was complicated, and I went to Pleiku to arrange for funds to complete the leper village.

I took the courier aircraft from Cheo Reo and rode all around the II Corps area in a Caribou, finally winding up in Pleiku.

That night in Pleiku I went downtown. There were about three rich families in Pleiku. They all had big houses surrounded by spacious grounds, with coils of concertina on top of the walls and guards on that. Surrounding them is a whole city of poor jerrybuilt shacks squatting in mud, filth and flies. It was easy to see how a kid could go Cong. After two months in the jungle and seeing the way the Yards lived I hated those rich people in Pleiku more than I've ever hated anybody before or since. A kid that had no knowledge of communism or what the Cong wanted to do to Vietnam would join anything that was against such bastards.

Whatever the faults of the Cong, at least their leaders lived in the jungle with the rest of them. If the Viets had done that there wouldn't have been any Cong.

Our attitude toward the Jarai began to change too. Ken was the only one in the team who had come to Buon Beng with any affection for them. The rest of us had reasons of our own; to get off Okinawa, or for the love of adventure, or the desire to prove something, or make a little extra money, or enhance a military career. There were a lot of reasons that had nothing to do with a hatred of communism or a humanitarian love for primitive tribespeople.

But you can't fight alongside people for months and not develop some feeling for them. My first day at our Forward Operational Base, when old Ay charged past me going down to the creek into a VC ambush, made me an admirer of his. A lot of the other old French soldiers were good too.

I think one thing that did it for me was watching Ksor Yul bicycle past the Mess Hall every evening with his two year old son on the handlebars, riding him two kilometers to the river for a bath.

The reasons that had brought us to Vietnam faded away and were replaced by an honest desire to help the Jarai.

Once we got the go ahead I started working with Bob Reed, the missionary, on getting the leper village going. The first thing was to go out there and find out what the old leper village chief needed.

Going out with Bob presented a transportation problem. The VC allowed him to drive the roads unmolested, but he couldn't afford to be seen driving out as part of a group of armed men in the service of the Vietnamese government. The Cong might decide that he was spying for us and ambush him the next time he came out alone. Conversely, no immunity was extended to American Army officers, and if I rode out with him in uniform we were subject to ambush.

Finally I said to hell with it and put on my Bermuda shorts and a sport shirt, left my pistol at home and we rode out in his Land Rover. It wasn't really taking much of a chance. The odds were very much against us being stopped by the

Cong. If we were I would try to carry myself off as a missionary.

"Bob," I said, on the way out, "why don't the Yards and the Vietnamese get along?"

"Sometimes they do," he replied quietly. "In Lieutenant Linh's district they get along splendidly. But that's an exception. He treats the people in his district well and makes an effort to understand them. That's the basic difference, really.

"That's what's wrong with the whole American program. It is all designed to prove to the Vietnamese citizens, including the Montagnards, that the government really cares for them, but in most cases the average Vietnamese is under tyrannical local officials who don't give a rap for him, and he knows it. You can't win trying to sell a flat lie.

"It's not just that they steal everything that's not nailed down and act like arrogant pigs. It is actually dangerous for the citizens to help the government.

"About a year ago six VC came into a village in Captain Dinh's district. The villagers were loyal and two of them went to Dinh. All he had to do was take some soldiers out and capture the VC. They had only one weapon between them. Instead he reported it to province and province reported it to Corps and so on. Finally three days after the VC had left the village a group of fighter aircraft flew out and bombed it level."

"That was sure smart," I said, shaking my head in wonderment.

"It's typical," he shrugged.

The leper village was about a mile back from the highway. thirty or so kilometers up toward Pleiku. It was just a collection of grass shacks that the Lepers had thrown together in a little clearing by a large stream. It had a very pretty setting there in the woods and that made me unprepared for the sight of those sad, filthy Yards, squatting desolately in the dirt with feet withered into scaly pods or hands doubled into shriveled claws or stumps.

"I got some rice from Albertson," Bob said, "and brought it out here, but it's too easy for them to say it's hopeless and give up. We are going to have to insist that they work for everything they get from us. Not work for us, but work for themselves."

I nodded agreement.

The old village chief came up. His feet were withered, but not so badly that he couldn't walk, and his hands were all right. He wore a loincloth and an old khaki shirt. Aside from leprosy his worst health problem was dental. He had very few teeth and even those he would have been better off without.

He bowed and extended his hand. I had no great desire to shake it, but didn't want to offend him. We bowed towards each other slightly and I shook his hand.

"He wants to show you something," Bob said. The old chief turned and headed back towards his little hooch. We followed. "I've told them not to shake hands with people," Bob said. "But he didn't want to hurt your feelings."

"I wouldn't have been in the least offended," I said, grinning sickly.

The old chief ducked through his door and came out a moment later with an ancient folded square of black plastic. He unfolded it and brought out some papers which had just started to yellow with age. He showed them to me proudly. There was a picture of him in uniform and a discharge from one of the French Montagnard battalions. He carefully folded the papers back up in the sheet of plastic, brought his bare rotted feet together, grinned around his black snaggled teeth, and saluted me palm out.

What can you do? I stood at attention in my sneakers and bermudas and returned the salute American style.

"*Oui, mon Captaine*," he said. For a minute there I thought he was going to kiss me on both cheeks.

He didn't but he did break out a *numpai* jug. One jug and one straw, and we both sat down on little blocks of wood and split that jug, passing the straw back and forth between us. I offered Bob a sip. "He knows my religion forbids me to take alcohol," Bob said.

"And aren't you glad?"

The rest of the visit was a little blurred. We saw there was no soap and no more food and a bunch of the lepers' kids sang the Old Rugged Cross in Jarai and then we went home.

It took me quite a while to work up nerve to go back.

41

One of our first acts on arriving in Vietnam was to order that there be no shooting of unarmed civilians. Generally the order was obeyed. But our CO, Captain Crews McCulloch, finally put an absolute stop to it in February. Nay Re killed a baby boy the same age as McCulloch's youngest daughter.

The company moved through a village and the Old Man, as we called the captain, stopped as he heard some firing up ahead. A minute later Nay Re came back, grinning from ear to ear. "We get two VC," he said, "wound one, kill other."

The Old Man moved quickly to the scene to check the two vicious communists. The dead one was a little boy and the wounded one was the boy's mother. She knelt on the ground in her black skirt, holding the boy in her arms and rocking back and forth. The round had clipped her rib cage, gone in through and out her left breast and still had enough punch to kill the boy. As she rocked back and forth, blood from her breast mixed with blood streaming from her baby's heart. Her face had no expression.

Captain Mac was filled with a cold fury that never really abated. Almost a year later, when all this was over, when he had transferred to the 173rd Airborne Brigade and I was back down with my own team, my wife went to dinner at his house. Somehow the conversation came around to this story and he told most of it. He couldn't finish it though because he started to break down and had to leave the room.

At the time, though, he didn't cry. As soon as he saw the mother and child, without time for conscious thought, his right arm snaked out and jerked Nay Re off the ground. The Old Man held him by the collar; they were nose to nose. Nay Re's feet dangled a full twelve inches off the ground. "Tell your men," Captain Mac said tonelessly, with measured cadence, "that the next man who shoots any unarmed person, I will kill myself. On the spot. Do you understand?"

I have seen the Old Man when he was displeased. I would not care to see him as Nay Re saw him that day. His little Montagnard body was shaking from head to foot. He made the head shake up and down.

Later, after he had time to think it over, Captain Mac realized he couldn't go around shooting his troops out of hand. They would have understood, but the U.S. Army would not. But he didn't tell them that, and they never tested him.

They were only one day out of the camp and the woman had a punctured lung. Bill Foody, our junior medic, bound her chest and covered her wound with an airtight bandage. Then while she watched silently, tearlessly, they buried her child under the trees beside the banks of the Li Piao river. Ken Miller was the radioman on that patrol. He put his set together and beat out a message to Mike Iten back in the camp. Get a chopper for the woman.

While Ken got out the message Bill supervised the construction of a litter. Then they started marching.

They marched all night down narrow jungle trails, over hills, through rivers. The Old Man gave no rest. They went too fast for security. The Americans were moving as fast as their long legs would go and the Yards ran. The Old Man was riding his fury, and he was determined that if the child had died the mother would not. We had come to save these people, not slaughter them.

The message came in at two in the afternoon. George Stogdill and I were working to get out the Monthly Operational Summary. I had just about finished writing the basic document when the message came in. SECURE MED EVAC FOR ONE CRITICALLY WOUNDED MONTAGNARD WOMAN, PICK-UP TOMORROW MORNING AT FOB.

"Well, okay," I said, "put in a med evac message, operational immediate."

"Has to go through Vietnamese channels sir," Mike said. He was a fine soldier, but at nineteen with one trip already behind him he couldn't miss a chance to show off superior knowledge.

"I know that," I said, "but it'll go faster if it goes simultaneously. While you get this out I'll go over and get the Vietnamese to send out another."

"It's not going to work, sir. They just won't send a med evac out for a Montagnard civilian."

"Mike," I said, glowering, "you know Captain Mac as well as I do. When he says get a med evac he does not mean try to get one. He means that we *will* have a helicopter out at the

FOB tomorrow morning. If this doesn't work I'll try something else."

He went back over to the commo shack and I grabbed Kpa Doh. We went to the Vietnamese team house to put the message out through their channels.

There were four or five Viets sitting around the office of their shack when we came in. They were turning out quintuple copies of some form or other and stamping each copy with four or five different seals in red ink. The new Second Lieutenant, the XO, sat disconsolately behind his desk staring off into space. He was about the third XO Khue had since we got there. No Viet, after all, is going to work long under a Montagnard if he can help it.

He was a slight, pleasant looking boy with long hair. He had been commissioned apparently without any training at all, and there was nothing about him that even vaguely resembled a soldier. He was, of course, not qualified for airborne.

Through Kpa Doh I explained the situation to him and he readily agreed to send out the message. Then there was nothing to do but go back to the Ops shack and do some more work on the monthly Opsum while we waited for the reply.

It was five-thirty in the afternoon when the message came in and the answer was negative. I got in the jeep and went to town to see if Major Judah could help.

The MAAG advisors were in their mess hall eating supper when I arrived. Seated next to the Major at the center of the table was a civilian in a checked sport shirt whom I had never seen before. He was a big man with a long civilian haircut and a mournful face, eyes staring out at the world through deep sockets. His mouth held something of a wry, petulant humor. He did not look too much at ease with the Advisory Group people.

"Sit down, Morris," the Major said, looking up pleasantly. "Have some supper."

"Thank you sir," I said. "But I've eaten." I hadn't. I just didn't want to get tied down to a plate of chow. "We've got a problem and I wondered if maybe you could help."

"Glad to if I can," the Major said.

I explained the situation. The Major thought a minute and gnawed on his lower lip. "Morris," he said, "I'm sorry. I'd help you if there was any way I could. But the evacuation of civilians is a Vietnamese responsibility. It's a policy and I just can't buck it."

I poured a cup of coffee. Judah had been my last hope. I decided to wheedle a little. "Sir," I said, "the evacuation of this particular civilian is *my* responsibility. Captain McCulloch has given it to me. I don't know what I have to do to get a helicopter out there, but whatever it is I'm going to do it."

The civilian leaned forward and said, "Captain, I don't know if it'll help any or not, but I'll make a few phone calls after chow."

"Thanks." I held out my hand. "Jim Morris."

"John Albertson," he said. "USOM rep." He said it unsmiling and very serious. USOM stood for U.S. Operational Mission, the overseas arm of the Agency for International Development.

"Anything you can do, Mr. Albertson, we'd sure appreciate it."

"Call me John," he said, putting down his knife and fork with a clatter. "Floyd," he said to the Major, "mind if I use your phone?"

"No, no. Go right ahead." But he didn't look happy about it. After all, he'd just said it couldn't be done. Going ahead and doing it smacked of irregular procedure. In Major Judah's part of the army they were very strong against irregular procedure.

Albertson and I got up and walked down to the office. "What do you have in mind?" I asked. We pushed through the door into the office and he sat down behind a U.S. Government gray metal desk. The office was full of filing cabinets, maps, charts, desks, typewriters. They had no arms room or ammo of their own, but had to borrow from the Viets. As soldiers they were up shit creek without a paddle.

"A friend of mine commands the chopper company at Nha Trang," he said. "He owes me a few favors. And USOM maintains a surgical suite at Nha Trang. The surgeon is due there tomorrow and he'd like nothing better than to patch up a Montagnard broad."

He picked up the field phone and gave it a couple of cranks. The line ran to Pleiku, ninety-three kilometers north. From there on it was hooked into a single side-band radio and you could talk to anybody in Vietnam, just about, on it. In theory, you could call all the way to the States, but by that time it had run through so many switches the signal was lost. "Hello Llama," John said, "get me Condor. . . . Condor, I want to talk to 3398."

He leaned way back in the chair, propped his feet up on the desk and lit a cigarette. He was totally relaxed, but I was all knotted up in a ball on my chair and my right foot was pumping like crazy.

"Lemme speak to Major Dietrich," he was saying. "Hello Heinz, listen. This is John Albertson and I got a problem. You wanta get in some flying time tomorrow? . . . Yeah! The Special Forces here have got some Montagnard woman shot up, and they seem to feel it's important to save her. . . . Yeah! Tomorrow morning. She's got a bad chest wound. It's got to be fast. Even then it's going to be touch and go."

Then in an aside to me, "What's the coordinates of that FOB of yours?"

I gave them to him and he passed them on to his friend.

"How you going to mark the LZ?" he asked.

"Yellow smoke and panels," I replied.

"Yellow smoke and panels. Yeah, thanks a bunch. No. No sweat." And then he let out a great peal of laughter and finished with "Albertson out."

"There," he said when he had finished, "that's the way to do it."

After watching him I had an idea he had done the whole thing just to show off. But I didn't care why he did it. He was our kind of people, and I was grateful. "Thanks a lot," I said.

"Nothing to it, my boy. Nothing to it. Let's go have a beer."

The chopper came and got the woman the next day and from then on Albertson spent more time hanging around Buon Beng than he did at his desk at the MAAG compound. The first time he came out I was working on the Ops fund, and Cowboy came in with a small sad-looking Montagnard in

46

khaki pants and a sports shirt. He was the most mournful man I had ever seen, with a downturned mouth and great sad eyes. But they were very alive eyes.

"Who's that?" I asked Cowboy.

"This Nay Luette, my brother-in-law. He is interpreter for Mr. Albertson."

We shook hands. "Albertson come out?" I asked.

"He come. He is in Mess Hall with coffee. He wait for you."

I got up and said, "Hey George, I'm going over to the Mess Hall for coffee. You want to come?"

"Yes sir, I'll be over in a minute."

My chair scraped back on the concrete and I rose to cross the dusty street to the mess hall. "Hello, John," I said. "Have a cup of coffee."

"Don't mind if I do," he said, grinning over the cup he had already half finished.

"Minh," I called, "*deux cafe!*"

I took a sip of coffee. It was too hot and too strong. My stomach was beginning to rot from all the coffee I drank with visitors every day in camp. "Man, that Interpreter of yours is the saddest looking guy I ever saw."

"He's got a reason to be sad," Albertson replied. "He just got out of prison. He was rounding out a three year stretch when he got loose in the general amnesty after the Diem coup."

"What was he in for?"

"All the Montagnard tribes sent a delegation with requests for equal treatment. Luette was the fall guy who took it in to Diem. Diem had him thrown in the clink out of hand. He was a damn good interpreter though. Damn good man to have around generally."

George's stubby form heaved across the road, and he squeaked through the door. After that I switched the topic of conversation, deftly, I hoped, to the subject of goodies for the leper village. John was damned obliging. I got everything we wanted. He said that was his job, to pass out the goodies.

6

I walked down the shaded portico to Albertson's room. He did not answer my knock so I crossed the grass to the MAAG office and walked in. Their Psy Ops Captain was working at his desk.

"Hey, Hal," I said, "where's Albertson?"

"Saigon," he said, looking up. "Left this morning."

"You know when he's coming back? We're ready to start on the dispensary at the leper village and we want to pick up the cement and tin."

"He ought to be back Monday or Tuesday."

"Well," I said, "there's no rush on it. They're not rotting any faster than usual. What's that you're working on there?" I crossed the room and sat on the corner of his desk.

"Report." He leaned back and chewed on a pencil, the swivel chair creaking. "Shows how many of these leaflets we've dropped in the northern area of the province this month. We've put out about a hundred thousand of them, all told."

"Lotta leaflets. You got any samples I could look at?"

"Sure, here." He handed me a stack of four different leaflets. I looked them over.

"You're putting me on," I said.

"No. What's the matter? They're beautiful leaflets, four color offset. Look at that art work."

"I'm looking. How long you people been dropping these leaflets up there in Bahnar country?"

"Around two years."

"Well, Captain, I hate to bust your balloon, but these leaflets are written in Vietnamese. The Bahnar up there are about two percent literate in their own language. I doubt if

48

anybody even speaks Vietnamese, let alone reads it. You've been providing the Cong with free toilet paper."

I expected him to look crushed, but he didn't, just annoyed. "As far as I'm concerned," he said, "my job is to drop leaflets. These are the leaflets they give me to drop, and that's what I'm going to do with them."

"Look," I said, "I'll give you leaflets. Give me some stencils and I'll write them up and have Cowboy translate them into Bahnar. You can run them off on your mimeograph. How's that?"

He shrugged disinterestedly. "Sure. That'd be okay. Thanks a lot." He turned to his clerk. "Boskins, give Captain Morris here a stack of stencils."

I took them and said, "It'll be two or three days before I have them back."

"Take your time," he said. "We won't get a chopper for another week anyway."

"Okay."

On the way back to camp I stopped in town and picked up some pictures at the photo shop and then dropped over to Cookie's Cao Nguyen for a Coke. Our chief cook, in addition to being contractor for the American Mess Hall, owned a laundry, a bakery and two combination bar-whorehouses in town.

I pushed through the colored plastic strips that shaded the inside of the bar and sat down in a rickety plastic sling chair at one of the tables. A girl in white silk bellbottom pajamas came over. She was very pretty and her long straight black hair drooped as she came to take my order.

"Bonjour, Captaine," she said.

"Bonjour, ma'amzelle. Donnez-moi un Coke s'il vous plait."

She swung away and brought back my coke a moment later in a large glass full of dirty chunks of ice. I held it, feeling it grow cold in my hand as the girl walked away. Cookie's was a filthy place, musty smelling, with patriotic posters on the wall and an old scratchy phonograph behind the bar. Through the windows, square holes cut in the rattan walls, I could see the dusty main street of Cheo Reo, the photo shop and the barber shop across the street, and the

Chinaman's hardware store next to the barbershop. I looked at the girl again and sighed. No time for that now.

It is a mistake to call the girls whores because that word has connotations that do not apply in Asia. Their services were offered in much the same spirit, and with no more shame, than bar peanuts or table napkins. A simple commercial transaction with no moral or personal implications.

I paid twenty piastres for the Coke, looked at the girl again, and walked into the sun.

Turning in through the gate I saw Ed Thomas work the big D-7 Cat we borrowed from the ARVN Engineers to doze the treeline away from the camp. Trees lay around him like felled soldiers, the great dirtclinging clumps of their root systems hanging on the ends.

The drone of the engine changed pitch as he mashed in the clutch and wrenched the levers. The Cat spun on its tracks, the engine changed pitch again, and he shoved a huge batch of felled trees toward the treeline, leaving a great scar of red earth underneath. It was not aesthetically pleasing, but it left a fine field of fire for two hundred feet out from the last strand of concertina.

The guard opened the gate and I drove through returning his salute, then spun the jeep in by the Ops shack and got out with the little sack of pictures and the psywar leaflets in my hands.

"You see Albertson?" the Old Man asked.

"No sir. He's in Saigon. But I got these leaflets from Jellicoe. They've been dropping them on the Bahnar for two years."

He looked at the leaflets and said, "You're kidding!"

"No sir. I'm going to write up a bunch of leaflets in Bahnar and he can drop those. I'll show them to you before they're run off."

We walked across the street and into the mess hall. Cookie himself had decided to grace this meal. He had a spectacular betel nut smile, a long scrawny body topped by a pork pie hat and three sons to do all the work. He scurried, managed and shooed the sons, bringing in more of anything that the Old Man wanted. Ass kissing has a long and honorable tradition in Asia.

50

The Old Man and I sat down across from Bill and Augie. I started to butter a slice of bread. "Hey Cookie," I said. "There's rat turds in the bread again."

His eyes flew wide and he snatched the slice of homemade bread from my hands and looked at it in horror.

"Mon dieu," he said, *"merci, mon Captaine, merci."* He picked the rat turd out of the bread with his fingers and then, as an added gesture of conciliation, reached down and buttered the bread for me and handed it back.

Across from me Thomas sat chuckling. The Old Man just went on eating, but he had a suggestion of a smile on his face, too. It was a typical meal, fried water buffalo with canned green beans, local corn on the cob and bread with rat turds, washed down with strawberry Kool-Aid, served from empty whiskey bottles. Augie and Bill put so much chlorine in the water that we couldn't drink it straight.

"Rat turds in the bread," I said. "No wonder everybody gets the shits."

After lunch it was *pok* time, the two hour siesta, and I usually took the time to read something. But I was interested in the problem of the leaflets and so stopped at my desk, rolled some paper into the typewriter and started working.

"Bahnar friends," I wrote, "if you are sick, if your children are sick or dying, come to Buon Beng and we will give free medical treatment."

I signed it Lieutenant Khue, Commander of the Buon Beng Strike Force.

Cowboy was messing around in the front office where the Interpreters stayed and played receptionist.

He had his American bush hat in a cowboy roll on his head and that was scrunched down over his eyes. Under that he had a pair of Renaud wraparound shades over his eyes and a Salem dangled from his lips. Slowly and with infinite care he read through the *Riders of the Purple Sage*, trying to make some sense of it. Frequently he put the book down and turned to the French-English dictionary on his desk. As a matter of principle he refused to learn to read and write Vietnamese, or at least admit that he could.

"Hey Cowboy," I called out. "Come here a minute, will

you please? I want you to look at this."

He came in and I handed him the propaganda leaflet. "You reckon you could translate this into Bahnar?" I asked.

"Oh sure," he said, "but I no think leaflet bring them out. Must be talk, face to face. They no trust leaflet."

He cocked the hat back on his head and sat on the corner of my desk while he rewrote the message in Bahnar.

I nodded. "I don't expect it to have much effect either, but it's bound to be better than this." I held out one of the MAAG leaflets.

His lips curled. "They drop this on Bahnar?"

"Yeah!"

He sighed and shook his head, continuing to work on the leaflet, while I rolled another sheet of paper into the typewriter, and started on the next one.

"Bahnar Friends," I started, but my mind wasn't really on the leaflets then. I was thinking how lucky we were to have Cowboy. Not just as an interpreter, but because he was a valuable advisor to us on his people's customs and habits. He had proved to be brave on patrol. Of course he had a phenomenal ego, but who doesn't in this business?

As I thought over all of his qualifications something clicked. I stopped writing and looked at Cowboy, thinking hard. After a minute he stopped writing and looked back at me. We needed intelligence, but had no Agent Handler. The Agent Handler needs to be brave, resourceful, clever, loyal, and most of all, he had to be able to mix with the background.

"Cowboy," I said, "go hire some spies."

I had visions of him putting on a loincloth and skulking around from village to village, so the VC wouldn't catch on. Or taking off his cowboy hat and riding the bus.

"Maybe I can go Saturday," he said. "I take three-quarter and squad for security. But let me pick men for squad. All volunteer."

That wasn't the way I had thought it would be at all, but, already committed, I agreed to let him go.

I started working again on the leaflet, but hadn't got very far into it when the field telephone in the front office went off. Cowboy and I both pushed back our chairs and went for it, but it stopped ringing before we got there. I could see the Old Man talking on the phone across the street in the mess hall. He was over there with the adding machine doing the final tally on the Operational Fund for the month. He motioned me to come over through the screen of the mess hall.

"That was Major Judah," he said when I got over there. "The Cong came into the village of Plei Ksom last night and took every soul there with them. He thinks they're taking them into the mountains to help out with the rice harvest. The Viets don't have a company they can spare to try and trace them down. So, he wants us to send somebody."

"The odds are pretty much against finding them," I said.

"We need to try though, if only for psychological effect." He paused for a moment. "Jim," he said, "it's my turn to go, but we've got to get this Ops fund out for the month, and I have got to start getting Operation Bat ready if I'm going to run it."

"You're really going ahead with it, huh?"

"Yes," he nodded seriously.

"You're the boss," I said, "but I'd be doing less than my duty if I didn't tell you." I sighed. It's not easy to tell your commanding officer, especially one you respect and admire as much as I did the Old Man, that he's dead wrong. "I think, and every other member of this team agrees with me, that a lot of people are going to get killed if you run that operation. Besides you're risking almost one hundred percent of our truck transportation."

When he gets serious he starts talking in a stilted, formal way. He was very serious as he said, "I appreciate your concern, but I have weighed all the factors involved and am convinced that the operation will succeed."

I shrugged. "Like I said, you're the boss."

"Fine, now round yourself up a platoon and take off after that village tomorrow. Take Cowboy with you."

I shook my head. "I'd rather not, if you don't mind. I've got him set up to do some intelligence work Saturday morning. I'll take Yul with me. Between his bastard English and my bastard French we usually make out."

"Suit yourself."

I was off and running. "Hey, Cowboy! Get Yul down

53

here."

We got the patrol rounded up and issued some ammo and chow that afternoon. As usual we didn't tell them where we were going or what we were going to do until we left. The VC were bound to have spies in camp.

We spent two days poking back and forth across the Ankhe Road and the Song Ba river, looking for footprints, campfires, anything. The river was beautiful, wide and shallow. It generally ran four or five feet deep and about two hundred feet wide. The water was perfectly clear and on either side the trees came to the water's edge, except for a few spots where the road ran adjacent to the water.

The Viet Minh had done a very thorough job on the Ankhe Road. The last vehicle to drive this stretch had belonged to the French Mobile Group 100 and that was in 1954 or thereabouts. The roadbed was solid enough. The French had done an excellent job of putting it in. There were lots of signs that Montagnards used the road frequently. It was the widest trail around after all. And it was easy for a man on foot to walk over the great hundred-foot felled trees that lay across the road every fifty feet or so. Where the culverts and bridges were out a man could walk around. The Ankhe Road was no bar to foot traffic, but it wasn't any freeway either.

That was the Old Man's Operation Bat. He planned to open it to vehicular traffic using nothing but our own organic transportation. Two and a half ton trucks with winches.

I thought it was suicide. The trucks were trailbound. That would mean the Cong would know where they were every second. It takes the Cong about three days to gather up a company, scattered out in little groups as they are, and maybe a week to put a battalion together. That's how the French Mobile Group 100 got itself annihilated on this same road. But the Old Man said he had it figured out. I sure hoped he was right. I wouldn't have tried it for anything.

It was hot. The rucksack weighed at least fifty pounds when we started out and wasn't getting any lighter. It dragged my back until pain became a permanent part of my vertebrae. On breaks we lay panting like dogs, while the sun

54

beat down, burning around the shade. The sweat ran down our backs and legs in rivulets and we didn't care, just planting one foot in front of the other, just doing the job, just walking and . . . Oh man, take a break. Throw the rucksack down, feel a sudden lift to the thighs and let a trickle of hot water from the canteen flow down your throat. Then drag on a filter cigarette, not because it tastes good. It tastes dry and acrid. But a civilized people smoke filter cigarettes and it's nice to remember that at one time you gave a fairly convincing imitation of a civilized human being.

"Aw Ri! Off and on. Let's go!" Back up, throw the pain back on your back, feel your feet start to smoke once more and start planting them in front of each other again.

By the third night, what with crossing and recrossing the river and doubling back and following false trails and dying in the heat, we made camp on a hill only fifteen kilometers north of where we started. I took my boots off and let the breeze blow between my gummy toes.

Except for firefights, the best time on patrol was after supper when you're smoking your last cigarette, before you put out all the fires. I enjoyed my favorite patrol meal, C ration beans and franks mixed with boiled rice, boiled chopped onion, chopped with the same knife that cut sticks and cleaned fingernails, and tabasco sauce, followed by canned C ration peaches and coffee. C ration coffee tastes like iron filings. The taste of the canteen cup didn't help too much either, although I made an honest effort to get the last of the beans, franks and rice out before making coffee.

Ray Slattery offered some instant tea. His wife sends it to him along with Norwegian sardines and other little luxury items to take on patrols. He is a man of many moods and contrasts, of contradictory traits. For a while back on Oki I thought the Old Man was going to throw him off the team. No matter what we did, Slats always loudly proclaimed it was a crock of shit. He said so frequently and didn't care who heard him. I talked it over with Ed Thomas who knew his reputation from Laos. Then we both went to the Old Man separately and requested that he be kept.

Now in Vietnam he worked harder and turned out more good ideas than almost anyone on the team. One of my worst

55

faults was youthful impetuosity. I knew it and tried to make it a point never to go on patrol without either Slats or Ken along to provide some good sense. In retrospect, maybe they held me back a few times when it would have been better to charge on. But you've only got to screw up once, Jack, and they plant you forevermore.

Mike drank the instant tea also. He was a less complex personality, nineteen years old going on twenty-five.

We learned a lot about each other during those long talks after chow, before rolling into our sacks for the night. I learned that the nuns where Slats went to school were free with a rap to the knuckles and that Mike's father was a German soldier, killed in the last days of the war, and his stepfather was a U. S. Army sergeant and a better father than anyone had a right to expect.

"What you going to do when your hitch is up, Mike?" I asked.

"I dunno, Sir," he said. "I'll either get out and go to college or I'll re-enlist for the 10th Special Forces Group. My German's pretty rusty, but it'll come back fast enough I reckon. How about yourself?"

"I don't know either," I replied. "I love the Army, but it's not what I do best. And this trip down here has been the best thing I've found in the Army. Once they find out you're literate the army wants to keep you in administration. I reckon I'll get out and try for a master's degree. Maybe try college teaching, maybe do a little writing. That's what I'd like to do."

We talked until it was too dark to talk any more, then kicked the fire apart and crawled into the sack. The breeze was soft and the trees rustled with it. The Yards on guard were coughing out low conversation when we went to sleep.

We had enough chow left to operate for one more day, so I left a squad to watch the rucksacks, took the other two squads, and with Yul, we hit the road after breakfast. Even with the heat it felt good to be moving without rucksacks. About a kilometer down the road we came to an area sown with punji sticks.

Slats was up ahead and he started to go up the side of the hill and work his way around the punji area. I decided to

56

move through them. It's pretty easy once you get the hang of it. I managed to sidestep all of them. The belt of punjis was only about twenty meters thick across the road. Six Yards followed me through and instead of watching the punjis they all watched me. Every one of them got stuck at least once and we had to send them back, gimping along using their carbines like canes. That ran the strength of our patrol down to fourteen men including Yul and the Americans. Another kilometer down the road we ran into more punjis.

It was lunch time anyway so we took a break. We crawled into what shade there was and ate. Then we crossed the river.

It was about two hundred feet across and around four feet deep. The cool water was refreshing. We held our rifles over our heads and I watched the water swirl up toward the pocket with my cigarettes. But they were still dry when we reached the other side. The heat made our waterlogged uniforms clammy as we climbed out, and the drying, steaming socks rolled up in the bottoms of our boots.

The land on the other side was like a well-kept public park. It was flat and the mountains on that side were a quarter of a mile back from the river. The trees were tall and well separated. The shadow made an agreeable shade and breeze stirred the moisture on our bodies. The grass was long and slender, of a delicate light green. The effect was marvelously pleasant.

We should have been in Bermuda shorts and sport shirts, with portable record players and girls. We should have spread a picnic basket under the trees and lain back and put the girls' heads in our laps and loved the afternoon away. But we had no girls and no picnic baskets. Only ammunition and hand grenades, rifles and knives.

We walked away back from the river and found a neat path, filled with fine grey gravel winding through the trees. On the theory that all paths lead to somewhere we followed it until we came to a fork. One fork was blocked by punjis and the other was not. We went around the punjis and followed the path that was blocked. Slats had one punji go through his left boot, but it didn't touch the foot.

We came to a small hooch, up on stilts, which had rice and corn and some tobacco in it. Rather than give our position away with a fire we chopped it apart and scattered the contents. A few minutes later we came to a small depression in the ground where the grass was high, and there was a split rail fence to cross. The fence could only be to keep in water buffalo. After that and the small hooch there must be a village nearby. We spread out in a line of skirmishers and moved cautiously forward.

Yul materialized by my side. "VC, VC!" he whispered. He motioned with his head. I followed him through the trees and we peered out at a clearing on the edge of the river.

There were three young men working a dry rice field. They wore loincloths and had no weapons. They were bent over cutting at the stubble with handmade scythes. It was hot work and they bent low in the sun, sweat glowing on their slender brown backs. We could see a small village clustered in the trees beyond them.

They were working by a bend in the river and water surrounded them on two sides. It was a simple matter to move through the trees and surround them on the other two sides. I motioned to Yul to form an encirclement.

Five minutes later he nodded to me that the encirclement was ready. I said, "Okay!" and stepped out of the trees into the hot open clearing. My troops followed me out and we and the river formed a ring around the three boys.

No one but a fool would try to make it across two hundred feet of clear water when confronted with fourteen armed men. It would be suicide.

They ran off the bank and into the water.

I ran after them screaming, "No *G'pow*! No *G'pow*!" at the top of my lungs. *G'pow* in Jarai is gun. There was no need to shoot them. We only wanted to take them from VC control. I ran off the six feet of bank and dropped charging into four feet of cold water. I lunged through the water that cloyed and dragged. They were ahead and gaining, me weighted down by boots and ammo, my rifle. They were barefoot in loincloths and they knifed cleanly through the water.

The scene was agonizingly slow, like the nightmare it has become on so many nights since, and behind me I could hear the crack of rifles and carbines firing. I screamed again, "No *G'pow*! No *G'pow*!" but it was no use and I could see the water kicking up little splashes where the rounds were hitting near them. I surged forward through the water.

When I was halfway across one of them gained the bank and scampered over the edge. The second was not far behind, but the third, the smallest, was slow and I saw him waver and soon red blood was cascading down his neck and shoulders like long hair. I gained on him now that he was staggering and I was only a few feet behind him when he stumbled up on the sloping bank. I reached him and grabbed his arm. He looked at me in horror, still holding his sickle in his left hand.

One of our Yards ran up behind me, took the sickle out of his hands and whacked him on the head with the flat of it. The boy collapsed to the ground, his eyes beginning to glaze. Water from the river mixed with the blood which ran all over his back and he lay in a little skinny brown heap.

I winced inside.

"No goddamnit, you stupid fool!" I yelled at the Yard and took the sickle away from him. "Get out of here!" He went on with the others, chasing the other two.

Mike ran up. He had some cross-training in medicine and I hoped he could patch up the kid's head wound. Mike's face was anxious, strained. "We were firing over their heads, sir. Slats and I were firing over their heads to get them to stop."

And of course when the Yards saw Americans firing they shot to kill. But what could I do, chew him out? His reprimand was lying dying on the ground and I could add nothing to it.

"Where's Slattery?"

"He ran down after the others."

"Okay, get the Yard medic up here and see if you can put a pressure bandage on this kid's head. You think you can save him?"

"If we can get an evac, stop the bleeding and get some albumin into him, maybe." He started calling for the medic. In a few moments the Montagnard medic slouched over with the aid bag slung over his shoulder; Mike took it away from him and started to paw through it.

He came up with a large pressure bandage and popped it open. Long flesh colored strands of gauze fluttered down like octopus tentacles. He put the pad on the kid's head and started tying the tentacles under his chin. "Put your finger right here," he said, and I held the knot for him.

"How about morphine?" I said.

"No. Not for a head wound. That would kill him in a flash." Mike had spent his spare time in the dispensary while I had to fill out stupid forms and bullshit with people in the mess hall.

I had never felt so helpless. Mike started pawing through the aid kit and found a can of albumin. He got it out and popped it open. "Goddamn!" he said.

"What?"

"This can doesn't have albumin in it. He's got it filled with APC's."

"Son of a bitch," I stormed. "Where's the radio? Maybe we can raise an evac."

"The Yard operator went on with the rest," he said. A cluster of about five Yards was standing around. Mike would be all right.

"Okay," I said, "you stay here. I'll go find them."

The mountains had flattened out and a broad flat plain stretched out before me, full of dry, waist high grass. I took off alone running, ammo pouches thudding against my pelvis. The watersoaked uniform weighed a ton. It must have been over a hundred and ten and soon I was panting. I slowed to a walk. Then I heard some firing ahead and took off toward it. Running, my whole insides revolted against the unexpected punishment. I hadn't run since we left Okinawa.

I came into a village in a clearing. Slats and the rest of the Yards were setting fire to it. It was about twenty houses.

Slats hammered upon the split bamboo door to one of the houses and was just crawling inside when I came up. "What was all that firing?" I demanded, panting. "Did you find those two guys?"

"No sir," he said. "I was just shooting some horses. Them two got away."

"Okay," I said. "Where's the radio? I want to see if we can raise an evac for that kid."

"He's around here somewhere," Slats said. "But you ain't going to raise no evac unless a chopper flies over. You better wash that blood off. If that gets in an open cut and he had anything you'll catch it."

"Okay, listen, round up all these Yards and get back over to the river. I want to see about that kid."

We got hold of Yul and he gathered the patrol. Then we started for the river bank.

A few moments later we heard the sound of a helicopter. We ran to the river. Mike was already on the radio. "Army aircraft, army aircraft. This is Bolen Patrol, Bolen Patrol." He talked for the whole time while we watched the Huey track in the distance, all the way across the horizon without ever once answering. They must have had their radio turned off, or been on a different frequency. It was a clear line of sight transmission.

The kid was lying a little way down the bank in the shade of a bamboo clump. I walked down there to look at him. The pressure bandage was a bloodstained rag now. Mike had moved him into the shade of a bamboo clump and put his feet higher than his head. That's the accepted treatment for shock. But not for a bleeding head wound. It didn't matter. There was nothing we could do to save him. We watched him die by stages. He was breathing in short panting breaths now and his eyes were beginning to glaze. His skin turned waxy. The loincloth was turned back where he lay, exposing his genitals. I wanted to turn the loincloth back and allow him to die with at least that much dignity, but I didn't want to touch him. Like what he had was contagious. He was just a little kid.

"You better come back up here, sir," Slats said from behind me. "You ain't doin' yourself no good nor him either."

I looked around. Slats and Mike stood on the bank above me. Slat's shirt was off to catch the breeze. His chest was skinny and white in the sun. Most of the Yards were flaked out under the trees, smoking. Yul looked at me with something like contempt. *"Il est Bahnar,"* he said. *"Il est VC."* To him or any other Jarai this kid, any Bahnar, was just an animal to be hunted down and shot. Had the tables been reversed the kid would have felt the same about Yul. The two tribes had been trying to kill each other off for

61

centuries.

"Yeah, yeah!" I muttered. I started up the bank, passing behind the bamboo clump.

An automatic weapon cut loose.

I took the safety off my rifle and said, "What the hell was that?"

"That was an automatic weapon, sir," Slats replied sarcastically from his prone position in the dirt. Everybody on the bank was prone. I was the only one standing, hidden behind the bamboo tree.

"I know that," I said. "Was it the good guys or the bad guys?" I thought maybe we had some hunters in our outfit.

"It was the bad guys. They fired from across the river."

"Jesus Christ, sir," Mike said, "the rounds hit only six inches under our feet on the bank."

"I bet they was aiming at my chest," Slats said. "I'm sure glad he was a lousy shot."

Just for laughs I poked around the bamboo and squeezed off three fast six round bursts ranging along the river bank. Then I had to change magazines. The answering burst whistled by just over Slats' and Mike's heads. He hadn't seen me yet.

I walked backwards up the bank and over the slight rise that fell away from it, keeping the bamboo clump between me and the sniper. I called to Yul to follow me: *"Un groupe, suivez moi!"*

"Oui!" he called back, and motioned for one of the squad leaders to take his squad and follow me.

"Slats," I called. "I'm going back down to that bend in the river and try to sneak across using those rocks for cover. You lay down a base of fire to cover our crossing."

"You're going across down there?"

"Yeah," I said, crouching low and motioning to the squad. Once far enough back from the bank I could move undetected. But my squad just casually got up and strolled back. He must have seen them. Goddamn it. We moved rapidly parallel to the river to the crossing site. The Yards followed me without enthusiasm. We splashed across the river hidden behind big gray boulders, water burbling past. I could hear firing from back down the river.

Once on the other side I formed my eight Yards up in a skirmish line, and we moved through the woods. I assumed that he had seen us fall back and was bugging out in one direction or the other. The Yards moved all spread out about five meters behind, with me all alone out front.

I walked slowly through the woods, more exasperated than scared. I was mad at the Yards for leaving me in front by myself. I motioned but they would not come up. The woods that had seemed so lovely earlier did not seem so now. They were dark and sinister. I assumed the sniper had bugged out, but did he bug out in my direction or in the other direction? If he came my way I would probably not see him moving until he opened up. All I could do was hope he missed the first burst, because on the second burst of the engagement he would be dead.

But I was scared then, babe. Let me tell you I was scared. My heart was pounding, and my asshole was puckered so tight you couldn't drive a needle up it.

He must have gone the other way. We never saw him. I moved the squad past where we had tried to catch the three and into the village. We burned it out. Crossing back through the river I went into a chuckhole over my head and lost my map and ruined my cigarettes.

"Is the kid dead yet?" I asked when we got back. "The sniper bugged out."

"Yeah!" Mike said. "He's dead. You want to bury him?"

"We'll leave him for his own people to bury," I replied. "Leave the bandage on though. If nothing else they'll at least know we tried to help him."

Across the river I could hear the *whoooooooo* of a Bahnar noisemaker, a slitted section of bamboo whirled on a three foot rope. "They're calling the clan together," Mike said. "We getter get out of here. You know what these barbaric mothers would do if they caught you?"

"Same as the Apaches," I said. "Let's go!"

It took us two hours to get back to the campsite. We stayed west of the river most of the trip, on the Ankhe road. To get there we walked through one solid kilometer of scorched field that had punjis planted into it before it was burned. They were about eighteen inches long, angled into

63

the blackened earth, and razor sharp on the ends. There was one every eighteen inches in any direction. Even though we could see them, we picked up three more wounds.

That night there were no fires and there was no carefree chatter. Across the river we saw fires burning and heard the ghostly *whooooooo* of the bamboo whistles. The next morning we made it out of there. On the way we killed about twenty more water buffalo.

That's about all except it was four years before I could sleep without watching that boy die in technicolor, widescreen panavision and full stereophonic sound.

We came into camp directly, having met the trucks again up by Plei Mnang. It was just before supper and I dismissed the patrol without coment. Then I wandered into the Ops shack and threw down my rucksack, streaked now and covered with mud, and my still soggy patrol harness on top of that.

George sat behind his typewriter, clean and fresh, fat and sleek, with a stack of clean white paper on the left and a stack of final copy reports on the right. "Welcome back, sir," he said, "how'd it go?"

"So so. Cowboy around?" I asked, leaning on the railing.

"He went home early."

"How'd his intelligence gathering mission go?" I pushed my hat back on my head.

"He got a tip and set up an ambush on a trail down there. He said they ambushed a company."

"He only had a squad."

"Yeah, I know. They had to split up and bug out. They met back at the truck the following morning. But he swears they killed at least one Cong, probably more."

I nodded. "Sounds like fun," I said. "Sorry I missed it."

I bummed a cigarette off him and went over to the wash house to wash off the outer layer. I went to the mess hall, face still bearded and filthy, with my hands in my pockets. I was just beat and didn't care about anything.

The Old Man was eating. I made myself a Scotch and water and went and sat across from him.

"How'd it go?" he asked listlessly.

I told him. "I wasn't going to count the kid as a VC kill,"

I said. "But after his buddy opened up from across the river I guess it'd be okay."

He listened with a distracted air and when I had finished said nothing.

"You reckon that's all right?" I asked.

"Yeah," he said, "that's okay. Herb Hardy got killed yesterday."

I didn't know him well. The only time Hardy and I ever talked was one day coming back from Pleiku. Our chopper landed with some mail at his camp. Plei Do Lim. I remembered him as a tall, quiet, blond captain of impressive action and few words. A good man. He and the Old Man had been to both the Artillery and Special Forces schools together.

"How'd you find out?"

"The chopper crew that hauled his body out came in here today," he said. "They said it was one round through the head. He was dead before he hit the ground."

The Old Man sat there talking, staring straight ahead. He wasn't looking at me. I think he was talking to himself. "They're going to put him in for the DSC," he continued tonelessly. "It's funny. If he'd lived nothing he did out there would have ever come out. And now he's dead and they're going to put him in for the DSC."

I wondered what good it would do him. I wondered how many sons grow up without fathers but only a small bit of ribbon and gold to live up to.

I refilled the scotch and water. I didn't bathe that night. I didn't shave. I didn't go down to the MAAG compound. I sat in our mess hall and listened to Miles Davis's Porgy and Bess album. It is the saddest music I know. When that was played out, both sides, I played all three Joan Baez albums straight through, and then I started the whole thing again. I drank the whole time. It was one of those nights when no matter what you do you can't get drunk.

I sat there drinking one after the other, thinking about the kid out there and about Hardy, and Jim Brodt, and McIver and more people than I can count who have died for what they believe in. Even the Cong. Because it doesn't matter if you're mistaken, just if you're willing to stand up and die for it.

65

I felt pretty lousy and I thought, deciding it was time to get serious about this thing.

So I started thinking about ways and means, and I thought of some. Then Ken came in and put his hand on my shoulder and said, "Time to go to bed, sir. I'm going to shut off the generator." He had the M-79 slung over his shoulder.

"S'all right, Ken," I said. "I can go to bed now. I got it all figured out."

"What's that?" he said.

"Death wins all the battles, but life wins the war."

"That's very profound."

"That is an axiom," I said with upraised forefinger. "A corollary is that since everybody dies, the important thing is the manner of our dying and not necessarily the timing of it. In other words the important thing is to go down fighting, not to wait for death to come to you . . ."

"And a stitch in time saves nine. Go to bed, sir. I have to shut off the generator."

I stumbled off to bed, mumbling great philosophical thoughts.

I was still filthy the next morning, but after cleaning up I went looking for Cowboy. "Hey," I said when I found him, "the next time you go on one of your intelligence missions, how about taking me along?"

"Okay," he said, "when you want go?"

"How about day after tomorrow?"

"Okay, we go day after tomorrow."

7

There were thirteen of us in the three-quarter. Cowboy drove and I sat beside him slouched down in the front seat, left foot on the windshield, right foot propped into the gas can bracket. My AR-15 poked across the hood, while my eyes searched the mountains around us for VC ambushes. I didn't expect any. It was just a reflex by now. They can't ambush you if they don't know you are coming, and nobody but Cowboy and I knew about this trip until he alerted his squad that morning. Therefore no VC ambush was likely.

The road wound and wound down through the mountains until it broke out on a broad flat plain. Then it straightened out.

"Hey, Cowboy," I yelled over the wind. "When we get to District Headquarters, stop. I got to coordinate with the District Chief. We can't operate in this district unless we tell him."

"Okay, no sweat," he said.

We pulled up in front of the low bamboo Vietnamese structure and got out. The district chief was out and we had to talk with his assistant, a second lieutenant. Through Cowboy I told him where we were going to set up our ambush, making a vague wave at the map. I didn't want him to know too much. His headquarters was undoubtedly infiltrated.

He said that he had ambushes in that area himself and that I would have to set up mine here. He waved at the map an inch or two from where I had. I nodded and said sure we would, and I smiled and he smiled and we had coordinated.

"Let's get out of here," I said.

Once outside the building and heading back to the three-quarter Cowboy said, "We cannot go where you said. No VC there."

"We'll go where we bloody well want to."

"Ahhhhhh!" he replied and nodded. We got in the three-quarter and drove off.

We stopped at noon at a big village on the road. Cowboy asked me to go with him to the house of a friend of his. A notched log leaned against the porch for stairs. Cowboy scooted up it with ease. I lumbered after him in considerably less agile fashion.

The lady of the house asked us inside, and I ducked under the door. The effect inside was very pleasant. Away from the windows the light filtered softly through the bamboo walls. There was a square raised section in the middle of the floor that served as a fireplace, the smoke simply rising to the roof and slowly working its way out the thatch.

The lady of the house gave us a friendly smile and offered us the floor to sit on. I leaned my AR-15 up in the opposite corner and sat down too. He put his cowboy hat and wrap-around shades on the floor beside him. The split bamboo was resilient and pleasant to sit on.

"Where's your friend?" I asked.

"He work in fields now, come back soon." He dived into his pack and brought up a couple cans of C's and pulled his canteen out of the carrier. "Let's eat," he said.

I got out two small C ration cans, sliced ham and bread, and the little C ration can opener. The C's and a couple gulps of water make a pretty fair meal.

While we were eating, a little boy about six years old came in through the door. He was wearing four bracelets on his left arm, an anklet on each leg, an earring, and a Hopalong Cassidy T-shirt.

I said, "Hi, kid."

He ran and grabbed his mother's skirts, looking back over his shoulder in apprehension. I guess he'd never seen anybody that big or blond before.

I rooted around in my pack and came up with a can of cookies and cocoa. I got up and opened the can and tried to give it to the kid. He grabbed his mother's skirts again and buried his head in her legs. I gave one of the cookies to the kid. He took it and ran off, unsmiling.

I took the little envelope of cocoa and threw it back into my pack. Then I bent back the lid of the can and turned the edges under in a three way fold. That way you can use it as a cup without cutting your fingers on the edges. I gave it to her. Later she would probably weave a wicker holder for it and throw away the lid altogether. She smiled and nodded thanks.

I always feel like some kind of condescending jackass giving my castoffs to the Yards. But they take the gift as it is intended. They have marvelous dignity and never beg, but offer the hospitality of their homes, their food and their rice wine.

I went back over and sat down. "What time you think we ought to leave?" I asked. I was beginning to think his friend wasn't going to show up.

"'Bout four," he replied.

It was one-thirty. "Okay, listen," I said, "I'm going to flake out for awhile." I'd been up late the night before writing my patrol reports.

I awakened about three-thirty. Cowboy's friend had returned. He had changed into formal attire to meet the *Captaine*. He wore a loincloth and an old U.S. Army olive drab dress blouse. I supposed it had been lend lease to the French and from there to one of the Montagnard Battalions.

"Bonjour, Monsieur," I said.

He cut loose a tremendous stream of guttural French, which Cowboy interpreted to mean that he wanted me to join him in some rice wine. My mind skittered desperately at the prospect, but I assented.

He brought out the jug and set it on the floor. Then he took out the long straw, but he siphoned off the *numpai* into a couple of *Biere La Rue* bottles.

I tried to chug it all down at a gulp, not breathing during the process. I couldn't kill it at once, but had to try it again. Then I belched and smiled approval.

Naturally he offered more, but I informed him through Cowboy that I had a delicate stomach condition and could not continue. Then rather more forcefully than was necessary I said, "Let's get started, Cowboy."

His grin was like a baby wolf's. He got up and put on his wraparound shades, his cowboy hat low on his nose. Then he took out that greatest of all Southeast Asia status symbols, a Salem cigarette, and lit it. He held the filter in his teeth, James Dean fashion.

Once he got his image intact we walked out into the sunlight and went down the notched log.

The squad was good, handpicked without regard to rank or unit. Their faces were calm and their eyes were ready.

"Cowboy," I said, "how did you explain these soldiers to the village?"

"I tell them we go hunting."

I looked at Big Stoop with his front teeth out and his thirty caliber machine gun in his arms. "With that?"

"Oh! They know that the soldier must take what gun he have."

It seemed a poor cover to me, but the Montagnards are not used to questioning things. "Okay, let's go."

We went out the bamboo gate and past the long spiked fence, the defensive positions and punji stakes and watch towers and turned left to head back toward the rice fields.

Moving through the fields, we automatically took up a kind of loose diamond formation, although we still carried our weapons slung. Once across the field we moved into the woods and waited. I unslung my rifle and leaned against a tree. Most of the others did likewise. We faced outward into the trees, weapons ready. I lit a cigarette. After we had waited about ten minutes, I asked, "Any idea how soon he come?"

"Maybe ten more minute. He must wait so nobody know we go same."

"Uh huh."

Another cigarette later Cowboy's friend came across the fields carrying a Jarai ax for protective coloration. Once he was in the trees we grinned and shook hands all around. Then the point man moved out, then Cowboy's friend, Cowboy, me, and the rest of the squad.

The way was fairly rough and for the first kilometer I felt it. The woods were open and green and the light was golden. We crossed a fair sized stream, jumping from rock to rock, trying to keep our feet dry. I missed the last rock, slipped and

70

my right leg went in the water up to the knee, making me feel like a graceless fool in front of the Yards. That sort of thing never happened to John Wayne.

After we had gone about two kilometers, Cowboy's friend, the agent, pointed to the ground. I went up to look. There was a small trail, a path, really. It was covered with fine gray gravel and wound along a slight rise through the luminous green wood. It looked like a path I had imagined Hansel and Gretel taking when I was a kid, pretty in the day-time, but scary and dark at night.

"He says every day, almost, one squad VC come by here."

"They come by day or by night?"

"Sometimes day, sometimes night."

"Does he see them?"

"Sometimes. Sometimes they make greeting."

I thought that was jolly.

"This is not good place for ambush," Cowboy said.

"True. Let's get back away from the trail and walk along until we find a good place."

Cowboy nodded and gave instructions to the squad. Keeping the same order we set off through the woods moving parallel to the trail. The country was not good for ambushes. There was no commanding terrain. There was very little cover, but there were tall grass and some trees to hide behind. Finally we set up in the least ridiculous location.

Cowboy asked if I wanted to position the squad. "You are Captain. I must do as you order."

"You've set this thing up. As far as I'm concerned you're running the show. If I see something I don't like I'll let you know and we'll work it out."

Then I asked how he planned to set up.

"AR's on flanks, machine gun in middle. All spread out with maybe five meter between each and get cover."

Aside from the Automatic Rifles and the machine gun every man in the squad had either a grease gun or an M-1 carbine, all automatic weapons. Cowboy and I had AR-15's. It was a hell of a lot of fire power for thirteen men. We could take on anything up to a VC platoon with ease. Anything bigger than that was trouble.

I suggested to Cowboy that he put a one man outpost

behind us so we wouldn't have any unexpected callers coming in from that way. He agreed.

Cowboy placed each man in position behind the best cover he could find. We were pretty concealed by some tall grass. I chose a spot by a V-fork tree about fifteen feet from the trail and sat down cross-legged.

I took off my patrol harness and put it down on the ground in front of me. Then I opened the ammo pouches. I took a magazine out of both pouches and laid them on the open lids. That left them free to grab. I had two magazines taped together in a U on the weapon itself and eight more from the pouches, two hundred rounds in all. Then I unsnapped the snaps on the canteen carrier to avoid making the noise later in the night. The canteen itself was wrapped in a wool sock and would make no metallic noise against its cup when taken out.

Everything was ready. It was five-thirty. I opened a can of peaches with the P-38 and ate them with the dirty plastic spoon in my pocket. When I finished it was getting dark. I rammed the can into the ground, olive drab side up, so the bright metal of its inside would not show. Then I turned the selector switch on the AR-15 to full automatic and laid the weapon beside me.

You have to sit perfectly still and make no noise. None. So immediately you want a cigarette and you have to cough. Your throat starts to tickle and your nose itches. Your back aches, then your legs, then your shoulders, then your neck. When you do not react to this but continue to sit still, the mind casts about for thoughts to amuse itself and pass the hours.

The moon rose to our front.

I started to shake uncontrollably. It was not cold and I was not afraid. It was a flat rush of adrenalin and the sudden knowledge that the ambush would go. I have had the same feeling since, and it has failed, and sometimes I have not had it and scored. But this was the first time, and I was sure. Then the shaking passed and my mind was coldly detached.

My aching shoulders were hunkered for a long wait. I did not expect to see anything until three o'clock the next morning. The moon was high now, and full and gold in the blue sky with clouds turning to silver as they drifted across its face. The breeze rose and then died and the clouds flowed past the moon, and the black silhouettes of armed men were passing quickly, quietly, down the trail. I couldn't believe it. It was too easy. Not after crashing around in the brush for four months.

It had to be Village Defenders or the Civil Guard. My God, if it is Civil Guard, where'll we hide the bodies?

We were all firing. One faded from my sights. Tracers from the thirty caliber weapons were ricocheting so high I thought the Cong were sending up flares. I fired up one magazine and then another. I kept firing. We all did. I wanted nothing to live out there. I felt nothing, neither elation nor horror, just the cold astringent calm.

I fired up five magazines before I stopped. Then everybody stopped and I called out, "Cowboy, let's check the stiffs."

"Yes, sir."

We got up and moved onto the trail. The bodies were lying to the left, to the right, on the trail, cut down running, alive. There were six bodies in all. Three had moved through before we opened up and got away. Later we learned that another died in a village the following morning.

I moved from one dark shape to the other, making sure they were dead. I fired a round into the ground by each man to see if he would move. None did. Cowboy moved beside me, covering.

When we came to the last one I moved in on him and he raised up his arms extended, eyes wide. He had no weapon. I said, "Good, we got a pris . . ."

Cowboy stitched him up the middle with his AR-15. He didn't even twitch.

"Goddamn it," I said, "we could have got some good information from that guy."

"Sorry," said Cowboy. "I get, you know, excited."

Nothing to do but shrug it off. I said, "Get their weapons and packs and we'll move out."

Cowboy was looking fearfully down the trail. "Maybe better we just get weapons. Must move fast now."

That sounded okay. When we got a report that the

weapons had been picked up I said, "We'll come back for the packs tomorrow." Cowboy didn't say anything. He just started moving. He really wanted to get out of there.

We cut straight cross-country through the brush and the creek, moving quietly and taking no known trail. We were back in the village by ten o'clock and the villagers loaned us a half-completed longhouse to sleep in.

I hadn't brought a poncho because I expected to be all night in an ambush position and didn't want to be comfortable and go to sleep. One of the Yards had a spare poncho in the truck. He offered it to me. I declined. He insisted. I assented. I rolled up in the poncho and wished for a pillow. Never satisfied.

The next morning we hired some villagers to go with us to carry back the Cong's packs and equipment. The bodies still lay across the trail in their black shorty pajamas and their black sandals made from old truck tire treads. Rigor mortis had set in and ants marched in straight lines across their bodies. They were so stiff we had to cut most of the equipment off.

I wanted to take the stiffs back with the rest of the gear. I figured it would make quite a stir when we kicked them out in the front of the Ops shack. Cowboy pointed out that there was scarcely room for thirteen men, all those packs and six stiffs in the back of a three-quarter ton truck. Besides, it might make some of the boys a bit twitchy. I said okay and we left the bodies on the trail.

Back in the village we gave each of the porters ten piastres apiece, which is about twenty cents, and Cowboy slipped his buddy, the agent, one thousand in small bills when nobody was looking. Then we thanked everybody, shook hands, exchanged smiles, said *Bonjour*, and *Merci* a few times, jumped in the truck and drove off.

We had to stop at the District Headquarters and report. The lieutenant there was afraid we had ambushed his ambush, so I had to show him the VC equipment. Then he wanted to examine it. I told him sorry about that and we drove off.

There was no rush. We stopped for a beer in Cheo Reo and still made it to camp by noon.

8

"Cowboy," I said seriously, "I've been thinking." We turned off 14 to head down the last kilometer to camp.

"What, sir?"

"You reckon Luette could do some intelligence work for us when Albertson's in Saigon?"

"I will ask him," Cowboy replied. "He is very good intelligence agent."

"Fine," I said. "When we get in, tell Sergeant Stodgill these men are to get five hundred piastres apiece and a three day pass."

He nodded, grinning. "That is very good."

We pulled up in front of the Mess Hall and the squad vaulted over the side of the three-quarter. I was smiling when the Old Man came out of the Mess Hall. "How'd it go?" he asked.

"So so," I replied. "We killed six, took three weapons and all their packs and equipment."

"Wha-what?"

Ken Miller, who had been doing this for more years than anybody, came grinning up and shook my hand. "Congratulations, sir," he said.

Not that a kill of six was such a big deal, but to be managed at night, which the Cong theoretically rule, and for us to ambush them on one of their secret infiltration routes, that was good. I congratulate me. It was very good.

In a minute half the team was surrounding the truck, gawking at the Cong's packs and equipment, laughing and talking. Captain Mac said, "Let's get this stuff over in the supply room and lay it out on the counter."

The packs were almost identical. Each had a white tin box,

75

about the size of a cigar box, filled with medical supplies, mostly from East Germany. Each contained civilian clothes and a uniform, blue Czech beret, blue turtleneck sweater and grey uniform pants. There was some German 7.65 mm pistol ammo, a lot of Laotian money and some Vietnamese money. The best thing was a complete courier log and a list of contacts, with pictures. There was a lot of little stuff, too, fountain pens, watches, mess kits.

Bill Foody appropriated a small yellow button with Ho Chi Minh's picture on it and wore it proudly for the rest of the day.

After awhile I went over to the wash house. I was sleepy and stiff from trying to sleep on that cold hard bamboo. I felt more filthy than after a six day patrol. After six days you're used to it.

Then I was going to have a drink and a good lunch.

Before I finished, a Huey landed on the pad, sending up the usual shower of red dust, chickens scurrying around in the trenches. By the time I got on a clean pair of boots and beret, the Old Man had our visitors looking at the stuff we had brought in. His offhand manner indicated that it was an everyday occurrence. Practically all we ever did, as a matter of fact.

The American was Major Rick Buck, our B Team Commander from Pleiku. The Vietnamese were Colonel Lam Son, the Commander of the Vietnamese Special Forces, his XO and an aide, a Vietnamese first lieutenant.

Colonel Lam Son was a sharp looking officer. So were his XO and the aide.

Buck pranced around fingering the stuff. He wore a spit-shined shoulder holster with a forty-five and a British camouflage scarf. He had a scar running from his left ear all the way around to under his jaw. I think he got it in a car wreck, but his whole body was crisscrossed with scars from Korea. He had so many clusters on his Purple Heart that you have to look twice to see what it is.

His intelligence came from divine inspiration and his operations plans read like scenarios from old Mike Todd movies. He wanted to be a general, bad.

But for all his faults, if you held that one big brigadier

general's star on one side of him and started a firefight on the other, Buck would be off screaming and yelling to get in the fight.

Once at Fort Bragg, we were all getting ready to go out on a field exercise. It was during the '62 Cuban crisis. Buck sat in front of the supply room on his rucksack looking like a little boy that had just had his toy taken away from him.

"What's the matter, sir?" I said.

"I just came from the 82nd," he replied, "and now we're going to be screwing around in swamps in Georgia and the eighty-deuce is going to be in Cuba, killing people. It's not fair."

Buck was an intelligent man, without any common sense whatever, but he was a soldiering son-of-a-bitch.

"They must have been pretty important people," he was saying as I walked to the supply room.

"I think maybe regimental headquarters group, infiltrating separately." Colonel Lam Son spoke English very well, without accent, but some of his locutions were a trifle stilted.

His deputy, the Lieutenant Colonel, was leafing through the courier log. "Very interesting," he said. "They leave Hanoi ten days ago. That means they fly into Laos and walk, from very close to border. It is four months walk from Hanoi to here. I think maybe they very important people indeed."

Buck confiscated all the stuff to take back for intelligence evaluation and naturally we never did get a report on what it was. All intelligence in Vietnam flowed up, and none flowed down to the people who could use it. But the maps in Saigon were gorgeous.

Once our distinguished guests had finished pawing over my haul, Buck asked to see our mortar positions. As they were walking away Buck hung back for a moment and gave me an arch look. He reached under his shirt and brought out a stack of paper with a red bordered SECRET cover sheet over it.

"Take this somewhere and read it," he whispered to me.

"Yes sir," I whispered back and tiptoed off to the Mess Hall to read it while they made their inspection.

The helicopter crew was in the Mess Hall drinking coffee. "You guys had chow yet?" I asked.

77

"Nope," said the pilot, a first lieutenant. "When old Buck gets started he don't like to stop for chow or anything else."

It was about two o'clock, but I hadn't eaten yet either. "Hey Cookie," I called out. He came a minute later, followed by two of his sons, wiping their hands on their aprons. Cookie bowed two or three times very fast and treated me to an Ipana ad view of his rotting teeth. *"Oui, Mon Captaine."*

"How about making up a bunch of sandwiches, about two dozen, half bacon, lettuce and tomato, and half peanut butter and jelly, okay?"

He bowed three or four more times and scurried off, fluttering his hands at the sons. In a minute we could hear pots and pans clanging and banging in the kitchen.

"Sounds like you guys eat pretty good here," the co-pilot said. He was a Warrant Officer, a dewy-eyed kid who couldn't have been a day over nineteen. Compared to him Mike was an old man. It didn't matter. If he lasted out his year in Vietnam, he would go home with the dew off him, with a tightness around the eyes and mouth.

"It tastes all right," I replied, "but it's not too sanitary." I indicated a small brown bottle on the table. "Take some of those before you eat. It'll save you the trouble later." It was a combination of bicarb, charcoal and peppermint. For the past few days I had been stuffing them like popcorn, but I still had a small pain in the belly that wouldn't go away.

"Excuse me a minute," I said, "I've got to read this here highly classified document."

I read it but it didn't mean anything. It was just an intelligence resume of the possibilities of Chinese intervention. I had read a better documented estimate in *Time* the week before. Old Buck always gets hopped up on that stuff though. He had a Masters in Poli Sci. Besides he hoped the Chinks would come pouring over the border and he'd become a Major General overnight like George Custer. I couldn't read the whole thing. It seems an inflexible law that the more highly classified a document, the duller it is.

So I got a cup of coffee and sat talking to the crew. In a few minutes the distinguished guests and the Old Man came back. They were still talking, outdoing each other in an orgy of mutual congratulations and "We're All In This Together" camaraderie. I shoved the SECRET report in the front of my shirt, got up and joined them.

Watching the group, there was one brief instant when everyone's eyes were averted but Buck's. I whipped out the SECRET jazzer and handed it to him. His eyes bugged and he shoved it down the front of his shirt a millisecond before they looked back. Then a moment later he said, in an aside to me, "Did you catch the significance of that?"

It was my turn to look arch, and in a conspiratorial tone I answered, "Yes sir."

He gave me a look of smug self-satisfaction.

"Gentlemen," I said, "I understand you have not had an opportunity for lunch yet. We have nothing formal prepared, but there are coffee and sandwiches in the Mess Hall."

This pronouncement was greeted with enthusiasm, and except for the First Lieutenant who had wandered off somewhere, we all trooped into the Mess Hall.

Inside the guests attacked the platter of sandwiches that Cookie had prepared. I had another one and a cup of coffee. The talk turned to the implications of the intelligence net we were just beginning to organize. I was getting ready to put in my comment when there was a shout from the supply room across the street.

It was thin and far away and I don't think any of the VIP's heard it. At least no one's eyes flickered. Faintly, but distinctly, I made out the words: "Geddada heah, you sorry mutha fucka."

I rose. "Gentlemen," I said, "I must excuse myself for a second." I went across the street just in time to see the Vietnamese Lieutenant run out of the supply room with two suits of camouflage fatigues in his hands, the legs fluttering in the wake of his exit. I walked into the dim interior of the supply room. Slats stood barechested with his hands on his hips, his expression more disgusted than usual. Obviously he had caught the lieutenant stealing fatigues. I went over to chew him out for starting an international incident.

"Slats," I said, "did you just call that Vietnamese officer a sorry motherfucker?"

He favored me with one of his sardonic grins. "Oh no sir," he said, "I was just talking to Augie."

Augie stood over by the submachinegun rack with an equally sheepish grin.

"He looked pretty agitated," I said. "Could be he thought you were talking to him?"

"Could be, sir," Slattery said. "I can't help what he thinks."

I should have been angry, but I laughed. Slats has a habit of doing what everybody else would like to do but doesn't dare. I said, "Yeah! Yeah!" and left the supply room with my hands in my pockets.

The meeting was breaking up when I got back to the Mess Hall. The Old Man and I accompanied the visitors to the chopper and saw them off in a swirl of red dirt. Through the dust we got a genial wave from Buck. He peered at us from behind his dark glasses, but he had an AR-15 ready in his hands and before he was out of sight was already looking over the surrounding countryside for targets. He sure liked action.

The Old Man looked at me and I looked at him and we both grinned simultaneously at the impression we'd made. He slapped me on the back and said, "How about a beer?"

"Oh, very well," I replied. "Now that you mention it I could use a beer."

We walked back over to the Mess Hall.

I never thought about getting hit before Cowboy and I made the first ambush. After I saw how easily we did it to them, I realized how easily they could do it to us if they really wanted to. I began to think about it. At night I lay there, looking at the mosquito netting and thinking how easy it would be for one of the VC infiltrators to come by and lob a grenade over the side.

I took to laying the AR-15 beside the bunk so I could reach down and grab it. I lay there and thought about what course of action to take if a grenade did come over the side. The best thing I could think of was to reach down, grab the mattress and roll left off the bunk, using the mattress as a shield. If the Old Man was there I would yell, "Grenade!" The AR-15 was on the left so I would come down on top of it and come back up firing.

The pains in my stomach didn't get any better.

Nevertheless, the ambush made us all happy. I was happy, the Old Man was happy. Buck was happy.

Cowboy was probably happiest of all, because he had added another chapter to the Cowboy legend. There was no question that he was a super jungle fighter, but later as I got to know him better, and got to know other people who knew him, I realized the true extent of his ego. He was, for instance, not above shooting holes in his jeep when things were a little slow, and fabricating a story to match. At least so a sergeant in Pleiku told me.

And years later, I ran into a Captain at Fort Sill who had known him way back in his Chu Dron days. The captain had been a sergeant then, and said he had been out with Phillip when they had come upon a bunch of VC bathing in a stream. Naturally they shot them, but this captain said Phillip was literally jumping up and down on the bank, laughing his ass off, as he shot them with an automatic carbine.

He was really something, my friend Phillip, and it was a measure of my attitude at the time that I loved him like a brother.

Book Two

"The basic difference between
an ordinary man and a warrior is that
a warrior takes everything as a challenge
while an ordinary man takes everything as a
blessing or a curse."

— Don Juan
Tales of Power
by Carlos Castaneda

9

The night before they left on Operation Bat, Mike came in and sat down on the chair by the Old Man's desk, a little rickety affair, with just enough room for a stack of papers, some pencils and a pair of elbows. I was at my desk running through some supply requisitions trying to find out what had happened to our request for RUCKSACKS, INDIGENOUS (600). We had trained something on the order of three companies of Strikers for ourselves and for other camps, but we had no rucks to issue them. Everything else, but no rucksacks, one item you can't operate without for any length of time.

"Huh, what?" I said. Mike had said something, but I was so intent on the requisitions I hadn't noticed him. He was visibly nervous and his face was intent.

"I'm worried, sir, or to be more exact, I'm scared."

"What of?"

"I'm scared to go on this operation."

His face was drawn and worried in the dim light, drumming on his knee with his fingers.

"You tell the Old Man that?"

"What I told him, sir, I told him that I didn't want to go on Operation Bat, but if he asked me to I would."

"Well, you goin'?"

"Yes, sir."

"Think you'll make it back?"

"Oh probably," he said. "If we get overrun I can always make my way back by myself through the woods. Any of us could."

"If you live through the initial assault," I replied, grinning evilly.

"Well, you're sure cheerful." He looked shaken, then shook his head.

I laughed. "Don't worry," I said. "If the Old Man says you'll make it, then you'll make it. He's never let us down yet."

I said it, but I didn't believe it. Mike went away a little happier. I went back to my requisitions.

That night before we went to bed, the Old Man sat on his bunk for a long time. We all have our civilization-reminding gimmicks. For instance, I liked to wear sports shirts and Bermuda shorts around the camp on weekends. Well, the Old Man usually sleeps in silk pajamas. But this night he sat for a long time on the bunk in his underwear, the mosquito net rolled up above him, his stocky body tightened into a knot of apprehension.

"Something wrong?" I said.

He shook his head.

"I've figured this thing out from every angle," he said. "I know my men and I know my equipment, and I know the VC. There isn't any way it can't work."

"Good."

"But," he said, "what if I'm wrong? What if I've overlooked something?"

"Why then," I said, "you will lose **almost** all our truck transport, one company of Strike Force, get about four Americans killed, and, assuming you live through it, lose whatever chance you ever had of making Major, let alone Major General."

"We'll make it," he said. He grinned and lay back, let down the mosquito net and went immediately to sleep.

But I didn't go to sleep, not for a long time that night.

The next morning I stood out there in my starched, pressed fatigues and freshly oiled boots, watching the Old Man get things saddled up for Bat.

He wore the old camouflage bush hat he got in Thailand a couple of years before, and his .357 magnum. Mike wore an issue bush hat and a forty-five. Everybody was wearing big hats on this deal. The idea of riding had given an air of opulence to the operation. Bill had his Browning 9mm and

George and Pancho were wearing .357's like the Old Man's.

As usual the Yards were formed up across the street. They looked happier than normal because they were going to ride. Two trucks were drawn up to carry the troops and a third was loaded with chow, ammo, and demolitions. The three-quarter with the pedestal mount thirty cal. MG led the procession. And right after that the Old Man in an old jeep that he had mounted three-quarter tires on for more traction. Bill christened it Bigfoot the Jeep.

Just before they left the Old Man came over and we shook hands. "See you in a couple of weeks," he said.

"Yeah," I replied. "You take care of yourself, hear?"

He walked over to the odd-looking jeep and got in. "All right!" he called out. "Let's go!" He slipped in behind the three-quarter and they rolled out the gate looking like Okies going to California. "Good luck!" I called, "good luck!"

Thomas had been on the other side of the truck talking to Stodgill. He walked across the street and stepped into the shade of the porch beside me. "Reckon they'll make it?" he asked.

"If anybody can make it Crews McCulloch can," I said. "I just don't know if anybody can make it or not."

The convoy drove up the Ankhe road to the abandoned village of Plei Mnang, mostly torn down now to get uprights for the leper village. They drove through the site of our old Forward Operational Base, now a singed-out wreck surrounded by punji stakes the VC had put in after we had closed it out.

They didn't have any trouble at all until they got to the Li Piao river. It was almost dry and the three-quarter and the jeep went right across. The three big deuce and a halves had to be winched up out of the sand though. It was a steep grade, and very soft. They made thirty-eight of the sixty-three kilometers the first day.

The patrol was going so well the Old Man decided to settle in and patrol out around the convoy for a few days.

The day after that we started getting interesting messages back at Buon Beng. MADE CONTACT EST VC SQUAD, 2 VC WIA. FRIENDLY, CASUALTIES NONE. For the three days they were in that campsite they made contact about three times a day, and killed four VC.

"Here it comes," I told Thomas. "The Cong are gathering in battalion strength. They are going to try and wipe that convoy out."

Thomas shrugged. "Now take it easy, sir," he cautioned. "The VC are getting the worst of these little probes. Maybe they'll slack off for a while."

"That makes sense," I said, "or maybe they'll take their time, get an ambush really dug in and hit the column on the way back."

I wish I had been there. I couldn't get the time sequence right. I knew they got a herd of buffalo the first day. The Yards were ecstatic. For once they had all the meat they wanted.

"I shot one old bull," Bill said. "I hit him with two bursts, and he turned and charged me. I started to run away and tripped over a rock. Man, I just lay there for the longest time, it seemed like, while that old son of a bitch came at me. Finally he dropped dead, right at my feet."

The day after that a squad of Cong came into the woods by the camp. The Old Man and Mike led a charge into their faces and killed two. Mike took a punji stake in his right boot. It ran parallel to the bone for eight inches under the skin. He finished out the assault on the VC squad and came back to get it pulled out. It took Bill an hour to get it out without hurting the foot any more. After that Mike had to drive a truck. He couldn't walk much for over a week.

Bill told me this the night they got back, down at the MAAG Compound. This whole chapter was pieced together like that, over beer. "Mike got his truck stalled out. He tried for maybe ten minutes but it wouldn't kick over."

"So how'd you get it started?"

"The Old Man came up and fiddled under the hood for a second. Then he walked around to the front of that truck and talked to it real serious for a minute or two. Then he got in the cab, turned on the ignition and said, "You *will* start!" It kicked right over and we didn't have a bit more trouble with it for the rest of the patrol.

"You know what I think?" he said expectantly.

"What?" I asked.

"I think they were afraid of the Old Man."

"Who were?"

"The trucks."

After that short stay they made a straight shot into Plei Ta Nangle. It wasn't easy. Yards and Americans both worked hard tearing up VC roadblocks and repairing culverts. The roadblocks were hardwood trees at least two feet thick and over a hundred feet high, dropped across the right of way. Fifty or so Yards would get under one of them and wrench it off the ground, staggering and side-slipping to carry it out of the roadway. But they made it.

The patrol stayed in Plei Ta Nangle for two days, resting, having a few beers, and renewing old acquaintances with the Special Forces team there. The Yards spent most of their time fishing with hand grenades in the river. Dupont lures, they're called.

The night before they started back, in Plei Ta Nangle, Bill said, "I think we can make it back in three days, don't you sir?"

"No," the Old Man said. "It'll take at least five, most likely seven."

"To go back the way we came?" Bill asked, amazed.

The Old Man shook his head. "Figure it this way," he said, "the Cong watched us come all the way here. They didn't really have time to gather together in strength. They know the road by the river is blocked up ten times worse than the one we came up on, and they know we have to go back. They also know how many men we have and what equipment."

"And?"

"They expect us to go back the way we came. I think if we do we'll run into a dug-in VC battalion and get zapped. I don't think thirty percent of us would live through it."

"What are you going to do?" Bill asked. "Go to Ankhe and come back by way of Pleiku?"

"Nope," said the Old Man, "we're going to open the road back by the river."

"Sir," said Bill, "that's impossible."

"No, it's not," the Old Man replied, "I figured it out." And that settled that.

They found going back much harder than going out. The

terrain was much rougher, the trees thicker. The other side of the river was a haven for snipers and there were plenty of them. Half the force had to be out on reconnaissance patrols at all times and the road was so heavily interdicted that most trees had to be snatched out of the road bed by winches on the two and a halves. Where the trees were too rough to pull out or the culverts were too big to repair, the trucks were put in double low, four wheel granny and just by God went up the side of the mountain.

"We'd be standing on a hill, see," Bill said, "just dog tired, covered with sweat. The Old Man too. He did more physical labor than any other two men out there. The only thing that kept me going was I wasn't going to quit until he did. Anyhow we'd be standing there completely bushed and I'd say 'Sir, I think it's time to pack in today. The men are beat.' And he'd say"—and here Bill's voice dropped into an exaggeration of the Old Man's Missouri accent—"'Naw, I reckon we can make mebbe one more hill 'fore nightfall,' and off we'd go. We'd do it too."

The reopening of the Ankhe road was more of a psychological triumph than anything else. It was no problem for the Cong to close it again. But the ARVN Engineers had planned to take a battalion and spend a year opening it up and the Old Man had done it with one company in two weeks. Nonetheless it would have been a very successful patrol even it it hadn't been the first vehicular traffic over the road in ten years.

The Old Man also figured out how to sneak into a village and scarf up all the inhabitants, including any resident VC, without being detected, without firing a shot and without hurting anybody. And like all good new ideas it was so simple that everyone wondered why nobody had thought of it before.

It was one of those days on the march when everybody was beat out and the Old Man insisted that they make one more hill. After they had done that and were *really* beat he got hold of Nay Re and told him he wanted twelve volunteers for a night patrol.

Nay Re came back after a few minutes of perfunctory grousing around to inform the Old Man that he couldn't get

87

twelve men to volunteer.

Captain Mac told him that he would have twelve men, including him, Nay Re, ready to go on night patrol, or he, Captain McCulloch, would personally wring Nay Re's neck.

At seven-thirty there were twelve very frightened looking Yards, including Nay Re, lined up ready to go. The Old Man and Bill were ready to go with them.

The Old Man got them together with Kpa Doh and told them what they were going to do that night. Their round staring eyes were almost the only thing visible when he told them. It was turning into a very dark night.

As soon as the light faded enough they moved out, single file, Captain Mac in the lead. Nay Re followed him and Kpa Doh came after that. Foody brought up the rear. They wanted to arrive at the objective with everyone they started with.

Walking quietly, the long file of men crossed the river. Slowly, slowly they moved, water sloshing softly around the thighs of the Americans and the waists of the Montagnards. This was the most dangerous part. If anyone saw them going across the river the mission was blown. If someone out there had an automatic weapon, they'd be fifty percent dead.

Glimmers of moonlight shot back from the black waters rushing past their legs and on across to the shore a hundred meters away.

Then the sheltering black woods were seventy-five meters, fifty, ten meters away. *Schloop*, the water ran out of the Old Man's pants leg onto the slick mud bank. The squish of his boots sounded as loud to him as a tank tread clanking in the night. Slowly and carefully he moved, his pants legs now cold and heavy with the water they had absorbed. A Yard stepped on a branch and the resulting crack sounded like a felled redwood. He stopped. Nothing. They moved forward.

The Old Man moved slowly and cautiously. The long snake of men following him moved even more slowly and even more cautiously. He came across a trail, a thin ribbon of beaten dirt, running through the forest.

The Old Man's voice was low and hoarse. "Re, Kpa Doh, Bill Foody." In a moment they were beside him. He looked at his watch. It was 2018.

"Okay," he said. "We follow this trail until we see a camp-fire. Then we back off from the village until everybody goes to sleep. Then we come back and get them. Everybody understand?" They nodded that they did.

"Re, you explain it to your men."

Re nodded solemnly. He went back further in the column and called the squad together to explain what they were going to do. As soon as he had finished the Old Man heard two men break out in a violent coughing fit.

"These two men have cold, very sick."

"Funny they weren't sick before they knew what they were going to do." He motioned Bill up. "Bill, dose these men with GI Gin. We can't have any coughing."

Foody dug around in his pocket for the bottle of elixir of Turpin Hydrate. He made each of the coughing Yards take a good healthy swig. Then he nodded to the Old Man and the Old Man nodded back to him.

They set off again through the woods, the Old Man following the trail like a bird dog. The coughing broke out again.

When the Old Man got to the back of the file he said, "Okay, what's the trouble now?"

"GI Gin no work," Nay Re said.

"All right," the Old Man whispered, "leave these two men here on the trail. We'll pick them up in the morning when we come back this way." The eyes of the two men got very big indeed when they heard that.

The Old Man thought no more about it and plunged off once more into the dark. There was no more coughing.

They walked for forty-five minutes through the woods. Finally they could see campfires ahead through the trees, and hear the low gutturals of Montagnard conversation. He pushed the men back off about two hundred meters down the trail. They sat down on the trail. One of the Montagnards said something to his buddy beside him. Shortly thereafter he found the front of his shirt caught in a rigid grip and found himself eyeball to eyeball with the Old Man. There was no further conversation.

When the luminous dial of the Old Man's GI wristwatch showed twelve o'clock they were up and moving again.

It took them fifteen minutes to get back to the village. Again they walked quietly down the trail. The village itself had been abandoned, but the villagers stayed in the general vicinity continuing to farm their rice fields. There were forty or fifty of them, including men, women and children. They slept on straw mats under the trees and the Old Man could barely make out their forms as the patrol came into the clearing. The campfires burned very low, just a few embers glowing softly in the blackness. He stepped into the clearing and motioned for Re to come up. "Have the men scatter out through the village and cover the villagers so none of them get away."

Nay Re nodded.

"Okay," the Old Man went on. "Then build up the fire so we can see what's going on and we'll have ourselves a village."

Suddenly the Yards had become very adept at moving quietly. They fanned out through the village like professionals. The Old Man threw some more wood on the fire. He crouched down and blew on the embers to make the flames come up and in a moment the clearing was filled with a very respectable light. A few of the Bahnar on the ground started to stir.

"Tell them to get up and come in to the fire," the Old Man said, "and nobody'll be hurt."

Nay Re relayed the message to the villagers on the ground and they suddenly became very much awake. They looked around and saw the tiger-suited soldiers covering them. They did as they were told.

It was a complete village. Most of the young men were still there. They came out of the woods awake and staring, with the members of the patrol behind them, weapons ready. The men wore loincloths, and unlike the Yards who lived near Cheo Reo, none of them wore any cast-off Western style clothing. All the women were bare-breasted and barefooted, their only clothing black wraparound skirts. Little children wore nothing but rings and bracelets.

Bill looked them over carefully. They were all suffering from malnutrition, skinny and wan looking. There were a lot of open running sores and the body of one little girl was completely covered with a scab that made her look like she'd been fried in batter. The scabs were cracked where her limbs moved and the cracks were red.

He figured he'd have to wrap her up in bacitracin and bandages and keep her like that for about six months to heal her. Automatically his eyes flicked from one of the refugees to another, keeping tabs on their aches and pains.

One man tried to melt back in the crowd. Bill looked at him closely. He wore tire sandals and black shorty pajamas. They had not noticed him at first because he lacked the butch haircut the hard-core VC favor. His hair was as long and bushy as any Montagnard's there. "Sir," Bill called. "This one's a VC cadre. Grab him." The Cong looked wildly around, like he wanted to run. But there was no place to run. He relaxed.

"They don't work alone," the Old Man called. "Watch for another one."

Captain Mac started over to see what Bill had found. He grabbed the one VC cadre. Two of the members of the patrol came over and grabbed the Cong by an arm each. He gave them a very mournful look.

"Sir," Nay Re called out, "we find another one. He have carbine, but he no use."

"Right," the Old Man called back. "Get his gun and watch him."

They spent the rest of the night in the clearing with the villagers. The following morning they gathered everybody together and got ready to go.

"Okay," the Old Man said to Nay Re. "We go back up trail and pick up the two men we left."

"That okay," Nay Re said. "Cough heal up. They decide to come with us."

The Old Man grinned at that.

"Right," he said, "bring those two cadre up here. We want to keep a close watch on them."

Nay Re went away and few moments later brought back one of the two VC cadre they had captured.

"Where's the other one?" the Old Man asked.

"Oh, he run away," Nay Re said.

"Why didn't the guards stop him?"

"Oh, he run very fast."

91

"Then damn it, why didn't they shoot him?"

Nay Re looked startled, then hurt. "Sir, you say not to shoot man unless he have gun. This man have no gun. We take it away."

The Old Man shook his head.

10

While the Old Man and his bunch were out on patrol, Bob Reed and I got all the thatch bought and delivered to the leper village. Albertson delivered another batch of Bulgar wheat and Prell shampoo to the lepers. Training went on as usual, and we bit off a lot of fingernails waiting for the daily radio contacts.

About the third day of the second week they were out, Cowboy came into my office and said, "Three VC come in and watch flick last night."

"Beg pardon?" I said, looking up.

"Yes, they come in and watch movie. I think they come to check out defenses and I put my squad out to capture them by trench. But they no go to trench. They just watch movie and leave with everybody else."

"For God's sake, were they armed?"

"Maybe pistol, but no rifle. But they were VC. My men know them."

"Well, I'll be damned."

"I ask Nay Luette if he want to do intelligence for us. He say he like very much if Mister Albertson say okay."

"I already asked Albertson. He said it was okay."

About two days later Albertson and Luette appeared at the camp, and I got Luette off to the side. "Listen," I said, "Albertson's going to Saigon Friday. How about starting with the intelligence work on Saturday?"

"I think that is very good," he said.

My plans for Nay Luette were similar to my original ones for Cowboy. I envisioned him skulking around the province in his little green USOM Jeepster wagon, picking up rumors and rumors of rumors from the villages. You'd think a guy would learn after awhile.

"I want like Cowboy," Luette said, "three-quarter with machine gun and one squad security. Also for myself I want M-2 carbine and camouflage fatigue."

It didn't make sense to me that a guy would go out on weekends and run raids and ambushes on the VC and then drive around unprotected all week in a Jeep station wagon and expect not to get ambushed. But if he wanted to try it, it was all right with me. Maybe he knew something I didn't. After all, it was his country.

About ten o'clock the next day I looked up and saw the column of muddy, filthy vehicles from the Bat patrol roll in the front gate. The Old Man was in first and parked his little jeep with the big tires by the Ops shack. He got out, bearded and dirty as usual coming off patrol, and threw his gear down on the porch.

"Glad to see you back in one piece," I said.

He just grinned through the brush on his face and said, "Was there ever any doubt?"

The column of grimy trucks stopped in the street and the Yards started dropping off the back, throwing their packs down ahead of them. They wandered into the formation area, while the Americans got out of the cabs.

"I'll dismiss the troops," the Old Man said. "I want to tell them what a fine job they did and how hard they worked."

Then in an aside to me he said, "Fix up a bonus for the twelve men who went on the night patrol with Bill and me. They did lousy, but I want them eager to work at night. Then we'll see about making them good at it."

I nodded.

Bill and Mike appeared at the Old Man's elbow, bearded, dirty, in their grimy camouflage fatigues with pistols slung low, Mike's forty-five right-handed, Bill's Browning left-handed. Bill had his bush hat on and Mike was wearing an OD baseball cap, cocked way back on his head.

"Sir," Bill said, "do you mind if we don't shave until tomorrow? We want to dazzle the Maagots tonight."

The Old Man grinned. "Just as long as you shave first thing tomorrow morning," he said. "One more day won't hurt." He fingered his own beard. "But I've got to shave this thing off. Lord, how it itches."

"Yes sir." They turned and walked toward the wash house. "What do you say we go down to Cookie's after we leave the MAAG palace?" Mike said.

The Old Man looked at me and said, "Come with me, Jim, while I get cleaned up. I want to talk to you about something."

He dismissed the troops, then went to change clothes. He wrapped a towel around his waist and put on a pair of Japanese shower shoes. "I've been talking to the chief of that village we brought back," he said, "and I found out why they won't come out. I found out why your propaganda leaflets didn't work, why we can't burn them out and why we can't starve them out."

"Good," I said, "what's he say?"

He picked up his toilet kit. "Let's go over to the wash house."

I got up and followed him. He was tired. His shoulders slumped as much as those square muscular shoulders could slump. His feet dragged a little as we shuffled through the dust going across to the wash house. Bill and Mike had cleared out by then and he grabbed a tin washpan as we went in the door and filled it full of hot water from the tap. Then slowly and carefully he began to wash his hands.

"I asked the old chief of the village we captured why they wouldn't leave," he said. "I told him we had no quarrel with his people, but the VC made war on us and we had no choice but to hurt the people who grew food for the VC.

"You know, he didn't object. He said he understood and that was the way of people at war."

I sat on the bench, leaning back with my head on the corrugated metal walls and smoked a cigarette, nodding. "These folks are sure resigned," I said. "They've taken so much for so long they're resigned to anything. They don't even have the strength to resent it anymore."

"That's right," he said sadly. He had washed his face and was slowly soaking lather into his beard. "I asked him if his people liked the VC. He said no, they didn't like them or dislike them. They came and were something to put up with like the rains."

"If they don't like the VC," I said, "why don't they come out of the mountains? The government will give them land. Life is a hell of a lot better under the government than it is under the VC."

"I asked him that. He said, 'This is my land. This is my village. I like my village. I like my rice fields. I like my buffalo. I no change.'"

He looked at me sternly. "We can starve them. We can burn them out. We can shoot them. We can do anything we want with them, but the one thing we can't do is get them to move voluntarily. And if we herd them out at gunpoint they are as like as not to go back to the hills."

"Great," I said. I shook my head and slumped. "Just great. What you've told me is that we put in four months work for nothing, not just here, but the whole war in the central highlands has been for nothing. That we're either going to have to kill these people or abandon them to the VC. That's what it amounts to."

He hung his towel up on a nail, grabbed a cake of soap and got under the shower. He turned it on and then jumped to the side as it came scalding hot out of the fifty-five gallon drum with the heating element in it.

He had made the heating element himself, on one of those Saturday afternoons when everybody else was goofing off and he wandered around with a claw hammer, building things.

From the side he turned the mixer valve that let in the cold water from the drums above. He had installed the mixer valve too, figuring it out as he went along. When the temperature was right he edged slowly sideways into the stream of water. "Ahhhhhhhhhhh!" he said. He started soaping his armpits.

"You know," I said, "your face is sunburned everywhere but where the beard was and where the brim of your hat came down. It looks like you're wearing brown goggles."

"You're wrong," he said.

"Huh?"

"About that strategic hamlet program. It's worked fine in a lot of places. In fact it's worked fine everywhere it's been handled right and the people have been organized in place."

He gave me a significant look. "Get that, Jim, in place. That's the secret to the whole thing. These people aren't loyal to the government and they aren't loyal to the VC. The only thing they understand is the village, and I think as long as we organize them in place we've got it made."

"We organize them just like the Cong, huh?"

"Precisely, the Cong are winning the war because we've been fighting the problem instead of solving it. If we use VC techniques to fight this war we put ourselves even with them. They have no edge on us in technique anymore. And since we have the edge on them in materiel, we win. Because when the VC organize a tribe like the Bahnar, they can only take from them. But we can organize them the same way and give them what they need to survive."

I wanted to hug him. Old McCulloch had done it again. He had come up with a plan which would win the Vietnam war if implemented properly. The problem was to get it going in our area and then spread it around to the rest of the program. The great thing about it was that we could stop treating the people like shit and start treating them like people again. I don't think any of us on that team was ever cut out to be a marauder anyway.

"You figured out how you're going to do it yet?"

"I've given it a lot of thought in the last two days," he said. He reached up and turned down the cold water. Steam was rising off the floor and heating up the wash house. He had lathered so much he was wearing a soap suit and the water wa coursing down it in little rivulets. "I figure we operate with five man teams, a psy ops man, a medic, an intel special-ist, a civic action man, and a leader. They've all got to be either Bahnar or Bahnar speaking and they'll work in loin-cloths or black pajamas. No weapons except pistols for self-defense. We'll keep a company within three or four clicks of them to come if they need help."

I lit another cigarette. It tasted lousy. I put it out. "That sounds great. But do you really think after this Strike Force has been over two years up there looting and burning and shooting people that we can go up there and say, "Hey, fellas, we've changed our minds. We want to be friends."

He nodded. "We can if we go in with somebody from the

same village. And we've got refugees from several villages who want to go back to those villages."

"Sure," I said, "but they're afraid to go back, because the VC will kill them if they go and tell the villagers that life is better under the government."

"Right! But if our team goes in with them and there is help nearby and the man doesn't have to move into the village until the whole bunch of them is with him, then I think we can get some of them to go."

"Maybe you're right, but it's going to be a race against time. First you've got to get approval from Major Chi and then get approval from Colonel Leonard, organize your villagers and your five man teams and make contact with a couple of villages. Otherwise the whole thing will die when the next team comes in and that's just six weeks away."

He washed the last of the shampoo out of his hair and stepped out of the shower. "That's right," he said. "It's not going to be easy, but we'll do it. We've got to do it."

"Anyhow," I said, "Luette's going out Saturday to get the other southern district organized. That'll give us two out of three. If your plan works we'll be operationally effective throughout the province. If the next team exploits what we leave them, before they leave there won't be a single Cong left in Phu Bon."

"We ought to be hearing from the replacement team any day now," he said.

"Already have," I replied. "Team leader's Charlie Judge and the XO is Walt Swain. It looks like a damned good team. I've been gathering up stuff to send them. All our maps and patrol reports, operational summaries, and pictures of all the people and places. I'm going to write Walt a letter and give him all the information that doesn't go into reports."

The Old Man slipped his feet back into his shower shoes. "Well, Judge's had two trips to Laos and Swain was Rybat's XO in I Corps last year. That's more experience than we had."

"They'll need it," I said. "They'll need all the breaks they can get."

11

Saturday morning Nay Luette came out and picked up his squad and the truck. I was in the office working on the letter to Walt Swain when Nay Luette came in, all right angles; right angle cheekbones, right angle elbows, mournful and shy talking. "Sir, I have come to go for intelligence."

I got up and went to the supply room to get some ammo and a carbine for him. He was already wearing camouflage fatigues. His squad was alerted and they were hanging around under the trees across the street, waiting for him to get ready.

I wished him luck. He gave me a wistful smile and said with great precision in his soft voice, "I will try my best, sir." Then he walked at a funereal pace to the truck and drove away. He almost ran over the guard, going out the gate. Worst driver I ever saw.

I went back to my letter. With all of the reports and photos we were sending it made a stack about an inch and a half high. I started to proof it before sending it off. Walt and I had been friends since the Special Forces Officers Course at Fort Bragg, good friends. I liked him because he was a fine soldier and because he had the most sardonic sense of humor of anyone I have ever met.

Hey Old Walt,

I was glad to hear that you and Judge are bringing the team down to replace us. It's kind of hard to realize it's getting time to come home. We feel like we are just getting a toehold into the place.

We have racked up a little over thirty confirmed VC KIA since we arrived, although I think the number they have dragged off into the woods would make it maybe two-thirds more. That makes us high scoring team in II Corps now, and we're kind of proud of that.

Thirty is not a figure to awe the WW II vet, but it is pretty good for a Stage 2 insurgency. Also we have completely stopped the strike force from killing innocent civilians, which has more value in winning the people than stacking up Cong. I reckon that the most important thing, though, is the VC incident rate. The first month we were here the Cong committed over one hundred assassinations, kidnappings, arsons, and the like. Last month there were three. I have read that the Cong rule the night, but they don't rule it in Phu Bon province. Last month we ran over thirty ambushes, five of which scored, with over 17 VC KIA. Our best month so far. We have run almost as many ambushes this month, but so far have not killed any. The reason is they have quit moving at night. They are holed up. They are scared. If they poke their heads out again we'll zap them again.

We are running a counterinsurgency operation, but are using guerilla principles to do it. That is, we are operating out of our own safe area around Buon Beng and have the support of the people and from this we have intelligence. When the intelligence net is organized on down a little further south, we'll be able to take on company-sized units infiltrating Chu Dle Ya, but as it stands now both we and the Cong are working in Stage 2.

Not that the problem is by any means solved. In the Northern district we have no intelligence at all and are still crashing around in the woods. The Old Man has just come up with a new plan which may solve that. If it works I'll write you about it.

Another thing we are real proud of is that we have lost only two Strike Force KIA since we got here, and both of those were in the first month. For that reason Strike Force morale is high and these little Yards are beginning to believe they can do anything. Once they get to believe it they'll start to prove it.

These reports, maps and pictures will fill you in on the total picture. One thing I would suggest though, have your specialists write to their counterparts on our team. They can fill them in with more detail than I can about their particular areas of concern.

Good luck and love to Hilde and Kim.

As ever,
Jim

I crammed the letter and all the maps, reports and photographs into a huge manila envelope and threw it into the outgoing mail. Then I lit a cigarette and walked over to the Mess Hall.

Walt was a good friend, but it was still maddening to have to turn over our operation to him when we had spent two thirds of our tour putting it together and making it work. Theoretically the reason for the six month rotation policy was that living in the jungle was too hard on you and there was too much mental strain, some such crap as that. As for myself, I'd never been happier, and for that matter have never been as happy since, as I was those six months at Buon Beng. Never was I more in tune with myself and what I was doing. For four months I'd been involved in working on a problem so engrossing I'd forgotten all of mine. If there had been any way to stay there I'd have stayed forever.

Besides, no matter how good our replacements were, they were going to have a different style of operating and it was going to take them about four months to put it together, with only two months left to get good at it.

I was walking kind of slumped over because of the pain in my belly. Not that I was in agony or anything like that. It was just a small persistent pain centered around the breastbone. Most of the time I didn't even think about it. But the more I ate the worse it hurt, so I was losing weight fast. I went over to the Mess Hall and threw down a handful of the bicarb, charcoal, and peppermint pills. Then I had a cup of coffee and started looking through last week's *Time*. Work was piling up so fast there was never time to read anything but the book and movie reviews and the Vietnam section. Nothing of that ever seemed to concern us out in the sticks. The correspondents seemed to stay close to Saigon in case the government might change that day.

But Saigon was a world and many centuries away from

101

Phu Bon and most of the Bahnar had never heard of the Republic of Vietnam, let alone whoever happened to be premier on the morning shift that week.

I threw the *Time* down on the table, took a final sip of coffee and went back over to the Ops Shack.

The principal difference between Special Forces and the MAAG is that we managed to sandwich in some patrolling in spite of our administration.

I put the pencil in my mouth to chew on, rolled a sheet of paper into the typewriter and typed (letterhead) at the top, and then down and to the right typed (date). Down again and further to the left I typed SUBJECT: Monthly Operational Summary, and a little below that TO: U.S. Army Special Forces Vietnam; APO 40, U.S. Forces, and a little below that THRU: SF Det B-440, U.S. Forces. Then I skipped four lines and put:

I. GENERAL:

A. *Operations*: Operational effectiveness continued to expand. During this report period forces advised by this detachment have run one long range patrol of fourteen days duration and thirty-two ambushes, based on information gained from our intelligence net. These operations have resulted in four VC KIA plus the return to government control of seventy-eight refugees. Friendly casualties have been light. Fourteen Strike Force WIA and three USSF WIA.

The basic letter usually runs to about three pages, single spaced, and it took me almost four hours to do. I threw the draft in the drawer and decided to proof it Sunday. It wasn't due in Pleiku until Wednesday anyway. Normally I wouldn't have done the damned thing on a weekend except Cowboy and I wanted to go on an overnight ambush Monday and I didn't want to write the report while I was half asleep.

I got up to go back for more coffee. Anyway I wanted to read the Modern Living section and find out what a discotheque was.

Noon Sunday we were eating dinner. The field telephone in the Mess Hall rang and the Old Man reached back and picked it up. "Buon Beng, McCulloch," he said. He nodded four or five times to the anxious buzzing voice on the other end. The voice was low and I couldn't make out what was said, but it was agitated.

When the Old Man hung up there was some concern on his face. "It was Major Judah, Jim. He wants us to get to town right away. He won't say what it's about, just that it's important and that we've got some explaining to do."

"Okay, sir," I said, "let me get my hat and gun. I'll be right with you."

A moment later we were in the jeep, buzzing off toward the town. There was a three-quarter at the end of a big column of dust coming from the other way.

"Hey," I said, "that must be Luette coming back."

The Old Man braked the jeep to a stop and I waved. Luette's three-quarter roared by and stopped.

Luette jumped down from the cab of his truck and came toward us. His face was working and his forehead creased. His body was shaking with rage. The squad of strike force in the truck looked pretty grim too.

"Oh sir," he began, "that District Chief is very bad man. I have important VC prisoner. That District Chief take away from me. It is all for nothing. We work all night. Go in VC territory and it is all for nothing."

The Old Man placed a hand on his shoulder and said, "Luette, hold on a minute. Take it easy. Now just tell it slow, from start to finish."

Luette started talking. He'd start slow at first and then get excited again and start shouting. The Old Man slowed him down and the process would start over. The squad on the truck said nothing, but their expressions urged Luette on.

"We start out yesterday," Luette began, "to go for intelligence. But first I must do like you say and go to District Chief. Tell him that Major Chi say it is okay we get intelligence in his district. We go to District Headquarters to see Dai'Uy Dinh. He is there. He say okay we have come for intelligence. Then he say he have much good intelligence himself. He say he have VC prisoner with much good informations. I say, what information prisoner he have? He say are many VC hiding in village maybe eight kilometers from District Headquarters. This prisoner will take him to them

103

for capture, but District Chief say he no have enough men. He say he have company, but need two platoon for guard District Headquarters and whole company go on patrol, so he cannot go. I say, let me talk to prisoner. He say okay, so I talk. Prisoner tell me what is in village and everything. District Chief is too careful. I tell District Chief, if he let me have prisoner for guide I will go with just my squad. He say okay.

"Oh sir, we walk all night through many mountains and much dark. The woods are very thick and not much moon. Many times I think prisoner lies and he lead us to ambush. Many times I think maybe better we turn back. We just go on to where prisoner lead us.

"Maybe four o'clock in morning we come to small rice field. In field are two houses. We find two VC in houses. They have pistol and two small boxes with many paper. Other house is empty. Then we go back to District Headquarters.

"We get truck by gate and I give prisoner we use for guide back to guard at gate and start for Buon Beng. We are happy to have prisoner.

"We get back to just past Buon M'rok and behind come up District Chief very fast in jeep. He stop us and say give prisoners.

"I say no, we must take prisoner back to Buon Beng.

"District Chief say that he hear one prisoner have pistol. Can he see pistol. I give him pistol and he point it at me. He say now give me prisoner.

His man grab my arm. I shake arm and throw his man in dirt. My men in truck point gun at District Chief and say if he shoot me my men will kill him. I say he can have prisoner, but first I must give prisoner to you and you will give to Major Chi. Then I get in truck and we go.

"Must be that he radio to province and tell them that I come because they have roadblock by Major Chi's headquarters. He make me pull in compound. They take away prisoner, two box, with paper, everything. It is all for nothing. I have nothing to give you, sir."

He was close to tears.

"Well, that's it," the Boss said. "That's what Judah wants to see us about."

"Probably is," I nodded.

"Luette," the Old Man said, "it will be all right. You go on home and get cleaned up and have lunch. Come back this afternoon and we will talk. Now we must go to town and get straight with Major Chi."

Luette went, still glum and bitter.

"Let's go to town, Jim," the Old Man said to me.

We bolted for the jeep and roared off. I yelled over the wind, "That's all we need, a Mexican standoff between Luette and a District Chief in the middle of the road."

"Jim," the Old Man said, "no matter how we get out of this, from now on none of our intelligence agents goes out alone. At least one American goes also, preferably two. These Vietnamese officers will jack them around every time. An American can just tell him to go to hell, in a polite way, of course, and drive off."

"You're right," I replied. "I wouldn't have let him go out alone in the first place if I thought he was going to do anything but recruit agents."

"Well, from now on they always have an American," he said.

By that time we were at the MAAG compound.

Major Judah was waiting in his gorgeous office, surrounded by maps and acetate and tapping his shiny jungle boots on the floor. He was, as they say, grim-visaged.

"Sit down," he said, and we sat. He was, after all, a Major. "Now tell me," he said, "what is Albertson's interpreter doing out in one of your trucks with one of your squads, taking prisoners by force away from a Captain in the Vietnamese army?" His voice rose a little in pitch and volume along toward the last. "Chi is so mad he's about to blow a gasket."

The Old Man didn't blink. He gave Judah a level unperturbed look and said, "So am I."

Judah cooled off immediately. When two hundred pounds of granite Missouri cotton farmer gives you that ice blue stare, you cool off fast, Major or no Major.

"Now, sir," the Old Man said sternly, "perhaps you'd be good enough to give us Captain Dinh's version of the story and we will correct any errors of fact."

The story Judah relayed to us was quite different from the one we'd got from Luette. In Dinh's version he had organized the patrol, led it, and then at the last minute Luette had taken away the prisoners by force.

The Old Man said, "Well then, there's no problem."

Judah's eyes widened. This whole thing was placing a considerable strain on his equanimity. When I saw the Old Man was master of the situation I began to enjoy it.

"Everyone in the province knows that Captain Dinh is a liar, a thief and a coward. Not even Major Chi will believe, for a moment, that this man would expose himself to the danger of moving at night through VC territory with only a squad. He'll go along with Dinh for the record, and we'll have to share the credit for the capture with Dinh. But after all it was his prisoner who led Luette to the other VC. It should be a fairly simple process to smooth it over."

A lot of tension went out of Judah's face. "Give me a fifteen minute head start with Chi," he said, "then you two can come on down to his headquarters. I ought to have it pretty well fixed up by then. He can't afford to kick up too much bother. It would mar the credit for a capture of this importance."

"I thought this was quite a bit of fuss over two garden variety VC," the Old Man said. "Who were they?"

Major Judah paused in the doorway. He was just adjusting his baseball cap to the correct military angle. His mouth had the firm confident line cultivated by professional officers. His belt buckle gleamed over his flat belly and jungle boots glowed under his carefully creased fatigues. "One of them was a body guard. He was a Master Sergeant in the North Vietnamese Army."

We nodded.

"As for the other one," he went on, "the Viet Cong National Liberation Front has the country divided into six regions. This guy is the commissar of one of them. He is the equivalent of the governor of about eight states in the United States," he smiled. "He is also the most important VC prisoner captured in the last two years. That's why Dinh wanted to hog all the credit."

"Outstanding!" said the Old Man, beaming.

When the fifteen minutes had gone by we got up and wandered down to the sector headquarters, a large wide-based U-shaped building, yellow stucco. A yellow Vietnamese flag with the three red stripes stirred listlessly at the base of a crooked flagpole.

Vietnamese military, civilian cops and all sorts of people you never saw were now barging in and out of doors with sheaves of paper in their hands trying to look like they were at the center of action. The guards outside the prisoner's cell had been told they'd be shot if the prisoners escaped. Their eyes were huge. For a second I thought they might shoot us.

Major Judah and Major Chi stepped out of the Province Chief's office. Judah gave the Old Man a wink behind Chi's back. Chi treated us to a nervous smile.

We walked up and shook hands. "I think Major Chi understands the way things happened now," Major Judah said.

"Yes," said Major Chi. "I think maybe I move Dai'uy Dinh to another district where he will not cause so much trouble." He giggled. "I was confused. Suddenly comes my friend the USOM Interpreter with prisoners. In one of your trucks. It is very confusing. But all right now." His hands fluttered. "Come, I show you prisoner."

We walked over to the heavily guarded doorway. Inside was a hallway with two doors and more guards. We looked inside the doors. In one a Vietnamese was sitting. He had long hair and wore black pajamas. His nose was bleeding and his eye was puffy. He looked sullen and dejected.

"I see your interrogators have been at work," the Old Man said drily.

"Oh yes," said Major Chi, "we get many good informations."

The Old Man nodded. "You should get some pretty good stuff from the document chests, too."

"Document chests?" Major Chi said.

"Why yes," the Old Man said. "Captain Dinh took two document chests and a 7.65 millimeter pistol from Luette."

"Excuse me," said Major Chi, excitedly. "I think I must have long talk with *Dai 'uy* Dinh." He scurried off, skinny, slew-footed, fluttery, intelligent, and mad as hell.

107

"I think the *Dai 'uy* is going to have some more explaining to do," Captain Mac said.

"We should have hired somebody to shoot the son of a bitch three months ago," I muttered.

Major Judah pretended he didn't hear me. We started walking back up toward the MAAG compound. "Anyhow," he said, "I think the heat is off you guys for awhile."

"It is," Captain Mac said, "but we'll never have the same old cordial relations with Chi again. We have disturbed the even tenor of his war. He survives by not drawing attention to himself."

"It seems a funny kind of war where you get in trouble by succeeding," I said.

But I got to thinking about it later. When I was a kid, about eight years old, World War II ended. I didn't understand it. I couldn't remember when there hadn't been a war and I didn't know the idea was to get it over with. I was terribly disappointed. To me the war was maps in the evening paper and Keep 'em Flying posters and heroes, and it seemed a shame to end all that.

The Viets had been fighting for over twenty years, and for the ninety-eight percent on the bottom war is hell, but for the two percent on the top the war was a good deal. Winning the thing didn't fit into anybody's plans but the Congs' and the Americans'. There was no law against disturbing the peace in Vietnam, but we might get arrested for disturbing the war.

12

Five days after that the Old Man left on a long operation in the Chu Dle Ya area, our first venture into the high concentration VC area to the south. Down there they ran in Company and Battalion strength.

With the pressure of final reports building up and only three weeks remaining until our replacement detachment arrived it looked like my last prolonged patrol had passed. Captain Mac left me curled around a typewriter in a semifetal position. I planned to run a few night raids and ambushes while he was out though. There was a directive which stated that an officer would be in the camp at all times, but I figured I could afford to leave for periods of less than twenty-four hours and still cover any emergencies.

Before we could get out on one of these though, Mike brought in a message from the B team.

CONVOY OF STRIKE FORCE DEPENDENTS FROM ANKHE TO PLEI TA NANGLE AMBUSHED BY EST REINFORCED VC COMPANY. THIRTY FOUR STRIKE FORCE DEPENDENTS KIA, TWO USSF WIA, SEVENTEEN WEAPONS LOST INCL ONE THIRTY CAL MG, ONE M-79 GRENADE LAUNCHER, EST 25 VC KIA. ALL SF DEPENDENTS FRM YR AREA. WILL BE RETURNED BY HELICOPTER EST 1030. RTN ALL DECEASED TO VILLAGE FOR BURIAL.

HARPOON

"My God," I sighed, "those dirty sons of bitches."

For once all Mike's flippancy left him. He didn't say anything. He just nodded. I read it again.

That's real nice. They can't overrun Plei Ta Nangle so they

ambush a column of women and kids. That's what I liked about the war. It was run on such a clean set of rules. I sat there a moment brooding and then called, "Sergeant Stodgill."

"Yes sir."

"C'mere a minute." I grated the words through my teeth, forehead pressed into my hand.

George rolled in a minute later. I handed him the message. George has three kids. His face simply crumpled.

"I saw that bunch out on the Ankhe bus, sir," he said. "You know who was on it?"

"Women and kids."

"Wally's wife and kids were on that ride."

I sighed. "All right. Get a deuce and a half over to the chopper pad and a detail to help unload the bodies. It's not going to be nice, but it's got to be done."

George left and I could hear him calling the Strike Force Adjutant, a gargle of conversation and few moments later the grind of a two and a half moving slowly down the street.

"Anything I can do, sir?" Mike asked.

"You can do what I'm going to do," I muttered, grimly.

"What's that?"

"Kill all the Cong I can find before leaving here."

He nodded.

I sat at my desk and continued working on the After Action Report. There didn't seem to be anything else to do. It was about an hour later when I heard the helicopter in the distance. I got up and went out back, through the bunk area and jumped across the trench, walking on to the chopper pad. A half dozen Yards squatted in camouflage fatigues by the bed of the truck.

The helicopter appeared on the horizon, a huge cargo net slung under it, laden with the weight of the bodies. The pilot swung it over the chopper pad once to estimate the approach. I threw out a violet smoke grenade so he could judge the wind. The pilot swung around, came down through a cut in the tall trees and hovered about thirty feet over the pad. The cargo net hung twenty-five feet below that.

He came in lower and lower until the net made contact with the ground. The hook on the net worked something like a pair of ice tongs and came loose when touched down. The net collapsed over the bodies and the chopper swung away, out through a cut on the other side back toward Plei Ta Nangle.

It was hot as hell and the sickly sweet odor of death hung around the chopper pad. We all stood and looked at the bulging net for longer than necessary. "All right, all right," I bellowed. "Let's get this stuff loaded."

George started the truck, swung it around and backed it up to the bundle of corpses. The detail was tying handkerchiefs over their noses. I thought about doing it too, but decided it wouldn't help. The closer we got the worse it became. George knocked down the tailgate and a Yard and I undid the cargo net and laid it back.

The bodies were wrapped, thank God, in blankets or ponchos. They were neatly wrapped, tied at the neck, shoulders, knees, and ankles. They must have been wrapped fresh because blood had seeped through the wrapping, a sort of maroon on the gray blankets and black on the green ponchos.

They were new ponchos. I guess Plei Ta Nangle had plenty or they would have just used blankets. Our supply room was about out and I'd have liked to have had some of those ponchos. I picked up a small bundle, about thirty inches long, maybe forty, forty-five pounds, and swung it up to a Yard on the back of the truck. He took it and moved it to the front. They weren't heavy and except for the smell it was just like loading cement bags.

It took only five minutes or so to load the twelve bodies and we stepped away from the smell. George and I stood in the shade of the latrine, smoking and not saying much. Between the smell of the cigarette smoke and the smell of shit we got some of the smell of death out of our lungs.

Out back, on the other side of the Ops Shack I heard a woman crying and shrieking and looked around the corner of the latrine to see who it was. She was walking up and down the street carrying clothing that had belonged to someone. It was issue strike force clothing, so I guessed her husband had been killed and wondered how she found out about it. She was a tall, skinny woman about thirty-five

111

years old, bare-breasted, barefooted. Her hair hung disheveled over her shoulders. She threw her head back, uttered a long continuing howl and wandered off. Several other women followed along behind her, offering to help. She shrugged them off and turned, distraught, and went off again, shrieking. A combat boot dropped from her grasp. She let it lie in the dirt.

I felt sorry for her and slightly embarrassed by the public display of emotion.

We heard the sound of the chopper again as it swung in over the trees. This time when the net was dropped they swung in over to the side of the pad and landed, blasting the area with dirt. The crew swung down and flopped their arms and bent their knees in a few limbering-up exercises. It must have been a long day for them too. I walked over and introduced myself.

"We got to pick up our nets this time," the pilot said. "One more trip and we'll be through."

"How about letting me go with you?" I asked. "I'd like to find out how this thing happened."

"Sure, come on ahead."

"You guys want a Coke or something while you're here?"

"We'll pick one up at Plei Ta Nangle."

"Okay, just a minute. I got to tell that sergeant where I'm going."

By the time I came back the bodies were all loaded on the truck and the cargo nets were in the back of the chopper. All the way up I sat with my feet on them.

I strapped myself in to the red nylon seat. The rotor took a couple of slow turns, whining, and then started whipping around. Dust swirled and kicked up outside. George and the Yards turned their backs to us and bent over. Then they dropped away beneath the helicopter and we passed over the trees.

The chopper climbed fast to 3,500 and we were out of gunshot range. It was cold at that altitude. The wind whipped our clothing and made my eyes water. The chopper shook laterally, its body trying to counterrotate away from the rotor.

From altitude the country was Vietnam's usual green

gorgeous self. Only the one road was chopped out by the river and that was almost totally invisible. There was no sign that man existed except where the trees had been cleared for dry rice farming. What villages there were, were hidden in the trees.

It was hard to imagine what the tribespeople below thought of the war, even after these months. Most of them had never heard of Vietnam, they had never heard of Diem or Khanh, never heard of the Cong. Never heard of Communist China or America. All they knew was the Viet Minh came and told them how to protect themselves from us and in turn took rice. They told the tribespeople we were monsters, tyrants and killers and only wanted their death.

The ones who came out knew better, but there were so few of them. If the Old Man's plan worked it would be better.

The ground rose up beneath us, but the chopper wasn't descending. Then below was Plei Ta Nangle, high on a plateau over the river. A triangular fort on the old French pattern, with a wall instead of a trench. Harlow Stevens told me they built it that way because the ground was too rocky to dig into.

A yellow plume of smoke went up just outside the walls of the fort as we landed.

A three-quarter drove out from the main gate and came down to where we landed as the rotor slowly whined to a stop.

Behind that was a two and a half with the rest of the bodies. The three-quarter stopped on the green grass by the chopper and Harlow stepped out. Then the two and a half stopped and a detail got out to sling the last of the bodies.

"Hello, Harlow," I said. "How's it going?"

He gave me a sardonic grin. "It's been better."

Harlow is about my height, maybe six two, and weighs around two-twenty. He played college football somewhere on the west coast and the weight suits him. He's got a wild comic sense that finds some fun in almost anything. He was on the solemn side today, though.

We stood in a little knot beside the aircraft, he and I and the pilot and co-pilot of the chopper. The crew chief and door gunner were looking into little holes on the other side of the aircraft.

Harlow's team sergeant, Billy Waugh, came over, smiling a happy smile. It always materialized during disaster. He seemed always to lean forward like a starter on the block. "Sir," he said to Harlow, "the second company's going out tomorrow, with or without orders. Their objective is to bring back thirty-four heads."

Harlow nodded. "That's inhuman and barbaric and brutal," he said. "But I can't do anything about it. I'm only an advisor. You did advise them not to do it, didn't you?"

Waugh smiled some more and said, "Oh, yes, sir. I advised them most strongly against it. You mind if I go along?"

"Better not," Harlow said. "You guys want to come with me? I'll show you the trucks we got off the ambush."

We got in the three-quarter. Harlow drove through the main gate. The pilot and I squeezed in the front seat beside him. Sergeant Waugh and the co-pilot were in the back. "You knew Wally got it on this ambush, didn't you Jim?"

"No!" I said. "I figured about his kids, but I didn't know about Wally."

"Yeah," he said, "he was wounded in four places from grenade fragments, and he was down but still firing. The Cong swarmed the truck and shot him to death with his own forty-five. His wife had her head blown off by a grenade and the two girls were killed by small arms fire."

"I don't get it," I said, shaking my head. "The Cong use terror, sure. But usually they have sense to use it selectively. They haven't accomplished anything with this but to get the Strike Force mad at them. Like that thirty-four heads deal Sergeant Waugh was talking about."

We were driving down a long dirt road leading to an improvised junkyard. When we got there we got out and walked toward the trucks. Coming closer I saw bullet holes in the side. Some tires were blown and the sides riddled. The windshields were smashed by small arms fire. Harlow jumped up on one of the tires and looked down into the bed. There was a long trickle of dirty maroonish dried blood leading to one of the corners where the tire had blown and the truck collapsed. The corner was still red and wet.

"The way I figure it," Harlow said, "they didn't know it

114

was going to be dependents. There's only the one road from here to Ankhe and only the one road back. They must have seen the convoy go out and knew it would be coming back two or three days later. That gave them time to set up an ambush and they hacked us."

"Look here, they put a round through the engine block of this truck."

We jumped down and looked. Sure enough they had.

"Who were the Americans on this convoy?"

"Squires and Goble," he said. "They were on the second truck. The main force of the assault hit the third truck and that was the one with all the women and kids. Squires and Goble killed nine Cong between the two of them. The Strike Force got maybe fifteen or sixteen more. When they finally got out of the truck Squires had eight rounds left and Goble two."

"You guys want a Coke before you take that last load to Buon Beng?" Harlow asked.

The pilot looked at his watch. "I reckon we better be going if we're going to get the chopper back to Pleiku before dark."

Ten minutes later we took off with the last of the women and kids slung under the chopper. The smell of death still clung around the pad when we unloaded and I helped George throw the bodies on the truck after the Huey took off.

"Park this thing around under the trees away from camp," I said. "Put a guard on it and keep it in the shade until a detail can deliver the bodies home."

The woman was still shrieking and wailing out on the street as we crossed it. Her volume had diminished some though. And her entourage of assistant mourners was smaller. "I wish that woman would shut up," I said. "We've got to get some work done around here." Even as I said it I was aware it was a callous reaction, but I was choked up to here with death.

George went to get the truck moved. And I went to get ready for chow. But none of us ate much that night. Cookie couldn't figure out what was the matter. The smell clung around the chopper pad for days.

13

Cruising along in a jeep behind a deuce and a half is boring. So I cut out around the lead truck and hit the accelerator. I was laying myself wide open for ambush, but it takes a while for the Cong to set one up and we hadn't given any warning we were coming. It was fairly safe.

The Old Man's patrol down where the Cong were thick hadn't worked out too well for him. They had been ambushed and in the counterambush assault Bill Foody had had his leg shattered and been evacuated. Ken Miller had been shot in the hand. Not too badly, since he had beat out his own evac message with the wounded hand. We had been playing ambush and counterambush for almost six months, but these guys had got themselves in a real live battle.

Twenty miles later I found the Old Man and his patrol flaked out under some trees by the side of the road. I spun off onto a little side road and pulled up in front of Captain Mac. He lurched to his feet and came over. He had the stifflegged walk you always get when you've walked for hours and then rested for an hour or two. God, he was skinny, drawn, the creases of his face etched in and gray. His hat was propped on the back of his head and the rifle slung.

"Hello, Jim," he said, "you hear anything from the hospital? Bill going to be all right?"

I nodded. "They think so," I said. "He's going to lose a section of bone out of that leg, but he'll have a working ankle, maybe a lift in the shoe, but other than that he'll be okay. He says this has solved his problem. He's going to get out and finish up at the University of Maryland, and then go on to med school."

"That's good," the Old Man said. "I'm glad he's not hurt

any worse than that."

He swung in the truck beside me. "Where're the trucks?"

"Be along in about twenty minutes," I grinned. "I couldn't wait."

"Impatient XO," he said. "You hear from Buck?"

"Yeah, he's coming in tonight. The message didn't say what for. It was marked For Your Eyes Only. He oughta quit reading that James Bond stuff if he's going to take it seriously."

The Old Man smiled wanly. Five and a half months, seven days a week, twelve, sixteen hours a day without a break. He needed a rest.

"I sent for him," he said. "We have a problem. Maybe the worst problem Special Forces has had to face since we came into the country. The Yards are going to revolt."

I looked at him and reached for a cigarette. "They got a right," I said. "If anybody ever had a reason to revolt it's them. Only thing is it's liable to blow the whole war."

He propped his feet up on the hood of the jeep and pushed the hat down over his eyes. He scratched around some in his beard. "Figure it this way," he said, "the Yards are all that's holding the Central Highlands. Ninety percent of the population up here; most of the Special Forces camps strike forces, all the village defenders, almost all the Civil Guard. the Central Highlands is half the land area of Vietnam. The middle half. If the Yards stack arms it's lost. If it's lost the whole country is cut in half, and very likely there goes the old ball game."

"What are we going to do?" I asked.

"The first thing we're going to do is talk to Buck. Then I may take a little rest and recreation in Saigon and talk to Colonel Leonard. What else can we do? We can't stop it. Nobody can stop it but the Vietnamese. They have to start treating the Yards decently."

There was a grinding whine from the road behind us. "Here come the trucks," I said.

"Yeah, I'll go get the troops ready. Tell you about this deal when I get back."

I nodded. He got out of the truck stifflegged and stalked over to where the Yards lay under the trees, his rifle dangling

117

from his hand like a little stick. Tired and beat as he was, he was three times more man than anybody I ever saw before or since.

Over under the trees I could see Phin Getting up and the Old Man talking to him for a minute. Phin turned around and barked out a command and the troops fell in. The Old Man came back with the other Americans. They all had that tired look.

"Delucia," the Boss said, "you and Iten ride back on the two and a half. Sergeant Thomas and I will go with Captain Morris."

Thomas sprawled all over the back seat with his rifle in his arms and went immediately to sleep. I spun the jeep around in the road and headed for home. "How'd you find out about this revolt business?" I asked.

"Cowboy told me."

"Did, huh?" I looked at him and cocked an eye.

The Old Man shoved his hat down over his eyes again and threw his feet up on the hood. He laid his rifle in the bracket formed by his feet and his eyes started flicking from tree to tree.

"Yep," he said. "I've kind of had an idea that something was cooking for quite a while. You know Kpa Doh's got over fifty thousand p's in the safe. He's saving up to help finance this deal."

"Kpa Doh too? Who else is in on it?"

"Everybody," he said, "just everybody. Nay Mul is the figurehead for the Jarai, but the real Jarai leader is Luette. Cowboy is the liaison between the Jarai and Rhade tribes. There's a guy in Ban Me Thout named Y Bham. He and his family are the Rhade leaders and they seem to be the main people in the whole deal, but it's all the tribes that are under government control; Rhade, Jarai, Sedang, Koho, the free Bahnar, everybody."

I whistled in surprise. "They got it organized that tight?"

"Yeah!" he said in the same tired voice. "They want American backing. If they don't get it they've been in contact with the North Vietnamese."

"Jesus," I said, "you know the Americans can't back a deal like that. We've got to stay with the Vietnamese. There just isn't any choice. I'd love to support a Yard revolt. If we were free to operate without the Vietnamese we could have the Cong out of here in a month."

He gave me a tired grin. "It might take two," he said, "but not much more than that. If the Yards were fighting for the Americans instead of the South Vietnamese they'd run the Cong out just because the Cong are Vietnamese too. We wouldn't have to spend four months organizing an intelligence net. Everybody would be our intelligence net. The guerilla threat would evaporate."

"What are they after? Do they want to split from Vietnam and form their own country? That wouldn't work. They haven't the power to maintain it."

"No," he said, "nothing like that. They want a kind of semi-autonomy, but what it breaks down to is they want the same break everybody else gets. They want a better education. They want to be allowed to get a passport and leave the country if they so choose. They want more of the Province officials in the highlands to be chosen from the tribes rather than being ruled by lowland Vietnamese. They want semi-autonomous units within the Vietnamese army, recruited, trained and stationed in the highlands, and they want them officered by American Special Forces until they have sufficient trained people of their own to command the units.

"Get that, Jim. They specified they want green hats. They hate the Maagots. They think a Maagot is no better than a Viet. And they have some more demands that are mostly corollary to the ones I've outlined. And if they don't get them they're going to fight."

"It looks like they're going to have to fight then. I can't see the Viets promising any such thing."

"No," he said, shaking his head, "the demands are reasonable enough, but it's the face thing. The Viets can't agree to it. Making a Yard province chief would be like making a Negro the Grand Dragon of Alabama. It just isn't going to happen."

"Well, Coach," I said, "it looks like we're eye deep in it. When's this thing going to come off?"

"September or October," he said, "unless something can be done in the meantime. Our hands are tied at this level. We

119

can't make any promises. All we can do is go along with Saigon. I'm going to get out of here in about three days and report to Colonel Leonard. He'll have to take it from there to MACV and the Ambassador."

I wanted to talk more but the Old Man said, "I'm dirty and tired. You mind?"

"Nope. Go ahead."

A minute later he was asleep in the seat and I drove all the way into Buon Beng with the two of them like that, dead to the world.

When we drove in, Ken met us at the Ops Shack. "Got a message from Major Buck, sir," he said. "He won't be here for another couple of hours yet."

"Okay," the Old Man said, getting out and shouldering his rucksack. "I'm going to get cleaned up. Have Cookie fix chow for the Americans and lay on a meal for the Yards. Tell Phin when he comes in that his Company can have three days off. Then they'll go on alert."

"I'll tell Phin," I said. "Ken, see if you can get hold of Cookie."

The Old Man lurched off to his bunk to get a towel and I parked the jeep. Then I went over to the Mess Hall to see how Ken was doing with Cookie.

Cookie and all his sons fluttered around the Mess Hall, laying plates, getting out bread and butter. The stove was going in the back. I got myself a Coke and started making a peanut butter sandwich that I chased with four bicarb tablets. I walked around hunkered around the pain in my breastbone all the time now. Mostly I didn't think about it except when I ate.

Through the screen of the Mess Hall I watched the Old Man go across to the wash house in shower clogs, towel around his waist, a toilet kit in his hand. As soon as he'd had time to get good and wet I heard a helicopter in the distance. I turned on the PRC-10 and gave them a call. It was Buck. He was early. I said come on in, then went over to the supply room for a smoke grenade and on out to the chopper pad.

I threw the grenade and watched white smoke curl up. Then I went back and hid behind the latrine until the dust had died.

Buck bounced out alone. Right away the chopper wound up and took off so I got a good faceful of dirt anyway. I spat it out and threw him a salute. "Sir," I said, "good to see you."

"Hello, Morris," he said, grinning maniacally, "McCulloch back yet?"

"Yes, sir," I said. "He's getting cleaned up. Come on over to the Mess Hall and have a cup of coffee."

He grinned harder and his scar got red. "Got anything stronger?"

"Chivas?"

"Rog," he nodded.

We left for the Mess Hall. "Where'd your chopper go?"

"Back to Pleiku," he said. "I'm going to spend the night. Reckon you can find room?"

"Yes, sir," I grinned, "I'll give you my hammock and we'll find you a couple of trees just outside the perimeter."

"Nice guys, nice guys."

We went back over to the Mess Hall, and I poured a couple of Scotch and waters. We sat down facing each other across the table.

The Old Man came out of the shower, clean shaven, with a towel around his waist and waved. "Be with you in a minute," he called.

"Take your time," Buck called back, "anything up to three minutes."

He looked at me across the table. "Morris," he said, "you got a map?"

I had an old patrol map in my pocket, wrapped in a plastic bag. He pulled it out of my hand and motioned for me to come over and sit where I could see over his shoulder. I went around the table and stood behind him with my feet propped on a chair and the drink in my hand.

"What I wanted to see you and Mac about," he said, forgetting we had asked him to come, "is that I want this camp closed and you people moved out of here somewhere before your replacement team comes in." He waved his hand over about a hundred kilometers of territory.

"Sir," I said, "you gotta be kidding?"

Buck is not used to being questioned by subordinates. His eyes bored at me like the twin barrels of a shotgun, all that

121

easy-going banter gone. "Why," he said softly, with an edge in his voice, "do I have to be kidding?"

I wasn't in the habit of arguing with majors either, but when I know I'm right I don't back down from anybody. Not ever.

"First off, sir," I said, "we got three weeks before we leave. I can name a half dozen camps in the Corps area that were picked with inadequate reconnaissance and I can name casualties resulting from that. Plei Ta Nangle's one. They're up there on that high plateau with a fabulous defensive perimeter, but get shot at every time they go to the river for water. There's only one road out and one road in so that Cong know when they go they have to come back the same way. We had thirty-four women and kids killed a week ago just because of that.

"Now we don't know that area you pointed out. There's never been any VC reported in it and we've never patrolled it. But I can tell from that map that there's not enough water to support VC operations, so I don't think there's any tactical reason for going out there."

He opened his mouth to say something.

"Second," I said, "this camp has the highest incidence of VC kills in II Corps. That's because of our intelligence net and because we've got the roads to react fast to the intelligence. We go out there in the middle of the boondocks and we lose both. No roads and no villagers."

He pointed to the map and said, "Look here, Buon Mi Ga here, Buon Brieng here, Buon Beng here. We've got to spread these camps out. They're all concentrated in one area."

"Yessir," I said. "So are the Cong."

"This business of being right in town here," he said, "the concept is to set up in isolated areas and clear them. Your camp doesn't fit the concept."

I was close to shouting in his face. "The concept," I said, "goddamn it, sir. The reason this camp is successful is because of its location. Because of the intelligence and the road net. If the concept doesn't fit the facts we'd better change the concept. The bloody facts are a constant."

It broke. Buck smiled. These rough sons of bitches don't

respect you if you take unlimited shit off them. "Well," he said, "hmmmmm. You better run some preliminary recons out there just to see if you can find a good campsite. Maybe keep this as a main base and use that as an FOB."

That was as much give as he had in him. Hell, I knew why they wanted the camp closed. It was such a lousy place to inspect, with pig shit all over it. We'd drawn a lot of attention to ourselves because of operational success and all these field grade and general officers started coming out. They didn't want to inspect a camp in the middle of a filthy village. There's no way you can convince a conventional military thinker that the price of success in guerilla war is pig shit. They'll accept casualties, privation, hunger, death, destruction, murder and the CIA. But they won't accept unshined belt buckles and they damn sure won't accept pig shit.

Buck never mentioned the move to the Old Man, and when I told him about it later he just laughed. "Forget it," he said. "It's too late for that stuff now."

Cookie had chow on the table by the time the Old Man got over to the Ops Shack. Buck and I dived in with him. The team came in after a while. We talked about the revolt. The Old Man explained the whole thing to him from start to finish. Buck was as surprised as I had been, maybe more so. After all, he was an expert in International Relations, M.A. Georgetown '59.

We were still talking about it long after the rest of the team had discreetly left.

"Goddamn, I just can't get over it," Buck said. He had unbent to the point of taking off his scarf and shoulder holster and he sat there in an old suit of jungle fatigues like anybody else. "Here we are, a major and two captains out in the middle of the jungle and we get involved in a crisis of international diplomacy."

I guess he'd read history for so long he thought it only happened in books. He agreed that the Old Man should go to Saigon and report the matter.

The Old Man got on the courier flight for Nha Trang the next day. He took Khue with him to see if he could get him paid. I left for an overnight ambush the day after that. It was my twenty-seventh birthday, and all night I sat there beside the trail in the rain thinking, "It's my birthday, God. You gotta send some Cong down this trail." But he didn't.

Another week passed before the Old Man came back on the Caribou. The Viets had come out with an order promoting all lieutenants with over seven years in grade. Khue, our camp commander, was a captain.

They both jumped in the jeep and the Caribou started its run-up and swung around, almost blowing our berets off and vaulted back into the sky.

"Get paid, Dai'Uy?" I asked.

"Yes," he said, "Cap Mac, he make."

"Had to," said the Old Man. "He owed the Ops fund twenty thousand piastres. The Viets hadn't paid him for over a year."

I started the jeep and let out the clutch. It lurched a couple of times and we started bouncing over the dirt access road. "How'd you get the money?"

"I told them I was a personal friend of General Khanh."

"They believed that?"

"Yep, I got twenty thousand p's right here in my bag to prove it."

"How'd you make out on the other deal?"

"Tell you when we get back."

We drove the rest of the way in silence. When we got out of the jeep old Khue saluted the Old Man and said, "Thanks, Cap."

The Old Man nodded and returned the salute. Then we went into the Ops Shack and through the outer offices into the back. He flipped his bag open on his bed and started putting things away. It was good to see him come back. He must have got some rest, because he looked a lot more relaxed than he had when he left, but all those provisional bitter lines he'd had in his face when he left were permanent now.

"So how was it?"

"About like I expected," he said. "I'll tell you about it . . ."

It seemed strange to the Old Man to be walking down a solid corridor. The walls were white and lined with pictures of the generals and civilian secretaries in the U.S Army chain of command. Doors were neat affairs with brass knobs and crisp lettering on them. The tile floor was waxed and buffed in long gleaming semi-circular shimmers. The people coming out of the doors wore khakis and walked briskly with worried frowns on their faces. The long galloping gait of the mountains was out of place here, as were the Old Man's sweat stained fatigues and worn, scuffed boots. He had remembered to get a haircut just before leaving Cheo Reo, but somehow had forgotten to shine his belt buckle. All the people in the corridor had very shiny belt buckles.

Here it was, J-2, Order of Battle. He knocked on the door.

A voice said, "Come in!"

He opened the door.

The man behind the desk was a major in khakis. His haircut was as slick as a peeled onion on the sides, and there was only a little patch on top, like a divot. He wore two ribbons on his shirt, the National Defense Service Ribbon, and the Army Commendation Ribbon. "Ah, McCulloch," he said, "come in. Sit down. Now what's this about a revolt?"

The Old Man told him.

"Very interesting."

"What sort of action does your headquarters contemplate?" the Old Man asked.

"Well, of course," the Major said, "we'll have to check into it quite a bit further. Then we'll complete our report and refer it to the proper agency for handling."

"What is the proper agency?" the Old Man asked.

"That is not for me to determine," the Major said. "Actually this is rather out of my field." He gave a little laugh. "I'm not really sure who is in charge of preventing revolts."

Seeing that was all he was going to get, the Old Man excused himself and made his way down the gleaming corridor to another door. This was one he hated to do. He tried not to be obnoxious about it, but he was one of the biggest baby picture showers around. And he ached for Marge. Just to talk to her and see her let down all that bright red hair that nobody else ever saw except pinned back. But you don't risk your life to save people just to abandon them on the eve of success. He was going to stay in Vietnam.

"Captain," said the next Major, "I quite understand your concern but you see we already have officers in the correct grade, and with the correct schooling on requisition. If we accept your application for an inter-theater transfer it will throw the entire program out of kilter." The major leaned back in his swivel chair and put his fingers together forming a steeple. The swivel chair creaked as he turned. This one had the Combat Infantryman's Badge with star. Two wars, but it didn't make any difference in his thinking. "I'm sure you understand."

Sure, the Old Man understood. These people didn't realize that the Yards would only work with someone they trusted and it took a long time to earn that trust. Too long to change every six months. Now he knew for six months we had been fighting the wrong enemy. We had been trying to cure the disease by killing the patient. The real enemy was behind these doors, in the American bureaucracy, the communist state, any organization that saw people as interchangeable parts.

Ah well! At least you could get something decent to eat in this town.

The Old Man swung off down the corridor, heavy lug soles on his boots leaving small red clumps of dried mud on the gleaming wax. He walked strong, but tired, with a little bit of lope and a little bit of swagger, and the busy little clerks and the anxious staff officers looked at him with jealous suspicion as he passed out the door into the sun.

"To hell with it," he said, finishing the story. "I've had my fling. Now I'm going back to Oki, get in a line outfit and build me a career."

14

About a week after Captain Mac got back we knew his report had got to the proper authorities. Spies started showing up in camp. Cowboy came in the night before and told me they were coming. He came into the Mess Hall, and since he didn't like coffee I treated him to a San Miguel.

"Surete send out spies tomorrow," he said.

"How do you know that?"

"Malaria spray control crew land at airstrip this afternoon and go direct to Police Headquarters. Not even stop at Public Health."

"Great!"

The malaria spray crew arrived at camp the next morning, which was Saturday, at seven-thirty. No genuine malaria crew starts to work before ten o'clock, and none had ever worked on Saturday.

They swarmed over the camp, much brighter and more alert than any other malaria crew. Cowboy's security detail kept tabs on their progress. Their *modus operandi* was to go inside a longhouse, set down the spray can, whip out a notebook and start asking questions. Like, "Are you planning a revolt against the government?" The reply was duly entered in the notebook and, usually forgetting to spray the hut, the spy departed.

When the Old Man and I drove to town that day there was a truck sitting by the intersection of the road leading to camp and Highway 14. A little Viet in a yellow hat sat there with notebook and pencil taking down the bumper numbers of all vehicles leaving the camp.

They left as suddenly as they came.

The next day Cowboy came into the office and said,

127

"Police arrest Luette this morning."

"What for?"

"For question, I think. But they come for me this afternoon. You mind if I take couple days off? Maybe go to Pleiku?"

"Sure, go ahead. Stay as long as you have to. You got anybody in camp that can go between with your agents? Otherwise we'll have to cancel Thursday's ambush."

He named a man in the squad that the agents might trust and I told him to take off.

"You take care of my wife and little girl?" he said before leaving.

"Sure. They'll be safe. You go on and don't worry. I'll see if I can spring Luette, too."

"Don't worry about Luette," he said. "He will get free somehow."

About noon one of the white hatted Viet police came out and inquired into Cowboy's whereabouts. I told him I didn't know where he was, that he was on leave and that I didn't know when he was coming back, or if he was coming back. I softened the blow by letting him scrounge a full tank out of our gas dump. He went away more or less content.

A little later Luette came out in the USOM Jeepster. For once he looked fairly happy. I guess for Luette hoodwinking the Vietnamese National Police was a sort of nostalgic enterprise.

I was in the office when he found me.

"How'd you get sprung?" I asked.

"I tell them," he said, "if they no let me go Mister Albertson will come and take away all their money for police and they never get paid again."

"I guess they didn't keep you long in jail then?"

"Not after I say that. They let me go fast."

"So what can I do for you?"

"VC send note they will kill me. Now maybe Surete send man to kill me too. I wonder if maybe I can borrow pistol?"

"Okay," I said, "but why don't you move into the camp here? Then you won't have to worry about being assassinated."

"No," he said, "I will stay in my house. I only want to

borrow pistol."

I got him my issue forty-five. I never wore it anyway, because it was about half again as heavy as my personal weapon and besides I wasn't used to the way it fired. Luette thanked me, went back out to his little green jeep wagon and took off.

God, he was a lousy driver. He almost ran over the gate guard again.

Stodgill was sitting out in the front office up to his eyes in paper. On the left he had a stack of blank paper and on the right a stack of typed paper and in the middle my rough drafts of reports, full of x's and strikeovers, improper spacing and wrong headings. He was blasting away on the typewriter. It sounded like Thompson day on the small-arms range.

I sighed, leaned on the railing and fumbled around in my pocket for a cigarette.

George stopped typing and took a sip of cold coffee. "What was that all about?" he asked.

"Luette," I said. "He's on the Cong's hit list and the Surete's hit list. For all I know he's on everybody's hit list but maybe Captain Midnight's Secret Squadron's. Anyhow I loaned him my pistol."

George held out two fingers. I dropped a cigarette in them and lit it with my farewell gift lighter from the Fort Dix Marksmanship Committee. "What good's that going to do?" he asked.

"Make him feel secure, I guess."

"By God, if there was two different sides of a war out to assassinate me it'd take more than a pistol to make me feel secure."

"Reckon he's used to it."

A few days later an L-20 buzzed the camp. George took the jeep down and got the passenger. He was a civilian, masquerading as a cultural anthropologist. He told the Old Man he wanted to talk about something. They got up and walked across the street to the office. "Take a seat," the Old Man said. The visitor sat down behind my desk and the Old Man sat down behind his, shoving the chair between his legs backwards and leaning on the back.

129

"You've come to talk about the revolt," he said.

The visitor looked startled, but nodded.

The Old Man laid it out again. By this time his spiel was almost memorized.

The visitor took out a cigar, stripped off the cellophane, licked it and stuck it in his mouth. Then, carefully and precisely, he lit it. "Captain," he said, "we started checking your story because we had similar reports from MAAG and USOM. We traced the MAAG report back to the detachment in Cheo Reo and the USOM report to John Albertson. They got it from you. Just to make sure we put your camp under surveillance. Our agents report no evidence of a build-up for a revolt.

"Now, Captain, what I want to know is, what do you hope to gain by fabricating this story?"

The Old Man stood up. "The interview," he said, "is terminated. You will be escorted from Buon Beng by my Executive Officer and you will not be permitted to return."

He led our visitor back to the Mess Hall and told me what he wanted and why he wanted it.

"Come with me please," I said. We got in the jeep and drove down to the airstrip.

The pilot was squatting on his haunches in the shade of the wing. I helped our guest with his bag and he got on the aircraft. Then I went back and sat in the jeep until he taxied to the end of the strip, made his run-up and took off. They winged away low over the treetops, never to return.

I waved. "So long, Double-oh-seven!" I called.

For me the rest was just putting it down on paper. The Old Man organized his eight man group and trained them to go into the villages in the Bahnar area. He took them up one time and they made contact with the village chief of one of the refugee's villages.

He intended to go back and make contact with the old chief again before we left. But he was called to Pleiku for a Commanders' conference and some other stuff came up. The little time we had left slipped away and one day an airplane landed at the Cheo Reo airstrip with Judge's team on it. It was time to go home.

15

I sat hunched over the wheel, three-quarter parked on slick red mud. Heat shimmers danced off the pierced-steel planking hardstand in front of us. The somnolent guard moped around the fifty-five gallon drums of Avgas, just as he had on the day we arrived six months before. He was wearing a poncho because the rainy season had begun.

Dark gray clouds hung down to the mountaintops around us and away off in the distance I could hear the sound of the C-123 bringing in Judge's team. The Old Man was parked beside me in the jeep and across the hardstand John Watson had a detail of Yards waiting in the two and a half to unload their boxes. We waited for the 123 to break through the clouds.

I couldn't help but think about the all-American boy I'd been when we bounced off the C-47 that brought us in here. In six months we'd learned to kill people calmly and with precision. And had learned to care for the Jarai.

That was what we were worried about. We did not want to see everything we worked for flushed down the drain and we did not want the Jarai nation to go Cong. The revolt was sure to backfire and repressive measures by the Vietnamese were very likely to drive all the tribes the other way. The Army wouldn't let us stay, but at least we could pass on a functional operation to our successors.

But it was such a delicate thing, built on such a shaky pyramid of personal friendship. The wrong word on anybody's part could blow the intelligence net. Without that they'd be back walking the woods waiting to be ambushed again. Not to mention the Old Man's plan for Bahnar. I didn't know if anybody but him could bring it off.

131

It had to be somebody with the right combination of courage and sagacity, somebody the Yards respected. But how many people can gain that kind of respect in an alien culture? There were too many ifs. I swung down out of the cab and walked over to where the Old Man sat waiting in his jeep.

"Well," I said, "if anybody can take over this kind of operation Swain can. He's worked an intelligence net before in I Corps."

"Unh!" the Old Man said.

I lit a cigarette, nervously broke the match into twelve pieces and started grinding them into the dirt. The Old Man sat there not saying anything. Didn't move either. The droning grew louder. The 123 dropped out of the clouds and made a neat three-sided square around the airstrip. She dropped straight in on the runway and the sound rose as her props reversed. The pilot let her run out the length of the strip, then turned around and came back to the PSP hardstand. He made one neat pivot, revving one engine and stopping the other. Water in the puddles around the hardstand jumped, red with mud. We almost lost our berets in the spray. Then it stopped. The side doors popped open and the tailgate whined down horizontal.

John Watson started the deuce and a half, backing it up to the tailgate. Judge's people came off the airplane. He and Swain dropped out of one of the side doors. Sergeants boiled off the tailgate. Their jungle boots were spitshined and there was a gleam of starch in their fatigues. The Special Forces, Vietnam flashes on their hats were brand new. They all wore store-bought green T-shirts instead of the home dyed jobs that we had.

Charlie Judge was a little guy and he walked with that packed down tightness that hypertense little guys have. He chewed on a little cigar and a little pistol hung in a shoulder holster under his left armpit. An S&W .38, I think.

Walt Swain, blond and handsome, carbine dangling from his hand, loped over. His shoulders were hunched a little bit and his eyes were already scoping out the terrain. That guy was made for combat.

"Hello, good buddy," I said.

132

"The large, pink Dai'Uy," he replied. "God, you're a skinny son of a bitch."

He stopped and leaned on the front of the three-quarter. "Glad to be going home, Jim?"

"Not really, Walt," I replied, shaking my head. "But we're tired, man. There's no question about that.

"Listen, you and your NCO's go back with me in the truck here. Captain Judge can ride out with the Old Man and Watson'll bring your boxes in the deuce and a half."

"Okay," he said. He went to tell their team sergeant what the drill was. Judge got in the jeep with the Old Man and they drove off. A moment later Walt was back up in the cab with me. Six of his NCO's hopped in back of the three-quarter. The rest were waiting around to go out with the deuce and a half.

I started the truck and turned her around on the PSP, starting back up on the red mud road, the old truck slewing in the slippery ruts. It whined and straightened out as we hit the highway going through town.

"Town's growing," I said. "That Esso pump in the marketplace just went in here last month."

"Tell me about your operation," he said. "We've heard a lot of good things about it all the way from Oki to here."

"The Old Man has a complete briefing laid on for after chow," I said. "Then we've got an orientation patrol planned for the day after tomorrow. It'll probably be a five-day. We've had our eye on an infiltration route about thirty clicks south of here and with any luck at all we can ambush a company."

As soon as we dumped off their bags Walt and Judge and the Old Man and I went into the Ops shack. The Old Man drew off the target cloth that masked the map.

"To the south," he said, "is the high concentration VC area, known as Chu Dle Ya. We have run operations in it, and they have been successful to a degree. But our greatest success has been in the interception of VC detachments infiltrating the area." He whacked the map with a yardstick he was using for a pointer.

"To get into the area they have to cross either highway fourteen on the west or highway seven on the east. These

133

highways are lined up solid with strategic hamlets and the Cong have to pass through their rice fields. We have agents in almost every village and once the VC set a pattern we can ambush their infiltration routes.

"It's not as easy as it sounds, because it takes anywhere from two to six weeks to set up the ambush, and once a route is compromised they immediately close it down. But they are afraid to move at night now, and their activities have been drastically curtailed."

Walt nodded. This was the kind of deal he understood. Judge sat there with his right ankle crossed over his left knee, blowing smoke around his little cigar. He looked skeptical. I was anxious, hoping they'd understand how it worked.

"We have this other area to the north which works completely differently. When we started we were working a standard food denial program, burning out everything we could find, trying to get the people to come out of the woods and settle in the strategic hamlets. The thing is, though, they are just as stubborn as hillbillies anywhere. They'd rather starve than come out. So now we're trying to organize them in place."

The Old Man explained his plan, that it had approval from everybody from the ambassador on down.

Judge puffed on his cigar one more time and said, "So the shootin' and lootin's all over, huh?" He sounded kind of disappointed.

That was his first comment during the briefing.

"How about camp defense?" Walt inquired.

"Frankly," the Old Man said, "it could be a lot better. We were told to prepare to move within thirty days when we arrived and it's been put off thirty days every month since. We didn't want to get involved in something we couldn't finish so we've concentrated on operations."

"I think," Judge said, "that we'll probably spend the first month or so improving the perimeter, getting out more claymores and so on. This camp doesn't look secure to me."

I was alarmed; the operation would fall apart without momentum. "Physically it's not," I said. "But all these villages around here provide the best kind of early warning net. If you just build and don't operate you'll find that security disappearing, and the intelligence net will fold on you. It's got to be greased with money and an occasional personal appearance or the Yards will lose faith in us."

He didn't say anything, but didn't look like he considered it any great loss.

Then the Old Man filled them in on the revolt. They had got the bare bones of it in Nha Trang, but they were glad to hear all the details.

"When's this deal going to come off?" Judge asked.

"October or November," the Old Man said. "The Yards haven't decided yet."

"Looks like an eventful six months."

After the briefing I got the Old Man off to the side. "Sir," I said, "he's gonna throw the whole thing away. The intelligence net, your plan for the Bahnar, everything. They're just not buying anything we've built up here."

"Yeah, I know it," he said. "We need a good orientation patrol. One success to show them how it works. They may not buy it, and even if they do they may not be able to make it work for them. But we've got to try."

The Old Man and I gave Walt and Judge our bunks so I woke up the next morning in the supply room surrounded by M-3 submachine guns and fifty kilogram burlap bags of rice. The smell of the burlap and of rifle oil and the high bamboo sides of the supply room made me wonder for a moment where I was. Then I sat up broodingly and looked at the vast pile of my gear in front of me. It was packing day.

In the dim supply room the slick nylon feel of the camouflage poncho liner I had used for a blanket was cool on my bare legs. I slid my feet into a pair of Japanese shower thongs and brooded more. My watch showed seven-thirty, the middle of the day, and here I was in my underwear. Aw, what the hell. We were going home anyway. I'd have to give Walt my AR-15 and pack up that pile of stuff, right after this one more orientation patrol.

There was a wide square of light over the counter by the door. I could hear Slats in his little cubby behind me sputtering and sawing in his sleep. Then the light over the counter was cut off. I looked up. It was the Old Man, quiet as always, but there was enough tension in the way he held himself to show he was excited.

"Get dressed!" he said. "One of Luette's agents walked all night to get here. He's got some VC primed for an ambush. You've got to hurry. It's thirty clicks south of here and the ambush is for noon."

I grinned incredulously. "You're going to let me take it?"

He smiled. "It's your Intel net," he said. "Besides, Judge and I have to meet the Province Chief today."

"Yes sir," I said, "would you get Swain up and tell him to pick whatever troops he needs. He knows what the requirements are."

"I figure," said the Old Man, "that you have to get out of here in half an hour to get set up in time."

"SLATTERY!" I yelled.

"Huh, whazza?"

I hopped into his room with one foot in my pants and told him we had half an hour to move out for an ambush. He made no comment, just started dressing.

Five minutes later I stood outside the supply room in an old raggedy tiger suit, scuffy jungle boots, patrol harness, two hundred rounds of AR-15 ammo and the weapon. In my pocket were a can of beans and franks and another of pecan nut roll. I was ready.

It was starting out to be a nice day.

Two buildings down I heard a lot of yelling. Cowboy was bouncing troops out of the longhouse.

Slats came out of the supply room behind me, fully dressed in a suit of blank green fatigues and a bush hat. He frowned and said, "What's the deal?"

"Ambush on route 14's all I know. Luette'll tell us about it on the way down. Get a deuce and a half gassed up and grab a bite. We leave in twenty minutes."

He started walking toward the motor pool. I went into the Mess Hall to fill my canteen.

A few guys already sat there eating, and the rest were walking back and forth from the wash house with toilet kits in their hands. I filled my canteen from the sterile water jug until it started to overflow. The old black sock taped around it was beginning to rot and rust spots showed through.

"What's up, sir?" one of Judge's men, a big redhead, asked, walking over and pouring a cup of coffee. Then I picked up two slices of Cookie's rat turd bread and piled six or eight pieces of prehistoric pig bacon on top of that. I washed down four bicarbs with the coffee.

"Ambush!" I muttered.

"You mind if I go along?" he asked.

"It's okay with me if it's okay with Swain."

He was up and out of the Mess Hall fast. He made it across the street before the spring on the screen door stopped humming. I downed the coffee, jammed a slice of fresh pineapple in my mouth, picked up the sandwich and went after him.

Walt was already halfway into his fatigues when I got back to his bunk. "Better hurry!" I said.

"I borrowed McCulloch's AR-15. You got any ammo?" He sat there lacing his boots quickly.

"Yeah, there's eight or ten magazines clipped up in my desk drawer."

"Got any grenades?"

I took one off my belt and tossed it to him. "I don't think we'll need any," I said. "We usually set up the ambush from fifteen or twenty feet away."

He shrugged, standing up. "What's the setup anyway?"

"Beats me. It's Luette's show. He'll fill us in on the way down."

He flipped on his patrol harness, snapped the pistol belt and said, "Okay if I take Holland?" That was the man who had asked to go.

I nodded. "Yep."

"Then let's go."

Holland was coming up in his field gear when we got outside. Slats had the deuce and a half drawn up in the street and troops were getting ammo from the bunker. I checked my watch. "Twenty minutes," I said, "not bad, but we got to get out of here."

"You and me," I said to Walt, "we ride in the cab with Luette. I want to find out how this thing works."

"Yeah," he said tensely, "so do I." After all he had no

137

reason to trust Luette yet.

The troops started milling around outside the ammo bunker while Slats locked up. "Hey, Cowboy," I called. "Get 'em on the truck."

He waved, coughing out commands in Jarai. The troops swarmed onto the back of the truck.

Luette came up wearing his usual hangdog expression. "You are ready, sir?" he said. He wore a tiger suit, bush hat and carried his carbine. The pistol was sticking out of his hip pocket. Behind him was an old Yard in a loincloth and khaki shirt.

"I introduced him to Walt and they shook hands. "This is my agent," he said, introducing us to the old Yard, and we shook hands all around again.

"We got to go," I said. We got on the truck. The driver was already up there with the big rubber rimmed goggles on his face. Luette jumped in and I got in after him. "I'll get in the back," Walt said, "and monitor the conversation from there."

A moment later we were rolling down the road. I checked my watch. Twenty-five minutes. Not bad.

As soon as we got out on the highway I turned to Luette and said, "How'd this all get started anyway?"

"My man in Buon M'rok, he meet three VC in Buon Ba M'la. They come in for propaganda and to buy things."

"Where'd they come from?"

"One is company commander. They have company on mountain in forest. They are infiltrate into Chu Dle Ya. So they come to town. My man hear them make propaganda. He tell them he like VC and he know a place where they can stay night safely. He take them to our agent's house in Buon Ba M'la. Then they talk until late. They tell him they have Company in forest and go back today."

"He say how they go back today?"

"They say either this way or this way, and they tell him the two ways they may go."

"He tells them not to go one way, because District Chief have ambush set up and it is dangerous. They thank him. Then he say he must go home or his wife will miss him and make question. Then he leave and walk all night to my house."

"So that's the old man in the back of the truck?"

"Yes, we meet other man on road for check if everything is all right."

The wind was whipping over the front of the truck and Walt couldn't hear Luette's explanation. After it was over he leaned down over the front and yelled in my ear, "What the hell did he say?"

I turned around and tried to tell him, but couldn't make myself understood. "Tell you when we stop."

"Okay," he nodded and sat back down.

I slouched down in my seat and pointed the rifle down the road, relaxing, happy. With the windshield down there was too much wind to smoke. The ground whirled by beneath. I got a couple of Chiclets out of the C rations in my pocket and chewed that. I had a good feeling about this patrol. So many had gone sour, so many nights shivering in the rain, waiting for Cong who never came. But I had almost unlimited faith in Luette. Good as Cowboy was, Luette was better. He never let his ego get in the way of his operations.

We wound through the pass leading down over the next plateau, walls of the mountains steep and high around us. It would be pathetically easy for the Cong to ambush us had they known we were coming. Later we crossed the bridge over the Song Ba and passed the place where a French battalion had been wiped out. There was a neat concrete obelisk with a greenish brass plaque almost lost in the elephant grass to mark the spot. Five kilometers later there was an old Yard standing by the side of the road and Luette motioned for the driver to stop the truck.

"It is the other agent," he said. We got out.

Swain jumped down off the side of the truck, landing bent-kneed and compressing like a spring. "Aw right, now what is the deal here?" he said. "Is this it?"

"Ambush is maybe four kilometers, **sir**, off in the jungle. We take this trail here." He pointed to the trail. Then he nodded toward the old man by the side of the road. "This is my man sir. He wait for us here. He will take us to the right trail for ambush."

The old man stood off to the side of the road, his skinny brown legs wrinkled at the knee, like an old elephant ear, expressionless. His grey hair was cut in a homemade crew cut. A ragged loincloth was drawn up between his buttocks and he wore an old U.S. Army olive drab shirt with WW II T-5 stripes on it. God knows where he got that.

Cowboy was forming the platoon up behind us. One squad was already taking up security positions in the trees beyond. Luette spoke to the old man in Jarai. The old man came over and spoke.

Luette talked some more, pointing to me. The old Yard stuck out his hand. I shook it and we both bowed slightly. Hand shaking is not natural to them and his grip was limp. Then he and Walt shook hands.

"There are only three VC," Luette said. "They have only one weapon, a pistol, sir. Let us try to capture them?"

"Okay."

"There are two trails, sir. They come together like this." He made his arms into a Y-shaped trail junction. "We will make an L-shaped ambush. Then when they are in the middle, close the other two sides."

"Okay," I said, "but if we have to move four clicks we'd better go, and fast. It's ten-thirty now. We should be set up at least half an hour before they come. If you want to position your men we gotta move."

"Old man and I go with point sir, to lead. Maybe you get in the middle."

"I'll be right behind you," I said. "Captain Swain will be behind me. Sergeant Holland and Sergeant Slattery will be with the second squad."

I like the point. It's more dangerous, but you can see and react faster. This old jazz about not getting the commander killed is a lot of crap. These boys make out just fine without a junior Jesus in charge. The important thing is to have the decisions come fast and right. To me that means the point.

We cut through the woods fast. Too fast for flank security to keep up. We didn't put any out, and if we were ambushed that's all she wrote. It was more important for Swain to see a successful operation than for us to play it safe.

The trail was flat and smooth and green branches slapped wet against my face, splattering water on my glasses and leaving me half blind. It finally got so bad I could see better without them than with them so I took them off.

It was a cool morning, the jungle dark green. Wet branches slapped against our old cotton tiger suits and soaked through.

"I never thought I'd see terrain like this in Vietnam," Swain muttered, behind me. "This is like Fort Benning."

"You like this better than Hiep Duc, huh?"

"Jesus, yes."

Walt's body was dotted with leech scars from one patrol where he'd had to crawl three kilometers on his belly through the jungle to raid a village. I hoped I'd never work in terrain like that, but later I was to work in worse.

We came into a creek bed, the water rushing over the slick flat brown rocks, and on fast through the jungle. We made it in less than forty minutes.

It was a little trail junction in the woods. One young soldier started to step on the trail. I pointed to him and said, "Stop!"

He stopped.

"Okay," I said to Cowboy, "tell these soldiers not to step on the trail. All we need is for the Cong to see a bata boot print before we're ready to spring the trap." Cowboy relayed the word. They stepped back respectfully into the brush. "How you going to set up?" I asked Luette and Cowboy.

"One half this way," Luette said, indicating lining up along one side of the trail junction. "Other half there."

"Okay, fine," I said, glancing at the watch. "It's eleven thirty-three now. They might be early. Let's get set up."

Luette gave the commands in a hoarse whisper. Half of the platoon melted into the jungle beside one leg of the L. The other half swung around and hid back away from the trail that intersected at a ninety degree angle.

We could see some arms and legs and the barrel of a carbine so we moved those men further back into the woods.

I said, "Walt, you and Slats go over there with Luette. Holland and I will take this leg here." They left and soon the jungle closed around them. I couldn't see them any more. "Okay Mike." He walked over toward our leg of the path and wet bushes swished as he went back into them. He hopped over the trail and faded into the green darkness.

There was a little rice hooch back there that provided an unimpeded view of the trail, but had good cover. And something to lean on. I unsnapped the canteen carrier and unbuckled my harness, letting it hang by the suspenders on my shoulders. Then I sat down cross-legged. Immediately the wet ground soaked through my shirt. I switched the weapon selector to full auto and draped it across my knees. My watch said eleven thirty-five. Nothing to do until they came.

A few minutes later I caught a flicker of movement to the left. Somebody walking on the trail. Then there was a break in the trees and I saw an old man in a loincloth, followed by an old woman with a rice basket on her back. I hoped to God nobody would shoot. They got past our leg of the L. When they came even with Luette's, he stepped out of the bush and motioned them in. Good, if they had seen anything they would get no chance to report it until after the ambush. I relaxed back against the tree.

It was pleasant and the birds sang until it started to rain.

It came in a solid sheet, and I thought about moving back under the little rice hooch, but it was leaking. Besides it was not well to move. It was the right time for the Cong to be coming by.

But they didn't. I sat in the rain, wrapped around the pain in my belly; miserable, fidgety, glasses fogged over again. I wiped them clean and put them back on. Chill from the rain soaked through all my clothes and skin and what had been the layer of fat between my skin and bones. I started to shake. Amoebae gurgled through my lower colon once more. If dysentery came it was just going to have to come. I had to sit still.

Wouldn't that be great to be taking a crap when the Cong came? I scooted on the ground to squeeze my buttocks closer together. My body was starting to get feverish.

Still they didn't come. It rained for an hour and a half and they didn't come. Steam was forming under my watch crystal. I could barely make out the hands. It was almost two and they didn't come. Then it stopped raining.

Half an hour later they came. We wonder how the Cong survive in the jungle. They do it by doing sensible things like coming in out of the rain. They walked down the trail in close file, making fast choppy little steps. They had moved like that the night Cowboy and I had made our first ambush.

They weren't even disguised. They wore black shorty pajamas and tire sandals. Briefly they walked across my field of fire in perfect file. I could have taken all three with one burst. It would have been fun, but Luette was right. Dead they were just dead. Alive they were information. I got up, signalling the men on my left to swing around and close the encirclement. They hesitated and then got up raggedly, moving not fast enough and too noisily.

The Cong stopped in mid-stride and looked around. They were surrounded on three sides by tiger suited Jarai. They broke for the open side.

"HALT!" I yelled. "DOH!" No, that was halt in Jarai. What the hell was it in Vietnamese? Son of a bitch. A machine gun opened up. I figured if anybody was going to kill somebody it might as well be me, so I opened up too and squeezed off twenty rounds in five fast bursts.

It was silly. I was just firing in the jungle. I changed magazines and fired again. The weapon went *schlug* and jammed on me, the bolt half home. "You rat-bastard son of a bitch!" I screamed at the rifle, crouching over it, trying to work the charging handle. I couldn't shake it loose.

Holland and the others moved on around me. In a minute it wouldn't do me any good to get it fixed. I'd be firing at our own men. I moved forward with them. Finally the firing stopped and everybody started milling around.

"Cowboy," I called. "Shape these cats up and get some security out."

"Yes sir," he called back through the woods. Then he barked something in Jarai and all milling stopped. The men moved next to the trees and faced into the woods. That was better.

"They try to run away. We have to shoot them," Cowboy said.

"You're telling me. You better get a squad out looking to find the bodies. If one of them gets away Luette's agents are in a strain."

"Yes sir," he said. He started moving again.

"Here's one over here," Holland called. "He's not dead yet."

He was over by a tree, about fifteen feet away from the trail. I started walking that way. "You reckon you can save him?" I asked. I took a look. He had leg wounds, head wounds, chest wounds, and belly wounds. "No, I reckon not," I muttered.

Holland kneeled down beside him. He was already getting the waxy look they get just before they die, and his breathing sounded like a kid's bubble pipe. It occurred to me that now it was over I could smoke. I reached for a cigarette.

Slattery walked up through the trees brandishing his AR-15. "This mutha jammed on me," he said.

"Mine, too," I replied.

"This sorry mutha," he said. "You shoulda seen the Cong over there. He was running right at me. His eyes was that big. He knew he was a dead mutha. That's when this mutha jammed on me. The machine gun cut him in half."

Then Luette came up through the trees. "We haff two bodies," he said, "but we must see if the other got away. Otherwise the VC will kill my agent. Will you move them into the camp if we do not find him, sir?"

"Sure," I said, "but let's see if we can find that body."

"Cowboy, he have squad out for to look."

I nodded. Mike was going over the Cong on the ground. He pulled a wallet out of his belt and handed it to me. It had a little money and some family pictures. The usual stuff you'd find in a wallet. The Cong had been watching, but now his eyes had gone glassy and he lay there, waxy and gurgling.

I heard one round fired off in the jungle somewhere and Cowboy called, "They have found the other one. He is dead." I wondered briefly what kind of shape they'd found him in, then forgot it.

"This one must have been the big cheese," Holland said. He reached in his belt and pulled out a Walther PPK, which only an officer would have.

It needed bluing real bad. He handed the pistol to me. I released the magazine and jacked back the slide. A 7.65 mm round popped out on the ground. I reached down and picked it up, shoving it back again into the magazine. Then I put the magazine back in the grip and shoved the weapon into my hip pocket. "You guys got six months to get yourselves some souvenirs," I said, smiling evilly, "I'm taking this home."

Mike stood up. He didn't look interested in giving me an argument about it. "I been waiting fifteen years for this day," he said, with wonder in his voice. "Fifteen years in the army to get into combat."

I laughed. "It takes two sides to make combat," I said. "This was just a slaughter."

Swain walked up through the jungle. He looked impressed. Even if this patrol hadn't gone according to plan.

I took my rifle and beat the butt one time hard against the bottom of a tree trunk. The bolt slammed home ready to fire. The Cong at our feet was dead, a little brown bloody mess. It was a shame. Outside of the Jarai, I liked the Cong better than anybody in Vietnam. What they believed in was wrong, but they sure as hell believed in it.

"Okay Cowboy," I said. "Let's get formed up and get out of here." He turned and started forming troops up on the trail, moving back toward the highway. I slung the AR-15 on my shoulder and looked again at the body of the Cong there beside the big tree. "Sorry about that," I grinned at him.

I fell in behind a little strike force trooper who was walking along happily, one of his bootlaces dangling in the mud. The strikers were chatting among themselves, already counting the bonus money for a successful operation.

Swain fell in behind me and I watched the feet of the little trooper ahead squish on the muddy trail.

Behind me Walt said, "This is getting off the pad kind of early."

"What?" I said. "Oh, yeah."

We walked on through the jungle, leaving the VC bodies to stiffen out in the rain that was starting to fall again.

16

The hall was about thirty feet long with three doors off to the right. At the end was a door painted in the same dismal green color as the hall. I drew in a sharp breath, marched manfully down to the end of the hall, and knocked on the door. A voice within said, "Come in."

Unconsciously, just in the last second before opening the door, I checked to see if my fly was zipped, my khaki shirt was tucked in at the waist, paratroop boots spitshined, belt buckle brassoed and all the rest of the military shinola routine complete. I opened the door and stepped gingerly inside.

Colonel Kelly sat at his desk. He glanced up and give me a look intended, apparently, to freeze my blood. I smiled inwardly. I went to his desk, stopped the regulation two paces in front of it and saluted. He was new and I wanted to strike the proper note. Almost no colonel now in the army expects his own staff officers to go through the entire, "Sir, Captain Morris reports to the Group Commander," business, not even the first time. But on the other hand I'd gone to one of those high school and junior college military academies when I was a kid, and those kinds of habits die hard. I never could get the feel of exactly how to approach one of these people. So I compromised, saluted, and said, "Sir, I'm Captain Morris, your public information officer."

"Relax, Captainnnnnn," Kelly growled, drawing the word out in a way that was intended to make relaxation impossible. I kind of liked Kelly hardassing me that way. It made him seem more human. I came to a liquid parade rest and took my first good look at him.

Kelly looked like a tough old Irish cop. I understand that

146

at one time he actually was a New York City cop. He was big with a body that tended to run to fat. His face had the defensive arrogance of a self-made man who had grown up among his intellectual inferiors and had not lost the habit of being smug about it. Besides, now that he was up here with some people who were as bright as he was he could feel smug about being self-made. I don't think Kelly was what you could call a genius, but he had a very good brain. Later I came to respect that. I have talked to a lot of high ranking officers about the subject of revolutionary warfare. He was the only one who knew zip shit about it.

"Oh yes," he said smiling, "I've heard about you!" It had an ominous sound. "You can relax, Captain. You aren't going anywhere."

Oh, you son of a bitch, I thought. How I would have loved to vault over his desk and strangle the bastard, fat squeezing through my fingers. He was condemning me to spend the remainder of my time in the army on this crummy little island in the middle of the East China Sea while my friends went to Vietnam and romped and stomped in the jungles, laughing at me when they came home, covered in honor and medals, while I sat pounding out tepid news release copy. Me, a public information officer, the most debased and despised creature in the officers corps. I was well aware that most of my comrades thought a PIO was some kind of military pimp evading real work. I wouldn't have minded that very much except I shared that opinion. It was my misfortune that I had the only journalism degree in the 1st Special Forces Group (Abn).

I could feel my words coming out all in a rush. Somehow I had to change this self-assured bastard's mind and I had to do it fast. "Sir," I said, and it was all wrong, because my words were just a little desperate, "there's a kind of fiction in the army that people are interchangeable parts. But I spent six months in my camp at Buon Beng and it took us four months to get squared away. We actually inflicted over sixty percent of our casualties on the Cong in the last two months. And the thing was rising in a geometric ratio. Sir, I want to go back to that area and capitalize on those successes. It doesn't make sense to send in somebody else who'll have to start from scratch."

I paused. He continued looking at me as though I were some sort of lab specimen. I plunged back into my pitch, hoping for some sign that he was beginning to see things my way. There was none.

"Sir, in the four months since Judge's team replaced ours they haven't been able to get a toehold in the area, just like it took us four months. Now I've got D Company to form up a team slated to replaced Judge's and it's got five members of our old team on it. They're holding the detachment commander's slot open for me. All I need is your release and I can go back to Buon Beng." In my mind I could see the Cong moving back in on the Jarai while I got fat on Okinawa.

He gave me a carefully practised sincere look, the kind they trot out just before they stick it in. "Captain Morris," he said, "I consider the constitution of my public information program more important than the organization of any individual A detachment."

Usually when I'm hit with something like that I just dig in. The man had just announced that he believed style more important than substance. He had also denied, with an airy wave of his hand, the thing I had lain awake nights brooding over, planning for, for the four months since returning from Vietnam, four months of hideous paralyzing boredom, official parties where I'd had parachute wings carved out of ice and placed in enormous punch bowls to melt while we all stood around in our mess whites, the ladies in long gowns, and drank ourselves senseless, the men congregated at one end of the room telling war stories and the women at the other end gabbling about baby diapers and bay leaves. The son of a bitch was condemning me to that. I started to put my hands on my hips, but managed to restrain myself. My reply, however, was almost a snarl. "Sir! I don't give a *shit* for your public information program. I just want to go back to Vietnam."

I didn't really expect him to change his mind; maybe throw me out of the Group, but not change his mind. I just wanted him to know what he had done.

He smiled slightly. "That will be all, Captain. You are dismissed."

I threw him an insolent salute, snapped out an angry about face and stalked out of his office.

Two weeks later, after the team I wanted was filled, I was put on another team and sent back. And I beat the team back to Vietnam by four days. It wasn't through any clever machinations on my part that it was done. It was simply that they got a rush requisition for four teams and had to scrape the personnel up somewhere. There is no authorization for a PIO in a Special Forces Group and there was no way to justify pulling somebody out of a real job to keep me in my fake one, no matter how important Kelly thought it was. So in spite of Kelly, I got sent back to Nam, but not with my team. My team was taken by some clown who was relieved of his command after two months. As near as I could figure from the guys who went back, Pancho, Slats, Augie, John and Ken Miller, they sat on their asses for six months. Except for Augie and Slats, they were transferred to Project Delta when it was organized. My own tour was more eventful.

Quite a bit happened before I left, though. I kept hustling for a job in Nam. Since the revolt was coming up I thought the B team in Pleiku might have a job for an intelligence officer with a knowledge of the country. I went over to see Major Ed Brooks who was putting together a team to replace Buck's.

"What can I do for you, young man?"

He was a thin man, saturnine, and he sat nervously moving behind his desk, picking up papers, fiddling with paper clips. I was being earnest as hell and launched into a prepared spiel. "Sir, I understand you are putting a team together. I've engaged in extensive intelligence work in your area of operations and know the country and the people pretty well." I held myself still, tried to keep the emotion out of my voice. I didn't want him to think I was some kind of nut. I wanted him to think I was the very model of a bright young officer.

He looked at me without raising his head from the pencil he was fiddling with, making his eyes go kind of round like

Eddie Cantor's. "You speak Vietnese?" he asked. I cringed at the pronunciation and shook my head. "No sir. I speak French a little, but most of the people in Two Corps are Montagnards and they . . ."

"I was looking for an officer who speaks Vietnese."

I mumbled respectfully on for quite a spell. Can't remember for sure whether I told him about the impending Montagnard revolt or not, because I knew he'd pick it up in a briefing when he got to Nha Trang. But somewhere in there he ventured the opinion that he wanted to get to Nam so he could get in his combat time before the war was over.

I was always startled to hear someone in a position to make decisions, presumably with access to the best knowledge available, mouthing these idiocies. I tried not to look too surprised, so I probably frowned instead of looking startled. "Sir," I said, "that war won't be over for twenty years."

His mouth dropped open in astonishment. "Twenty years. Captain, that's the professional life of an army officer."

I shook my head. "Sir, before this war is over it's going to take the professional lives of quite a few officers."

He got me out of his office pretty fast, not having any desire to waste his time with a raving lunatic.

The rest of his story is interesting, so I'll sketch it in. Nobody briefed him on the coming revolt, because Colonel Leonard had gone home, taking his staff with him and somehow in the changeover nobody passed the word that the Montagnards were going to revolt. They did, and in four camps killed all the Vietnamese Special Forces Personnel. Brooks was directed not to interfere, but anyway went out and personally talked an entire camp out of revolting. He had sized up the situation and done exactly the right thing. If I gave the impression that Brooks was an idiot, I didn't mean to. Nobody understands Vietnam until he has seen it. When Brooks saw Vietnam he understood. For this, and for disobeying orders during the revolt, he was relieved of his command.

I am not sure whether he retired or resigned, but he left the Army shortly thereafter.

17

My team, A-322, arrived in Nha Trang on the 24th of October, 1964, in driving rain that continued so that we couldn't get into our camp, Kham Duc, until Friday, the 13th of November. We had no changeover orientation. The team we replaced left on the same plane. We couldn't blame them. They were already two weeks overdue for rotation. So long, guys.

One mile of runway, out in front of the camp. I stood on the runway, the only outdoor surface in the camp not covered. I had mashed my beret down over my nose and stared pugnaciously at the mountains surrounding the camp. They were beautiful, gorgeous things covered with heavy jungle, and in the mornings the fog hung heavy in the mahogany and teak trees. The camp itself was large and, compared to Buon Beng, it looked like Fort Benning.

I turned to *Dai Uy* Anh, my counterpart, who stood beside me on the runway, looking like a four-fifths scale model of Sesse Hawakawa in *The Bridge on the River Kwai*. He stood wrapped in a ragged old French army overcoat, his own green beret mashed on the left side of his head in the VNSF style, and watched me warily. It was our second day. I wanted to strike a reassuring note. "This is a good camp, *Dai Uy*."

He looked at me and smiled as slick as linoleum. "Yesss!" he said, "very good camp, just like Dien Bien Phu."

He was exactly right, mountains surrounded the camp, which rested in a bowl, and the thought chilled me. He should know. He'd commanded a Viet Minh battalion there.

I got to know the *Dai Uy* very quickly. He had a reputation as a thief and a coward. To my way of thinking they

151

were both undeserved. He was forty-five years old and had a bleeding duodenal ulcer. It was no surprise he didn't want to go on patrol.

Insofar as I was able to determine, he stole no more than was normal for an officer in his position. After all most of his pay was stolen too. For my money Anh was a good man. He was a Nung, a member of a tribe of hereditary Chinese mercenaries who fight for hire all over Southeast Asia. Anh was from China and a graduate of the Whampoa Military Academy. He had been in some Chinese army or other, in the Viet Minh and now was in the ARVN. He would never be promoted and he knew it. He was old. He was tired. Nobody, but nobody, in the ARVN chain of command ever came out to see what he was doing.

There was no reason to assume that Anh didn't know how to soldier, but no one cared, so why should he.

"Would you show me the camp, *Dai Uy?*"

He nodded, wheeled and led me off through the mud. I followed respectfully behind. Anh had been an officer for over twenty years. I had been a captain for ten months. I had to play the new boy, for if I pushed and tried to tell him what to do he would ignore me. He knew what to do. He just wasn't doing it and there was no way I could force him.

At the time we arrived no patrols had been run from Kham Duc for about two months. The team before us had run one to the south, got shot up fairly bad, and never got another out since. From the appearance of the camp they were in no shape for offensive combat operations. So the first step was to get our strike force squared away into something resembling a military unit.

We slogged on through the mud, he proceeding briskly, the French overcoat swishing perilously close to the mud. I lurched along behind in the fine falling mist, great clumps of oozing mud collecting on my boots, then falling off when layer after layer built up until finally the mud would not support its own weight and slid in a viscous mass back where it came from.

We slogged through the mud, past the buildings with rattan walls and tin roofs. Vietnamese strikers in filthy tiger suits, which had been cut down so tight that they could barely move, straggled desultorily past. They were the scruffiest lot of presumed soldiers I had ever seen. A Fort Dix basic trainee would put them to shame. Some of them glanced up and threw the Dai Uy a ragged salute, most did not.

You must understand the position an advisor is in. He cannot give orders directly to his troops. He must go through his counterpart. He cannot give orders to his counterpart. He must make him wish to respond. This relationship drove a lot of U.S. officers nuts. I always looked on it as a challenge, for each of these people has his key, and once you find it it's like riding in an automatic elevator. Punch the right button and it'll take you where you want to go.

In the *Dai Uy*'s case I knew if I even gave him advice he'd ignore it, go out of his way to do the opposite in fact. If I told him what to do he lost face. But that was okay, because he knew what to do anyway. He wasn't doing it because nobody gave a shit. That is, except me. My role was to be his audience.

"My goodness, *Dai Uy*! What's this?" My face registered shock and a kind of numb disbelief. I pointed to a little pile of live carbine ammunition that someone had left lying in the mud by a well.

Anh stalked over and looked critically at the ammo, like someone had shit in his mess gear. He sucked in his breath, his eyes bulged and his nostrils flared. He shrieked in Vietnamese and strikers started scurrying around. In a moment the ammo was gone and he smiled at me. I smiled back and we proceeded with the inspection.

We went through the kitchens, where rice was cooked in great flattish iron pots like dishes, about five feet across the top. Great gobs of the glutenous stuff were being paddled over fires by Vietnamese cooks. Dogs ran openly through the kitchen and garbage lay in heaps throughout the cooking area. It was the most filthy place I'd ever seen. I said nothing, but made a note to check with Steve or Atomic Jones, my medics, about it.

We went on into the barracks. There were at least four men flaked out on the rattan racks they used for bunks. They looked pretty sick. "What's the matter with these men?" I asked.

It turned out they were sick with beriberi. We had no fresh vegetables because the camp was closed to air traffic most of the time by the rain. Aircraft couldn't get down in the mountains where we were. Later when I checked with Steve he said there were no vitamins in the supply system right then. All of Special Forces was out. Until we got some of either vegetables or vitamins we would have beriberi.

These guys were down, because they had no energy. But they weren't dead. I asked one to see his carbine. He eased off his bunk and walked over to where the pile of his field gear was leaned up against the wall. He picked the carbine up gingerly by the barrel and brought it to me. I had expected it to be bad, but not this bad. It had rust on the barrel and rust on the receiver. I jacked back the bolt and stuck my thumbnail in the receiver adjusting it so it caught the light and squinted down the bore. It was so rusty it looked like red velvet. Without a word I handed it to the *Dai Uy.*

He shot straight up in the air and came down screaming. In a minute there were sixteen soldiers in the barracks, cleaning carbines like a son of a bitch.

In this wise we proceeded around the camp every day I was in it. After a couple of weeks it began to bear some resemblance to a military installation.

There were other problems too. One day Squeaky Moore, my Commo man, came into the team house where I was reading. He stormed up to me and said, "Well, I reckon I'll be going home in a couple of days," in the high squeaky voice that gave him his nickname. He was redheaded and freckled, a thorough professional, on this third trip to Nam. Next to Slattery he is the most foul mouthed man I ever met.

I looked up and cocked my head. "How come?"

He put his hands on his hips and said, "We was unloadin' that C-130 out there on the strip with a bunch of them fag strikers from Ta Ko. They wasn't workin' worth shit and I told one of them to hustle up."

I nodded. "So!"

"So he shot me the finger and said, in perfect English, 'Fuck you!'"

I nodded. "And?"

"I hooked a finger in each nostril and rolled the little mother fucker down the runway like a bowling ball."

I went back to reading my book. "Forget it," I said without looking up. "If they send you home for that they'll have to send me too."

The team at Ta Ko had pretty much the same guys that had been at Plei Do Lim on my first trip: White, Edge, Worley, Cade, Stamm. They had new officers, of course, and a few new enlisted men. Their old commander, Herb Hardy, had been killed. For that matter, White, the team sergeant, had died of a heart attack while they were at Ta Ko, and he was only thirty-four. Finally they closed Ta Ko out when it was sort of embarrassedly discovered that the camp was probably located in Laos, through map error. No one knew for sure whether it was in Laos or not. These borders are very poorly defined.

When they moved that team they put them in to replace Roger Donlon's team at Nam Dong where he had won the medal of honor.

Plei Do Lim, where I met them, incidentally, was where Barry Sadler wrote the Ballad of the Green Berets, although I wouldn't hold that against the place. Ken Miller had helped open Plei Do Lim up. Oh, hell, it's all interconnected. For years the teams from Oki played leapfrog with each other all over Vietnam. It's a hell of a saga.

But I digress.

In the meantime, that team was stuck at Ta Ko, where the Strike Force had been for two years without going home or seeing a woman. Half of them had long hair and half of them had short hair and they were all very friendly with each other. But not with the Americans. Every so often somebody threw a grenade in the teamhouse.

There was no air strip at Ta Ko so they had their stuff flown in to Kham Duc and then into Ta Ko on helicopters.

And that's how Squeaky got mad at this kid.

Another time I was reading in the teamhouse when Les Nolan, my demo man, who was working in supply, there being nothing around Kham Duc worth blowing up, stormed in, grabbed a shotgun off the wall and started to storm out.

I glanced up from my book, and said, "Hey Les, where ya goin'?"

Les looked back over his shoulder, a slender, boyish man with curly brown hair. "Gunna kill me a Company Commander," he announced, turning toward the door.

I eased myself out of the chair and strolled rapidly out after him. "Reckon I'll go along with you," I said. "What seems to be the trouble?"

We had a very peculiar organization in that camp; every company had three commanders. First there was the VNSF Commander, a Vietnamese lieutenant who was detailed to be in charge of the company by the Vietnamese. Then there was the Nung Company commander who was a civilian instructor with military experience, who had been hired to train the company and somehow become attached to it, but remained a civilian and was technically a part of the camp staff; then there was the Strike Force company commander, who was the striker placed in charge. He functioned in fact as a sort of field first sergeant. Of these three the only one who had any military ability was the Nung. He was also the one who had no official status. It was a silly organization but was in effect when I got there. I hadn't changed it, or got Anh to change it yet, because I wanted to get a better feel of the camp, and have the ideal organization for this place when I did change it. A change throws everything into disarray for a while, so if you have to make changes at all it is best to make them only once.

At any rate, as Les explained it to me, the Strike Force company commander had marched his troops to the supply room in a state of high excitation because the recruits had been issued new uniforms, while his company still had the crummy old ones they'd been issued before, and felt they had lost face thereby.

"They what?" I strode along beside Les, simply amazed. I thought I had some grasp of the Oriental mind, whatever that is, but this was too much. It made no sense.

We walked in the back of the supply room. It was dark and

my eyes took a moment to adjust. I could hear a lot of angry murmuring out front. I wasn't conscious of it, of course, but I must have shifted into the same sort of emotional overdrive you get into in combat, because by the time we got to the counter which opened onto the front of the supply room I had gone completely past fear and was into complete . . . and . . . absolute . . . control. I had all the power in the world running through my body. All of it. Because I was absolutely right.

It was like a lynch mob scene in a movie. One hundred and fifty Vietnamese shouting and shaking their loaded carbines at me and Les, demanding new uniforms or they'd burn down the supply room. Right in front of them was their company commander. This kid was a natural leader, a handsome boy with a lot of drive who'd been placed in charge of the company by somebody or other before I got there. But he had no leadership training. Somebody had put him in charge just because he was a good kid. He really was a good kid, too, but he was in the wrong here, and because of that if I didn't act right a number of people would die—with myself heading the list, probably.

I could feel myself swelling up, welling with fury, face turning purple as I faced him. I towered over them all anyway, standing six foot two to their average of about five three, plus I stood on the floor of the supply shack which gave me an added foot, and I was large, 195 pounds, and blond and I looked professional, and old; combat had given me a look of gravity at least ten years older than the twenty-seven I was. On top of that I was now in a perfect controlled fury, riding that rage and in total charge of it. I must have looked murderous. Seemingly of its own volition my finger rose and pointed directly at the kid company commander. He quailed before it, even with those hundred and fifty guns at his back. He spoke no English at all, and my Vietnamese is almost nonexistent, but even though I spoke in English there was no mistaking my meaning. My voice went hoarse as I grated out: "You call yourself a company commander." Ominous pause. "This is the sorriest exhibition of leadership I've ever seen." My finger, still pointing at him, quivered

157

with emotion. I let the power of my outrage flow into my face, almost to the point of leaping the counter and strangling the little bastard, only there was no need to do that. I grunted, "Now you form this company up in a column of fours and you march them back to their barracks and you submit a requisition in triplicate and we'll, by God, *consider* the matter of new uniforms."

They did not straggle off shamefacedly. They were formed into a column of fours and marched off. Not exactly proudly, but more like soldiers than I'd seen them before.

It seems strange now, but I didn't think enough of the incident at the time to report it to higher headquarters. I went back to the team house and had a drink of strawberry Kool-Aid. The water again was too vile to drink straight, and my throat was *awfully* dry. I went back to reading my book, *V.*, by Thomas Pynchon. I recommend it highly.

They never did get around to making out that requisition, and were still in the same uniforms when I left.

Far from being satisfied with these little victories in human relations I was becoming frantic to get on with the mission. We had been given six months, only six months, to work in this area. We had been here something like two months and only got two patrols out and neither of them made contact. To me a no contact patrol was no patrol at all. All a no contact patrol proved was that you didn't know what you were doing.

And we were making little or no progress in turning the Strike Force into an effective unit. I had got myself all psyched up for contact, and all I was doing was talking us out of Mexican standoffs, filling out reports and reading paperback novels. As far as I was concerned this mission was turning into a drag. I could have done everything but the Mexican standoffs on Okinawa, and there wasn't much to them.

Two months gone. It was time to get it on, get out in the woods and move among them. Somewhere along in there I had become addicted to adrenalin, and I was thirsty for some.

Much as Special Forces guys wanted to go to Nam, though, I did have one incident of a man refusing to go out

158

on patrol. We set up a patrol to the south to check out reports of a big infiltration route and the location of an NVA regiment that was supposed to be twelve clicks, about eight miles, to the south of us. In that jungle that's a five or six day walk.

There was a rule in effect in I Corps, where Kham Duc was located, which was that all patrol routes had to be cleared in advance with the B team in Da Nang. We'd had the same rule in II Corps, but at Buon Beng we'd just ignored it. It was our contention that our Strike Force was infiltrated, and so was the Vietnamese B team, so their first clue that we were going out was a paragraph in the daily sitrep stating we had done so. We never told anyone, including each other, where we were going.

In point of fact I had always thought that the advance clearance rule was thought up and promulgated by VC infiltrators in the Vietnamese command structure. But it was enforced very rigidly in I Corps, where the B team had only six camps to worry about. There had been twenty-two camps in II Corps and we could do pretty much any damn thing we wanted to. But in I Corps they kept a close check on the A teams.

Anyway we sent in an area on the map that we wished to be free to operate in and the patrol went out. I'd taken the first one, and Squeaky and I forget who took the second one out. I don't know quite how it happened, but it turned out that we got clearance for the wrong area. The one which was cleared was free of enemy activity.

We got a message from Squeak on the third day that the VNSF patrol leader, a candy-assed lieutenant (we had three, a candy-ass, an idiot, and one young officer with whom I'd be proud to serve anywhere) refused to move out of the authorized area. We quickly got clearance from the VNSF B team to go where we wanted to, and radioed this information to the patrol. He still refused to budge. I got a written order from his B team commander to go on and flew over the patrol in an L-19, zinging the order in a message drop. He still refused to move into the area.

At any rate Squeaky came in the team house two days later covered with mud and field grime, hopping mad. He had gone out looking for combat, not because he likes to camp out. I was in my usual place, reading, and he stormed over to me and glared down. "I ain't going out no more. This is my third tour in Vietnam and I taken all the shit off these little bastards I'm goin' to. I ain't goin' on patrol no more."

Even my own NCO's were becoming infected with the spirit of the place. The older ones had all been to Nam three or four times and had been ground down by the nature of the war, the difficulty of getting the Viets off their ass. They had been here before and they would come again. It was all business as usual to them, and if they didn't make contact this trip they'd make it the next.

I couldn't take that tack. Ever since I was a kid I wanted to be a soldier, a real soldier, and in fact a guerilla leader. Those were the war stories I read, *American Guerilla in the Philippines, Never So Few*, stories of the Maquis, and the OSS Jedburgh teams. I first heard of the Special Forces in 1955 when I was a college freshman and read a story about them in the Saturday Evening Post. I said then that was the outfit for me, and it took six years but I finally got in. Vast armies moving across the plains of Europe, superweapons, rockets; that wasn't my style at all. But small groups of highly trained guerillas moving through the jungle at night to save their country from an invader; that was my ideal. That's why I loved working with the Yards. It was exactly made to order for me. But working with these Viets; if they didn't give a shit, why should we?

For one reason. All my life I'd wanted to be a soldier. I did not intend for my war to be the first one America ever lost. And if there was anything I could do it wouldn't be. I was prepared to die, not prepared to lose. They might get me, but there'd be a tall stack of dead ones around me when I went under.

Only I couldn't even move these fucking phonies out to make contact.

I looked at him for a moment. He was furious and I didn't blame him. What was I going to do? Here was a professional sergeant refusing to fight. I couldn't let him do that, but if I ordered him out in his present mood he would tell me to shove it and I would have no choice but to court martial him.

"Get some chow!" I said and went back to reading my book.

A couple of weeks later when it came his turn to go out again I went by his room just before we turned off the generator. He was lying in bed, reading, a glass of Kahlua on the nightstand. It was the only thing he drank, a nightcap just before retiring.

I leaned on the doorjamb and looked at him for a moment. He looked up at me. "It's your turn to go out again," I said.

He glared at me for a long moment, really glared. Then he nodded, "Okay!"

That was the end of that.

I sent the Americans on patrol a lot at Kham Duc. Most A camps sent two Americans with a patrol, and at Kham Duc they had sent two Nungs with each American as bodyguards. All our strikers were juvenile delinquents who had been recruited out of the Saigon jails and reliability wasn't their strong point. When my friend, Tom Kiernan, had been at Kham Duc, for instance, his technique was to take them out by helicopter to a point a couple of days march past the objective so they'd have to march, and if necessary fight, through it to get home.

I always sent four Americans on a company size patrol, and I was coming around to the idea of sending four Nungs with each American. That way, no matter what happened we'd have a small platoon that would fight. The concept I was evolving, as a matter of fact, was to use the Vietnamese Strike Force as bait to draw the VC in and then fight them with the Nungs and Americans, which represented a well-trained disciplined force.

There was a little desperation in my tactical planning for Kham Duc. We were responsible for patrolling twenty-six kilometers of the Laotian border. We were twenty kilometers in from the border, and this was in an area where you are moving extremely well if you go two kilometers a day. We had three companies to do the patrolling with and were very lucky to get one out at any given time. The Viets would stall on going out as long as they possibly could. Our mission was "Border Surveillance," but I interpreted this to mean Infiltration Interdiction. The war could never be won unless infiltration was controlled. It could not be controlled unless someone controlled it. Reporting sighting some tracks so that it could be plotted on some technicolor map in Saigon wouldn't do it.

So I interpreted our ultimate mission as stopping all that infiltration through the entire twenty-six miles.

My original plan, formulated on Okinawa, was to use highway fourteen, which paralleled the border, to move companies by truck quickly, so as to achieve surprise in any given area. But when we got there we found that the rains had washed the highway out.

In effect, then, our mission was impossible; Border Surveillance or Interdiction either one. It was impossible. But I thought if we just kept pressing, kept hustling, kept moving, took more chances, drove harder, pushed, pushed, pushed, we might make a dent in it. Or vice versa.

I got Al Smith, my XO, out on a patrol to the north. And he was able to go about six clicks on highway 14, which saved him three days march. They went quite a way up there. And found nothing but trees and elephant shit.

I later heard that Colonel Kelly had portrayed this expedition as some sort of daring exploit in Saigon. Turns out that no one had been up there in a long time and all their Intel maps carried that area as completely VC controlled. Actually it was controlled by anybody who went in it. Only, other than to check occasionally, there was no reason why anybody would.

That was good information. It meant that the enemy wasn't operating at all in the upper half of our area of responsibility, so we could concentrate on the south. And we knew there was no infiltration to a distance of about ten kilometers below us. Somewhere down there was that VC regiment, and probably all the infiltration that went anywhere near Kham Duc followed one or two major trails down there, right through that regimental area. The first step was to locate it. That part would be relatively easy. The next part would be to get these Saigon cowboys, the juvenile delinquents we had for a strike force, to go and operate in an area where they'd be outnumbered ten to one.

Oh well, one thing at a time.

162

I proposed a patrol to the south to Anh and he started going through the motions of getting it cleared, with something less than enthusiasm. None of his lieutenants wanted to go out.

After the incident with Squeaky and the Vietnamese lieutenant I had determined to either go myself or send Al Smith on every patrol that went out. That way the Vietnamese lieutenant patrol leader was not put in the ignominious position of having to accept advice from someone of inferior rank.

Before I could get the patrol mounted I was ordered to make a survey of the area to the south, with the idea of putting in another camp down there, right astride the infiltration route. It seemed like a good idea to me, except that I wanted to make a major change in the concept of operations.

What I wanted was to have the area to operate in, but not to build a camp. I wanted three companies placed under my command, two operating at all times, with the third, and three Americans, back at Kham Duc for rest, retraining and maybe a little R and R in Da Nang. Almost a real guerrilla operation. With some Montagnard support it would be.

To my way of thinking a camp was nothing but a nuisance anyway. The VC could watch the camp and tell when you went out on patrol and where you were going, but if you shifted your base of operations every three days you could never be hit by a planned attack, which was the only kind the VC used, and that would give you much more incentive than operating from a fixed camp. It was then, and still is, my belief that operating like that you'll make more contact by accident than you will on purpose operating from a fixed camp.

Anyway I determined to make a reconnaissance of the area to the south. I was thinking in terms of putting together a small recon patrol, just myself and another American and maybe ten Nungs. We had to take Viets on combat patrols, but maybe they'd let us go out alone if it was just a recon.

Before I could put in a request for such a mission I got word that the Nung company from Da Nang, a reaction force under the control of our B team there, was going to run a company strength patrol from Kham Duc to Dak Pek, the first camp to the south, and the northernmost camp in II Corps. Since these guys were going through the same area I wanted to recon, it seemed a good opportunity to go with them and take a look at the place. Besides I was going stir crazy from sitting around camp. And I'd finished reading *V*.

I sat in my jeep on the edge of the airstrip watching the Nungs bounce off the end of the C-130 they'd come on. It did my heart good to see them. Fine, professional looking troops. Once they were formed up and started to march off to quarters I went over to introduce myself to their advisor.

He saluted in the barbarous Australian manner. I returned it and shook his hand.

"Warrant Officer Baxter, sir, Royal Australian Advisory Training Team."

I was getting pretty good at listening to Aussies. I understood the first time. Baxter was a well set up man of about thirty-five. He was medium height and solidly built with curly hair, longer than they like it in the American army, and a weathered mug of a face.

"Going out with us, eh?"

I nodded. "Yeah, I want to get out of this place for a while."

He looked around the camp, grinning acknowledgment.

That evening, after I got my field gear ready, I went down to the team house and got a beer. I went over and sat down by Jack Cade, the commo man from Ta Ko, who had come to our place for a ride home on a chopper.

"Hello, Jack," I said.

He nodded, "Evening, sir."

I asked about the team at Ta Ko, most of whom I'd known before.

"Edge's got a new one," he said. Cade grinned like a panther. He was the most pantherish man I'd ever seen, medium height, very muscular with a strong graceful body and an evil grin, set off by a slight gap in his front teeth. He looked like a sort of cross between Warren Beatty and Warren Oates. And he looked mean.

"It's another biblical quote," he said. " 'Yea though I walk through the valley of the shadow of death I will fear no evil, for I know I'm the baddest mother fucker there.' "

164

I cracked up; I could just see Edge saying that. Before I was through I'd hear every soldier in Vietnam saying it, or variations on it. That's why I include it here. I'd like to see a great cultural innovator like Edge given due credit.

"You going out with them Nungs tomorrow?" He squinted an eye at me over the top of his beer can, smiling a little sardonically.

I nodded.

"That's not a good place, down there where you're going."

I shrugged. "Yeah," I grinned. "There's only one thing that bothers me."

"Yeah, what's that?"

I had a flutter in my stomach, because it really did bother me badly, even though I tried not to let it. "So far every officer in the First Group that's been killed in Nam has been a big blond captain from C Company."

Cade grinned a very evil grin, but said nothing.

It was true, too. Brodt, Hardy, Cordell. Each and every one a big blond captain from C Company. I hadn't checked it, though, but I did not believe that every big blond captain from C Company who'd come to Nam had been killed. What were the odds? Fuck it, I thought, and pushed it out of my mind. Besides, my hair is red. It just looks blond in a crew cut.

Williams, our tall skinny junior commo man, came into the team house, looked over in my direction and came to me, holding out a message form. "C-1 CO arr your loc 1030 hrs tomorrow, urgent discussion future plans," it said.

Not now of all times. "Shit!" I exploded.

"What's the matter?" Cade said.

"Major Allen's coming in tomorrow and he wants me to be here to discuss plans or some shit like that." Waiting for a forty-five minute talk with Allen would blow my plans for the next two weeks.

"Too bad!"

I had got a message like that at Buon Beng once, that Buck was coming in and I'd stayed in, sending George Stogdill out on patrol. Buck didn't show up and George got eight kills. "I'm going out anyway," I said. "I gotta get out of this fucking place for a couple of weeks. I'll come back from Dak

165

Pek through Da Nang and talk to him then."

Cade may have said, "Maybe they're trying to tell you something," or he may not. I wasn't listening. I was making plans for the patrol.

18

Baxter kept me well back toward the center of the patrol, a position befitting a visiting dignitary. I didn't like it much, but it was his company and I was just a straphanger. I could have ordered him to let me move forward, but I didn't like having high ranking officers coming around and telling me what to do, and I didn't suppose he did either. After all I was a guest here.

It was midmorning before we left and we walked parallel to the airstrip, as though we were going north, and then turned right into the jungle, so beautiful it could take your breath away, with the giant hardwood trees, mahogany and teak climbing up a hundred feet before the branches interlaced so tightly that there was no chance of seeing naked sky, just luminous green leaves letting a pale light through so that it was perpetual dusk, damp and hot. Down underneath, the undergrowth crowded close to the trail, so there was no possibility of moving cross country. It was either move on the trail or don't move at all. A patrol had gone out from one of our other camps nearby with orders not to move on the trails. They went one hundred yards in a week. They did not get out of the sound of their own generator. That ended that experiment.

Before we got all the way to the river, maybe two kilometers from camp, I heard the sound of an aircraft landing on the airstrip. Major Allen. My back stiffened as I looked over my shoulder, wondering if he would order me back. If he gave a direct order I would have to go. Otherwise I would stay with the patrol.

We received no message.

I had been in camp for a month, without exercise, and the

rucksack dragged at my back after the first click. It wasn't bad, but I remembered my first patrol here, struggling, all afternoon, mouth open as we climbed up the slippery, muddy trail for four hours, made camp, stumbled down the other side in the morning, ate lunch in a creek, and climbed up all afternoon. We'd been able to move maybe two kilometers in a day, sticking to the trails. Compared to that, this was fairly comfortable.

We wound down and down and down slowly toward the river. The walking was still fairly easy and I enjoyed it. On the first patrol before this I'd been winded and spent all the time we were moving in utter misery. Come to think of it, though, it hadn't been nearly as bad coming back, and since then I had hoofed it up to most of the little platoon sized outposts we had on the peaks around the camp. Maybe I was in better shape than I thought. I'd probably lost some weight too, camp food being what it was.

The map showed the river as a small stream that we should have been able to wade easily, but when we got there it was over forty feet wide, looked to be about ten feet deep and swift, rushing over rapids to a short waterfall maybe fifty feet downriver from the stream.

It was very beautiful, though, and I was filled with a curious mixture of pleasure and frustration at our difficulty. Most of these Nungs couldn't swim, I was sure, and I was equally sure the stream was too deep to wade. Moving with packs and equipment like this there was no way they could cross. About two weeks before two American SF men at another camp had been killed in a river crossing just like this.

The green luminous light of the jungle turned gold in the open air, and blue sky hung down over the burbling river. There was white water frothing around the slick, mossy rocks in the stream. It was fair to say I was a happy man; esthetically pleased. I don't know why, but I surged forward past puzzled looking Nungs in tiger suits bellowing, "Aw right. Goddamnit. What's the story here?"

By the time I got to the head of the column Billy Baxter, who had more time in the jungle than I had in the army, had devised a scheme to get across without ropes and without getting our gear wet.

There were long vines hanging from the trees. The Nungs pulled a bunch of these down and tied enough together to reach across the stream. Baxter had guards out both up and down stream, two man teams, I believe, each about fifty meters out from the company and facing out. I'm not even sure they waited for an order. Those Nungs were pros.

A lanky Nung kid had volunteered to take the vine across and stripped to the waist, tied one end of the vine around him. There were several of us gathered around the head of the company now, but then we sort of faded back into the jungle a little. The Nungs weren't the only pros out here. And we automatically hesitated to offer too tempting a target. There probably weren't any Cong around, but offering your sweet body as bait is a poor way to test that hypothesis.

The kid hung off a tree that jutted out over the water and lowered himself in. He started swimming across in sure, swift strokes. In a few minutes he was over and had the vine tied to a tree on the other side. A couple of other Nungs went down in the water. They had their gear on, but their carbines were slung high on their necks, to keep them above water. All the Nungs had M-2 carbines, incidentally, which meant that every man on the patrol had an automatic weapon, multiplying our fire power several times over what one of my little strike force companies would have. These special outfits, being more elite and working closer to the head-quarters, got first pick on the best gear. There was some justification to it though, because these fellows had some fire discipline. My strikers would just have shot all their ammo into the air at the first sign of contact and that would have been the end of our fighting ability.

At least with M-1 carbines my strikers couldn't waste their ammo faster than they could pull the trigger.

I asked Baxter if I could go over early. I wanted to get across so there would be an American (Australians were honorary Americans, or vice versa, in Vietnam) on the other side. Really I just wanted to get over there to get my adrenalin up a little. I think perhaps Special Forces guys and other people like them have depressed metabolisms and they have to be exposed to some sort of danger to feel normal. I do not recall a moment in my life when I was not bored before I got to Vietnam; very few since leaving there. Going to Nam was like trying on my first pair of glasses. Before the glasses I didn't know that other people could see clearly. Before going to Nam I didn't know that everyone wasn't paralyzed by boredom all the time.

I suppose that in any well-ordered society people like us would be locked up or shot. But then you would have to get people like us to do the locking up and the shooting.

I grabbed the tree and lowered myself into the water. The water swirled up to my chest quickly. But I had my rifle in the air and my pack had everything inside it in a waterproof bag. The only thing I was worried about was my Randall knife. It was my most prized possession, a beautiful eight inch number one. The design is very similar to Constantin Brancusi's *Bird in Space*, and to my mind just as beautiful. In point of fact there is a Randall knife on display at the Museum of Modern Art in New York on the same floor as the Brancusi.

I was a lot taller than the Nungs and got almost halfway across before my feet left the bottom. I had to hang on the vine and pull myself for maybe fifteen feet and then I was touching bottom again. It was a piece of cake. I could probably have made it without the vine, but the Nungs were too short.

Then the vine broke and two Nungs were swept down toward the fall. I quickly shed my gear and started downstream, hopping clumsily over the shining wet rocks to get out to them thinking of the guys who had drowned the week before. But it wasn't necessary. They both pulled themselves up on some rocks and we dragged them over to the far shore. Then some more vines were cut and the rest of the company came over.

The rest of the afternoon we spent moving up the trail to a high mountain peak where we were to make camp that night. Baxter told me it had served as an outpost for Kham Duc a few years back and there were some small bunkers and good visibility there.

Our uniforms were hot and steaming and my socks rolled up in my boots. Our uniforms never did get very dry during that period because there was a perpetual drizzle that hit the canopy above, slid down the slick trunks of the giant hard-wood trees, soaked into the ground and hung on the bushes, slapping at you as you moved down the old trails, wet-slapping, wet-slapping, until your entire body was soaked. My glasses were slapped and steaming all the time, until I finally gave up trying to see through them and put them in my pocket. My vision isn't all that bad, and you can't see farther than ten or fifteen feet in that bush anyway.

There were elephant feces on the trail, enormous grey turds with straw in them. I never did see the elephants though. As usual, on the trail I abandoned myself to musing, making a thousand connections, planning, scheming, always trying to figure some way to make this crazy assignment work. With the best strike force in the world this job would have been difficult. With the dizzy band of unfortunates which I had been provided it was impossible. There had to be some way to put some fire into these sleazy little creeps. There is always a way. The Nungs were good, though some of their organization and practices would have driven a conventional American commander into a frenzy. For instance half of them were burning joss sticks tied to the end of their carbines as we marched along. It was supposed to ward off evil spirits.

Well, I guess they figured if they got rid of the evil spirits with magic they could take care of the Cong themselves. Each platoon headquarters consisted of a platoon leader, platoon sergeant, messenger and witch doctor. I guess witch chaplain would be the correct term. We went along through the jungle burning joss sticks, the witch chaplains muttering incantations.

I was beginning to get a handle on how to work with Orientals. A lot of Americans believe the Viets are cowards, and this isn't true. But they have to be handled right. The Cong, for instance, are not cowards and they fight with considerable success. The difference, I believe, is in psychological preparation. It is well known that the Cong rehearse and rehearse and rehearse until an attack is automatic. Rehearsal is a part of the American doctrine too, but not to the same extent. Each of their rehearsals is run like a combination rehearsal and pep rally. The soldiers cheer so much and get psyched up so much that when the time comes for the attack they are too crazy to stop.

I don't believe this crap about the Cong believing so strongly in his cause that he'll sacrifice himself. No, what happens is that they are driven bananas before they attack.

Once *Dai Uy* Anh and I were discussing how we'd plan an attack against Kham Duc if we were the VC. I opted for sneaking up through the draws and crawling under the wire at a couple of spots I had picked out to beef up the guard. But the *Dai Uy* said no, they would come right across the runway. This seemed insanity to me, to run a battalion across fifty yards of flat runway, into the lights, with two layers of triple concertina wire and a minefield, and machine guns planted to give flat grazing fire. It struck me as the most stupid, suicidal plan I had ever heard of.

But the next camp they hit, that's how they did it.

And the reason, I believe, was that, psyched up, and sometimes doped up, as they were, their troops were in no condition to do any thinking about what they were doing. It had to be kept very simple or they would screw it up. And what was more simple than running forward, driven by the adrenalin and their own overheated imaginations, supported by having their buddies on either side, yelling and screaming until they either fell dead or made it.

With American ideas of respect for human life and conservation of casualties it was stupid. But to Orientals it made excellent sense.

Contrast this to the way we did it. We trained our Vietnamese troops in the basic military skills, but there was little or no attempt to indoctrinate them, and most attempts that were made were half-hearted and inept. On patrol they wandered through the woods, fat, dumb and happy, until they were fired at, then they lay on their backs and fired up into the air, hoping the noise would scare the Cong away. This went on until some American could get a couple of Nungs and maybe a striker or two with some balls, and run the ambush off.

With these kinds of odds it was a wonder we did as well as we did.

I was going to have to find some way to get our strikers

psyched up. One problem was that we never had a fixed objective. We just wandered around until we were shot at, so there was no rehearsal and no pep rally. I wondered if it would be possible to have the pep rallies without the rehearsals.

I thought about bayonet drill. First time I took bayonet drill at Fort Hood we were out there on the sand screaming "Kill! Kill!" thrusting and lunging, and I thought, how silly. But after fifteen minutes I got in the spirit of the thing and I was screaming, "Kill! Kill!" for real and I wished there was some (check one) (a) Kraut, (b) Jap, (c) Chink, (d) all of the above bastards out there for me to stick my blade through. Kill! Kill! Die, you zipper-eyed motherfucker. It really worked. And at the time I was a junior journalism student at the University of Oklahoma, down at Fort Hood for his ROTC summer camp; not killer material at all.

Maybe bayonet drill. My team would go bugfuck when I came back suggesting that we start bayonet drill.

In this way we marched, straggled, lurched, up this incredibly tall slick jungle covered mountain.

I have often wondered since if I was really so nobly dedicated to the cause of the war or if I just liked walking in the jungle like that, alone with my own thoughts. The war was a great puzzle, great to think about, great to plan, great to do. It was so incredibly peaceful out there in the jungle. There was none of the cacophonous jangle of television breaking for commercials, telephone calls, agitated messengers running in, fool colonels from headquarters insisting on the exercise of totally incomprehensible policies. There was only the perpetual green jungle, so close it hit you in the face thirty times a second, rifle slung like a guitar over your shoulder, maybe fifty pounds in your rucksack, and a Nung ahead and a Nung behind.

I liked the slow plod forward, up the mountain, down the mountain, the peacefulness of it, birdcalls, and monkey whoops in the morning, with the mists shrouding around. True, there was the danger of a firefight, but firefights were exciting and I was not afraid. I knew in a general sort of way it was possible for me to die, but I gave no credence to it. I was, after all, the hero of the book, and the hero never dies,

173

at least not until the end of the book, and then nobly.

So I was not afraid of the Cong, and I was not afraid of the jungle. We stopped for a break and I sank wearily to the nearest rock and lit a cigarette. Immediately the ground around me came alive with little buggy whips, hunching across the ground to get on me. Soon they were all along my pants and heading toward any break they could find on my uniform. But there were no openings for them. When we first got to Kham Duc a peppery little fellow from some Research and Development outfit flew in with a case of gadgets he wanted tested. They were all patently useless except one. That was the leech repellent. It was just like regular GI insect repellent except that its base was lanolin rather than alcohol. Cover the openings in your uniform: boottops, waist, fly, sleeve openings, neck, and they'd never get through. The stuff was good for six days and nothing could wash it out but a river crossing.

Only once did a leech get on my body at Kham Duc, and that was before we got the leech repellent. On the first patrol I woke up one morning and felt something on my back. When I pulled it off it looked like a large grape, or a small plum. I didn't know what it was, didn't connect it with the one inch buggy whips at all. I threw it down and mashed it and it squished red blood. My blood. Then I knew what it was.

Billy Baxter said the Brits didn't have anything like the leech repellent in Malaya. He said that many nights they'd stop on patrol, take their boots off and wring the blood out of their socks.

I never saw any more of that leech repellent after we left Kham Duc. I guess it wasn't adopted by the army, since it worked and didn't cost much.

Grinding and heaving we made it to the top of the mountain just before dusk. True, just as Billy had said there were some old bunkers up there and the trees had been cut down so that the area was defensible. Normally on top of those mountains you can't see six feet in front of you because of the undergrowth. But here, although the mountaintop itself was cut up and left ugly, we could see for twenty miles. I looked out across the valley, shrouded, gray green rain forest welling, diving, and climbing to another peak twenty miles away.

There is no way I can describe the beauty or majesty of that moment. I stood, the ranking man, king of everything I surveyed, looking over my domain, twenty miles of it, and the clouds drifted by in the valley below. A hawk soared across a hundred yards out and fifty below where I stood.

I had paid dearly for that moment, but it was worth any price which could have been exacted for it. It was like being given the world on a hot dog bun.

That night I slept in the rotting bunker, rolled up in a poncho, with the smelly feet of a Nung pressed against my nose. I would rather have been in the jungle in my own hammock, but still, I slept like a rock.

The next morning we groped down the mountain and ate lunch in the ever present stream at the bottom. We perched on a rock ledge over the rushing stream and I skewered meat out of a can of C-rations, drinking water with iodine pills in it and munching vile C-ration candy afterward, while Baxter sat twenty feet downstream, brewing tea and discoursing barbarously in Australian.

We continued that way for four days, without seeing any sign of the enemy, or any sign of human life. We knew there were Montagnards there in the area, the Katu. No white man had made contact with the Katu in this area. They were reputed to be headhunters, and the French had mounted a few punitive expeditions against them, without results. None of us had ever seen one. We saw no sign of them, although, in the distance, across the valleys we sometimes saw their rice fields through breaks in the trees.

The Cong were supposed to have made contact with them and to have used them as guides on infiltration routes. They must have spent a long time making friends with the Katu to be able to do that, for they were Vietnamese, and the Katu, if they were like other Montagnards, hated Vietnamese passionately.

But we saw nothing, only the perpetual jungle. We pulled ourselves up the slopes that were seldom less than forty-five degrees. I used my rifle as a staff a lot, for it was still hard for an old flatlander like me to push myself up in these mountainous jungles. I don't know which was worse, the climbing up or the climbing down. After five days we had covered ten kilometers. When I was getting ready to go to jump school I sometimes ran farther than that on my lunch break.

But at noon of the fifth day we found evidence that the other bunch was in the area. Spear traps. I heard a sound of *spong-g-g-g-g* up ahead and the Nung ahead of me pointed as we went by. There was a concerned look on his face. There hidden in the jungle beside the trail was a spear, made of a piece of split bamboo, pointed on one end and notched on the other, propped up on a Y-shaped stake. The notched end had a tied-down branch attached to it, bent back to form a catapult, hooked to a trip vine which ran across the trail, aimed groin high. This one had been sprung by the point man of our patrol. He had spotted it in time and no one was hurt.

I looked and nodded. "Uh-huh! Pretty slick." And every man wounded by one would require two others to carry him.

We stopped early that night, just after passing a little clearing which for some unaccountable reason had beer and coke cans lying in the grass, as though a bunch of Americans had had a picnic there.

I moved forward in the column until I came to Baxter, writing out his evening sitrep for the commo man. "What's the story?" I asked.

"We need some chow," he replied, "and this is the last clearing big enough to take a chopper between here and Dak Pek. We're going to stop here and get some tucker." That's where the cans had come from. Some other patrol had been resupplied here and the chopper had brought cold drinks.

I nodded, thinking again. "How's about I take a squad up ahead for a couple of clicks and check it out. I can see if there's any sign, and spring any spear traps we find. That way they won't slow us down so bad."

He agreed. I took the squad immediately and set off down the trail. As is my custom I put out a point man ten meters ahead of the squad and then I walked just behind the number two man. That way I could see the point and if any action started I'd be right on it. We were running on the trail along the top of the ridge line so we were able to move very rapidly

176

in comparison to our normal pace. We went for more than a kilometer and disarmed six spear traps on the way. That meant there'd be that much less chance of their tripping us up the next day when we moved out. With only ten men we moved very quickly and I had little time to muse on the events of the day, or plan for the future, but the germ of a plan did form in my mind and I talked it over with Billy Baxter when I got back.

"You ever try a staybehind ambush?" I asked. We were seated on our rucksacks. My AR-15 was leaned up against a tree and his shotgun sat beside it. He wouldn't carry an AR-15, said they were too prone to jam. I couldn't help but agree with him, since the last time I'd fired one in the rain mine had jammed. But they were such death-dealing little jewels when they did work that I preferred to chance it.

He nodded, chewing on a mouthful of rice and C-ration beans and franks.

"Okay!" I pointed my fork at him. "What I want to try is a go-ahead ambush."

He looked at me close, perhaps a little puzzled.

"Look! That chopper'll be in here tomorrow. When it comes in every Cong for twenty miles is going to know there is a patrol in the area. The odds are you'll be ambushed the day after you get resupplied, right?"

Baxter nodded agreement. "It could happen. That's the most likely time."

"Right!" I nodded intensely, pointing my fork at him. "Okay! They're trailbound, just like we are. So if they ambush you, they will have to come in on an intersecting trail. What I want to do is to take a couple of squads out tonight after the resupply, set up an ambush on the next most likely trail junction and maybe ambush the ambushers." I grinned, very proud of this little scheme.

Baxter looked at me closely. His face betrayed very little, but I think he thought the plan had some merit. It was kind of a long shot, but what, in that war, wasn't. At any rate, he agreed.

The chopper came in about three o'clock the next afternoon. But he only brought half the stuff we ordered. It was an old Marine H-34 that hovered and whopped around for an ungodly long time. There was no way he could do that and not give our position away with total accuracy. They would know where we were, what trail we were on and what direction we were moving in. If I ever saw a set-up for an ambush this was it.

They were supposed to bring in two loads of stuff, but there was only one chopper, and by the time he finished unloading there was not enough time to make any headway so we made camp for the night.

The next morning I went to talk to Baxter.

"We didn't get enough supplies to complete the patrol," he said. "I'm going to take enough to get back to Kham Duc on the highway, cache the rest and abort."

That blew my go-ahead ambush. If we changed directions, dropped down the side of this mountain, instead of running the ridge, and went over to the highway, they wouldn't be expecting us to come that way. I nodded, mildly put out, but a little relieved.

We weren't expecting to move very far that day so we got up late and started caching the supplies. It was noon by the time we were scheduled to move out, and as we got the company formed up the Marine chopper showed up again with the rest of our stuff. So we reverted back to the original plan, got the additional supplies, retrieved the supplies we'd hidden halfway down the slope of the mountain and started out again.

It made me a little happy and a little scared. I would get to go ahead with my original ambush plan, which wasn't really the safest plan in the world, when you thought about it. But I hate it when everything changes, and then changes back again. Continuity in planning, the ability to project your activities with some kind of long range control, is essential in a successful operation. True, it is necessary to be able to improvise when the situation calls for it. But this wasn't improvising. This was just fucking around.

And I was worried, too, about what the change in timing would do to the go ahead ambush. We were starting a half a day late, but not moving far. It was very possible that when I went ahead tonight with my ambush part I would find the Cong already set up. My two squads would have less chance in a counter ambush drill than the entire company. I lost myself in running out all the possible permutations of the situation.

But before we left there was one more idea I had that I wanted to try. Americans are so well supplied that when they leave a bivouac site they disregard all kinds of things Vietnamese peasants, or Montagnards, or Cong, whoever is in the area can use. C-ration tin cans, for instance, make excellent cups, or booby traps. There are plastic spoons, and many other goodies, including sometimes rations that have proven too heavy by the third day. Especially after a resupply, when some guys go through and cull out the food they don't like, ham and lima beans, for instance, or the crackers, which taste lousy and eat up a lot of space. Anyway, about three days after one of the sites is vacated, the scavengers show up. That is where the staybehind ambush works well. A small party is left behind on the fringes of a bivouac site, usually waiting about three days. The scavenger party is usually only three guys and it's three easy kills in an area where any at all are hard to come by.

It works best when the company can run in a loop and move back through the same area four or five days later.

But it's hard to train guys to lie still with a bare minimum of movement for four days, and sometimes it's hard to bring the company back around. In that case the ambush party has to catch up, which isn't safe.

So the staybehind ambush is rarely used.

Back at Buon Beng I'd dreamed up this nifty booby trap that I had wanted to use ever since. The idea is to take a hand grenade, pull the pin, and holding the handle down, slide a C-ration can down over the top, then place the can upside down in the dirt, packed in pretty solid. Charles scavenges through the bivouac area and picks up the can, which releases the handle, which blows the grenade. He's got four seconds to move, so he may get away, but in any case it gives him something to think about.

Turned out later that this idea had been done before, and the best thing is to replace the original firing mechanism with an instantaneous detonator. But I didn't have an instantaneous detonator.

179

We had never used this little gadget at Buon Beng because the scavengers were more likely to be Montagnards than Cong, but here there was no question. It would be bad guys.

So I got a can, pulled the pin, and, heart pounding a little, because I am afraid of grenades, I made my little booby trap. I was so proud. I had invented something.

Then we formed the company up and moved out. I stood with my foot on the tin can, so none of the Nungs would kick it over and blow himself up, until half of the company had gone buy. Then I pointed it out to the man behind me and made signs to tell him to pass it on what the can was and fell in behind a Nung.

We were able to move very quickly, running along the top of the ridge like that. It was just like walking, not mountain climbing. And I had taken the squad ahead and triggered all the spear traps for a kilometer ahead. We were going to move faster than I had figured, right through the area where I had expected to be ambushed. And since we had just finished getting the supplies I didn't expect to get hit until the next day. We would probably move through the area where we would get ambushed before the ambush party got there. We were really humping right along. Still though, it would be fun to take a party out to the next trail junction and wait and see what happened. Yes, it would definitely be worth a try.

Those are the things I was thinking as we moved along. It was very pleasant walking, although there was the perpetual drizzle sliding down the sides of the hardwood trees and the jungle pressed in thick around us. Funny, I can get claustrophobic almost anywhere in New Jersey, and submarines and elevators drive me bananas, but I have never felt closed in in the jungle. I have always felt secure and quietly happy in the jungle.

I was startled out of my reverie by the sound of a shot ahead, answered by several automatic weapons and the sound of a grenade. That was probably one of the Nungs. I was always dubious about throwing grenades in the jungle. About half the time they'd hit a tree branch on the way to the enemy and drop down among the friendlies. Also I was very chagrined about having misfigured the time of the ambush.

Outsmarted yourself again, eh, Mastermind?

All around me the Nungs were hitting the dirt, although there was not a sign of any gunfire coming through this far back in the company. It was the point which was under fire. The Nungs moved very professionally, but I saw several of them looking back over their shoulders at me with something akin to anguish on their faces.

I wasn't worried. I still thought of this as the kind of firefight we'd gotten into north of Buon Beng, being ambushed by two or three ill-trained Montagnards, with maybe one weapon and three rounds between them, more lookouts than ambushers. But I wanted to get up to Baxter and see what the story was. So I dropped my rucksack where I stood. Taking that fifty pounds off had somewhat the effect of saying SHAZAM! I felt free and able to fight again. Heavy ammo pouches thudding against my pelvis I charged forward toward the point of the company, startled Nungs looking over their shoulders to see what fool was up and moving around when that war movie soundtrack was playing ahead. They looked so scared it was funny and I could feel a grin forming on my face. Not the wolf grin I'd worn when we went out hunting action at Buon Beng, but a kind of silly grin as though I was caught in some Marx Brothers comedy.

I came upon Baxter, who was crouched on the ground. I heard a couple of rounds snap around my head and decided maybe he had something there. I got down beside him. "What's the story?" I asked.

"There's an infiltration trail ahead," he said, "and it looks like a beauty. The Cong are up on a hill overlooking it."

All this time the company was down and all this ammo was banging around. Lying there in the dirt like that wasn't the way to do it. If we didn't overrun their ambush they would pick us to pieces. Besides I couldn't get those Buon Beng ambushes out of my mind. I was much more afraid that they would get away without our killing any of them than I was that they would inflict serious casualties on us.

"Where's the Nung Company Commander?" I demanded of Baxter.

He pointed toward the rear of the company. "Back there.

I've sent for him."

Technically Mr. Hee, the Nung, was in command of the Company and Baxter was their advisor and I was an observer. The whole thing was far too cumbersome to work well and I was bored by the prospect of having to work through such an unwieldy chain of command. By the time Hee finished making out the morning report, or whatever the hell he was doing and Baxter made it clear to him what he wanted and we executed it, the bastards would have inflicted casualties on us and got away clean. A quick plan formed in my mind. The ambush was forward and to our left. We would move out to the right and through or around the point, with luck flanking the ambush. Fortunately the jungle was flat and open enough for that kind of maneuvering here. It was about the first place on this patrol where it had been.

I stood up and looked around. Snap! Snap! rounds around my head. I thumbed the AR-15 to full auto, took a deep breath and bellowed, "FUCK IT! LET'S GO!" charging off in the jungle firing short bursts from the rifle.

I was moving through heavy woods, going down a slight grade. The woods weren't so heavy as to impede progress, but I couldn't see much. Baxter was moving very cool on my left and the Nungs were up and following. They were good, very good. They moved automatically up on line with no commands or hand and arm signals at all. They were firing short bursts at the direction of the enemy fire. It was fine. It was a classic, textbook assault.

Somebody behind me said, "Punji's!" And sure enough the ground we were moving through was sown with them, needle tipped and sticking up at all angles. "Fuck a bunch of Punji's," I muttered and immediately got stuck in the leg. Ah well, it didn't hurt much. I ignored it. "COME ON! COME ON! COME ON!" I bellowed. "LET'S GO! LET'S GO! LET'S GO!"

Goddamn, it was beautiful. We went around them, moved back up the slope and overran their position without a single serious casualty. The Cong moved out leaving one man dying that I saw. I heard of another. We had done it. I had led a successful assault against a well-defended enemy position. Oh shit, it felt good. The adrenalin in my body was going *zinggggg* and *zinggggg* and *zinggggg* some more. Somehow it filled me with a fantastic feeling of calm. I felt totally in charge. It was as though my body were completely at the disposal of my will. I had only to think of what needed to be done and the body would do it instantaneously, without tiring or complaint. It was a very sweet feeling.

I had fired up one magazine from the AR-15. I changed fast and kept my rifle on the Cong who was dying. Baxter was there with his twelve gauge also, and a couple of Nungs were with us, but we stayed fairly well spread out in the clearing around the dying man.

I stood at the bottom of a perfect staircase of split logs, pegged into the side of the mountain. They were fairly new and well-maintained. We were standing at a major intersection of the Ho Chi Minh trail, only eight miles from my camp. I had flown over this place two or three times in light aircraft on recon flights, but there is no way I could have seen this through the tree cover.

The dying Cong was no amateur either. He wore a professional looking gray cotton uniform, sort of like what the attendants wear at a Derby gas station.

His hat was a darker blue brimmed floppy hat, like the fatigue hats the U.S. Army wore before World War II. He had a new pack, two or three Chinese grenades and a brand new SKS carbine. And of course, Ho Chi Minh sandals. He had the standard North Vietnamese regular haircut, a butch with white sidewalls, slightly longer on top than the American military version. He was a good looking trooper, a hell of a lot better than my strike force. But I was worried about the way he was lying. He was face down with his hands under him. He might have a grenade under there with the idea of taking three or four of us with him. Having to stand still and watch him was making me more and more nervous.

Billy nodded his head at him. "I'll watch him," he said. "Keep an eye on the trail, please!"

I turned and covered the trail.

Baxter's interpreter ran up. He was an intelligent looking Vietnamese kid, fairly well educated, and obviously considered himself too good for such rough usage. He was fairly hopping up and down with fear. "More VC on hill!" he jabbered, pointing excitedly. Then even more excitedly he pointed at the VC. "Kill him! Kill him!" he shrieked.

That was something of a temptation. The Cong was dying anyway, and we couldn't trust him. If I shot him he would be out of his misery and we could quit worrying about him. But killing prisoners has never been my style and I could tell that Baxter wasn't interested either. At this stage of the game South Vietnamese were great ones for killing and torturing prisoners. I think they knew they didn't have their stuff together and it frightened them. They worked off some of this fright by proving how brave they were on the helpless and infirm. The Cong in most areas were much more cool about it and never killed anybody unless there was a good reason for it. Morally there was no difference in their actions, but tactically the Cong version made much better sense.

I'd have been a lot better off if I had gone ahead and shot him, for then I'd have found out something I needed to know. But I didn't.

The interpreter's fear filled me with contempt and in reaction I was positively laconic. "Uh!" I said to Baxter. "This guy says there's Cong on the hill. What say I take a squad up there and check it out?" At this point I was thinking of two or three of them left up there to cover their retreat, and I wanted to get them before they got away too.

He nodded, turned, and did one of these You, You and You numbers with his finger. I wound up with six Nungs, turned and bounded off up the stairway; reminded me of a dance number in an old MGM musical, An American in Paris, I think, where Gene Kelly goes bounding up a set of golden steps supported by absolutely nothing but blue sky, singing, "I built a stairway to paradise, with a new step every day." White tie and tails he wore, and carried a cane.

It was really a neat set of steps. They were not weathered at all.

I reached the point where the hill started to flatten out some, the military crest it is called in tactics classes, and it occurred to me that I was awfully exposed running on those steps so I sidestepped to the left, off into the brush.

This was a fortuitous move for as I jumped left I heard a crack and felt a thud in my right shoulder. He must have had a perfect sight picture on the center of my chest. I squeezed the trigger on my rifle. The bolt went *ka-schlugg* and that was it, baby. Jammed again.

I have done a number of foolish things in my life, but none so foolish as to lead an assault against a defended enemy position with six guys and me with no weapon. I dived down behind a log. There was a lot of firing going on now and I looked and saw that all my Nungs were down too. I looked at my shoulder. There was a large black hole in my shirt, rimmed with red, drying blood. It was pretty nasty looking, but my arm moved just fine, and other than the initial sting it felt all right. I grabbed the charging handle on my AR-15 and tried to budge it. The handle went way back. The circumstances were the same as the last patrol at Buon Beng. It jammed on the second magazine in the rain. I couldn't bust it loose. We were taking all kinds of fire, and what we needed was to put some indirect fire on the enemy. I turned around and bellowed, "We need an M-79 up here." There was no reply, so I bellowed again, but there was no hearing over the sound of the firing, and nobody seemed to be coming up the hill for us.

That was when my thinking started to go awry. The rifle was jammed and I couldn't get anything going and I didn't have any means to get at the bastards at all. I could have whipped out my Randall and stormed up the hill with it alone, and I was almost, but not quite, angry enough to. I was in a cold fury of frustration. Mechanical devices have always hated me, but for my own rifle to malfunction at such a time transcends the limits of allowable fuckups for inanimate objects. "Aw right," I muttered, "gimme a fucking carbine!"

Some Nung in the bushes behind me, that I hadn't even seen, threw one at me. An M-2 carbine, with a thirty round magazine, and I had no idea how much ammo it had in it. I checked the safety and saw the switch was on full auto. Then I started looking back up the hill.

About twenty feet on up the hill a Cong poked his head up from where he was hiding behind a felled tree trunk. I squeezed off a three round burst at him and he ducked back down. I started counting. When I got to ten he poked his head back up again and I squeezed off another burst. Ten seconds, in ten seconds I could get up there and blow his head off. I jumped up to go after him and just as I got to the squatting position some son of a bitch that I didn't see shot me in the left nut.

It was a slapping sting, really hard, and then it went numb. The thing, I think, that stopped me from pursuing this matter any further was something I had read, or heard somewhere, about your testicles being made up of thousands of feet of tiny filaments all rolled up in a ball in your scrotum. I got this rapid mental image of my scrotum being broken and all those filaments rolling out as I tried to charge on up the hill. I saw them thick as thread, and pink and glittering, dragging down in the mud, and me charging the hill, stepping on them in my cleated jungle boots, stopping my own rapid charge with a jerk. Yes, I believe that mental image did it. I lost all interest in personally taking that hill at that moment.

I was still able to move pretty well, crawling. I started scooting back down the hill at a fairly rapid clip. When I got a little way down I heard my demo man, Bud Kelly, who had come along on the patrol, calling, "You all right, sir?"

I grinned. I couldn't help it. It was easily the silliest question imaginable under the circumstances. "Hey Bud!" I called.

"You all right?" he called back. To this day I don't know where I got this information. I certainly hadn't gone around and asked. But it was correct. "I've got one dead and one wounded and I'm shot in the right shoulder and the left nut," I called down. "Other than that everything is just swell."

I scooted down the side of the hill and was immediately ringed by anxious white faces. "Are you okay?" Baxter asked.

We skinned down my pants for a look. It was very strange. The trousers were covered with blood, but they were not broken. Apparently the round had just plowed a furrow across my pants. If I'd been wearing jockey shorts it wouldn't have touched me at all. But as it was there was complete trauma and the scrotum was swollen and bruised black all over. It looked, in point of fact, like a rather large eggplant covered with blond hair. My poor little penis, on the other hand, had shriveled almost to the point of disappearance. Another inch and it would have been concave. But although everything seemed fairly messed up, it was all there. I figured after six weeks or so it would be in working order again. Hoped so, anyway, for it was not a certainty. But in the meantime, there were more pressing problems.

As the Nung medic started bandaging my groin I called to Baxter. The Nung was doing a very professional job, I was pleased to note. "You're going to need everything you've got to get up that hill," I said to Baxter, "and you'd better put some indirect fire on it when you go up there."

He was listening very closely. "Got it," he said. "Now we've got to get you out of here, and the rest of the wounded. We're going to send for a medevac and take you back to the chopper pad. Can you walk?"

"Dunno!" I said. I got to my feet, profoundly grateful that I was not knockkneed. I was a little unsteady, but still able to navigate. "Yeah, I think so."

Billy turned his attention back to the job at hand. I went with a detail of the sick, lame and lazy, heading back toward the chopper pad, something like a mile, maybe more, back on the trail from which we'd come.

It was funny walking. I felt weak, of course, woozy would be a good word for it, and the woods seemed so peaceful as we walked away from the fight. I hoped they could take the hill and not take any more casualties.

There was another problem. It got dark early there and it was about four-thirty as we started walking. We had a half hour or so of daylight to get out and I was fairly sure that if we didn't get out that night I'd bleed to death.

It was a very peculiar feeling to be calculating the chances of my own immediate death, knowing that the life was leaving my body, for I could feel myself getting weaker and weaker. I figured the odds on my survival at maybe three to two in favor, but I didn't really like those odds. It was time to give some serious thought to the possibility of dying. I discovered I could do it.

187

I mean that I felt inside myself that if I were dying and knew it I could carry it off with style, with a smile on my face, if not a melody in my heart. I could, if necessary, make some smartass remark that would be talked about in Officer's and NCO Clubs for years when they got in one of those, "Remember old so-and-so", "Yeah, he got it in —————" conversations.

They're really pretty discouraging, those conversations. You sit around for hours, getting drunker and drunker and talking about how your friends got killed. I reckon I got to do that for about a third of my Special Forces Officer's class before it was all over. Us bloodthirsty warmongers, you know, we all like to die. It's right there on our Form 66, Hobbies: judo, sky diving, dying. That's why we start all these wars. We like to die so much.

Anyhow, I was strolling along, dying, and knowing I could do it if I had to.

Finally though, although I could die with aplomb, I couldn't walk anymore. I was too weak. I sank slowly to the jungle floor, bleeding from an unbandaged wound on the right cheek of my ass that nobody had discovered yet. It was just a little thing, probably from the same round that caught me in the nut, and I don't think anybody ever did discover it until I was on the operating table, since it was never sewed up. It's there now. The scar looks like I was kissed on the ass by somebody wearing purple lipstick.

If it had been bandaged with the others I could probably have walked all the way back. The Nungs made a litter by cutting a long pole and strapping a poncho to it. They rolled me into the litter. I felt kind of candyassed for being carried, when some of the others were walking, but I just couldn't hack it. Bobbing along on that litter, only semi-conscious, and the sharp intake of breath as the Nungs dragged that low slung litter with my long, fat American body in it over some little hillock. Oh, Jesus, and the sun going down slowly. Then I heard the chopper ahead, but didn't know if they would make it before the sun went down and the chopper had to go away. And if it did, would I make it through the night? And if we had to stay by that chopper pad overnight the Cong would be on our ass and the chopper would stand a strong chance of being shot down. Oh, fuck! If we didn't get all the wounded out of here tonight, there would be hell to pay.

It was the whole movie serial thing, the sun was going down, and the chopper was hovering and I was wondering if they would make it or not. Shot of sun going down, cut to shot of chopper going away, cut to shot of hero passing out. Fade. Be sure to come back next week.

Next week there's the synopsis, and the hero makes it in time. Which we did. I felt my body go over one last bump and we broke out into the fading sunlight. The chopper was circling around, but it circled back.

It was at this time that I did the only truly unselfish thing I can recall having ever done. I grabbed ahold of the nearest American, I think it was Bud Kelly, but I am not sure, and asked, "Have all the other wounded been evacuated?" It was my intention to refuse evacuation until all the Nung wounded had been got out. A lot of American advisors have evacuated their American wounded before their Viets. That is unacceptable. An officer, and every advisor functions as an officer, must lead by example. If he doesn't bend every effort to take care of his troops, placing that ahead of his own life, but not ahead of the mission, then he is a disgrace to the uniform he wears. This was particularly true in Vietnam where their own officer corps was so poorly trained and shot through with the idea of mandarin privilege. What the hell would the Nungs have thought if I'd been evaced first? You know bloody well what they'd have thought and they'd have been right.

But I got the answer I wanted. The Nung wounded had all been evacuated, although the dead had not. The Nungs were very picky about the burial of their dead, wanting it done on home ground and all that, but I felt that getting the stiffs out first would be stretching a point too far. I was all set to go.

The chopper eased back in over the little clearing, too small to land in. The downdraft beat the grass horizontal and fanned my fevered brow. Since they couldn't land they lowered a cable from a winch that hung outside the door. At the end of the cable was a gadget that looked like an outsize horsecollar. A well man can sit in it, and an unconscious one can be strapped to it, but how does a man with a pair of balls the size of an eggplant sit in it? The answer was that I had to hang from my knees and hold on to the little ring at the top that held it to the cable, weak as I was. Strong hands grabbed me and lifted me into the horsecollar. I grabbed the ring, weak and dizzy, and immediately the horsecollar started spinning slowly, *wzschoom——wzschoom*. I held on tight and the cable went up and the ground dropped away beneath as the thing spun around and I held on as tight as I could, which wasn't very.

"Hold on, sir," Bud Kelly called out, "hold on!"

I looked down and saw my chance to make some smartass gesture. I grinned confidently and called out, "Airborne!" Then a couple of Marines grabbed me and pulled me into the chopper and we were away toward Kham Duc.

19

I must have passed out in the chopper for the next thing I knew we were landing on my strip and the anxious faces of Al Smith, my XO, and the *Dai Uy* Anh were looking in at me. I was glad to see Al, but doubly glad to see the *Dai Uy*. There was real concern on his face, he really cared whether I lived or died. I count that as a victory in a war that has been marked by animosity among the allies. I liked the old *Dai Uy* a lot and he liked me. We respected each other. It made me feel that if I could have stayed there we could have accomplished the things I set out to do.

They put me on a litter and I was carried to a waiting C-130. A whole 130 with no passengers or cargo save your old Uncle Bunky. That was rather nice, I thought. The Nung wounded had already been taken by chopper to the ARVN hospital in Da Nang, but I was going to the 8th Field Hospital in Nha Trang. The American Special Forces doctor from Da Nang was there, gave me a shot of something pleasant, and some plasma, and poked around to see if there was a round in my lungs. I knew from the trajectory of the bullet when it hit me that there couldn't be and I told him so, but you know doctors; man, you can't tell them anything. They think you check your brains at the door.

I dozed off again and woke up being carried off into a spiffy little white ambulance with a red light on top. I caught a glimpse of the light revolving, but they didn't use the siren as we moved out. Then there were more glimpses of fluorescent lights and hallways that spun rapidly as we turned corners. Then we were in a large room, and a pretty nurse in a white uniform was cutting my grundgy tiger suit off and an officious blond kid medic came up and handed me a card and a ball point pen with U.S. Government stamped in white on the black plastic and said, "Here, Sarge! Fill this out."

I grinned and started filling it out. I was suddenly conscious of how scroungy I looked, six days of beard and totally filthy, surrounded by all these antiseptic medical personnel. Somebody new came up and said, "Sir, there's a Special Forces colonel out there to see you."

The kid who handed me the card actually blanched. "Gee," he said, "are you an officer? I didn't——"

I was amazed that he could be concerned about such a thing at such a time. "Forget it, kid," I said. "I don't give a shit."

The colonel was the deputy group commander and he just wanted to pass on a couple of words of praise and encouragement. It was nice of him.

A couple of days later Colonel Spears, the group commander, came over to hand me a Purple Heart. I took that as a chance to propagandize for my idea of a floating guerilla operation in my old area of operations. He seemed interested, but I never saw anything come of it.

All those medals I got are rusting away in a drawer now somewhere, but when things are really bad and my soul needs balm I remember three things. (1) Billy Baxter told Bud Kelly that I had more guts than any American he ever saw. (2) A few months later I was having a beer on Oki with one of the guys who had been in my team and he casually remarked, "You had a lot of respect at Kham Duc, sir," and (3) I had been stuck in bed for two weeks and finally I couldn't stand the boredom any more so I got a bathrobe and shuffled off to the officer's club there at the hospital. It was a half block and it took me a half hour to walk it. I just sort of meandered along, dizzy in the heat.

Coming up the sidewalk the other way was Jack Cade, grinning his deadly Cheshire cat grin. "Hello, Jack," I said. "What are you doing here?"

I believe he was in for an ulcer, but I don't remember for sure. At any rate we stood there and chatted for awhile. Then he said, "You won't make jokes about all the officer KIA's being big blond captains from C Company, now, will you, sir?"

"Huh uh!"

But I did fabricate this other joke about how I'd said I'd give my left nut for a thirty day leave before leaving Okinawa, and then got it as convalescent leave for losing my left nut. A lot of people thought that was funny and it had some currency around Group for awhile.

After leaving Cade I continued shuffling on down to the little officer's club they had set up there in the hospital, went in and sat down on a barstool. I couldn't sit right on top of it, but had to kind of park there on the right cheek of my ass. Even that hurt quite a bit. As I recall, my scrotum was still sort of wired together.

I ordered a Scotch and water and sipped it slowly, feeling the warmth curl around in my belly. It was quite a nice feeling.

There was a poker game going near the bar and one of the players was Jack Morrison, a crusty old Australian warrant officer. Jack had the reputation of being the most foul-mouthed man in the Australian Army, which, if you're familiar with the Australian Army, you'll realize is no mean accomplishment. He's a sort of beat up old duffer, Jack is, with a lot of pride and a lot of style. He was in the hospital for about eighty pieces of shrap he'd picked up in the successful defense of the battalion he was advising. Before I got up he'd shuffle by my bed in U.S. jungle fatigues, Japanese shower shoes—he couldn't wear boots because of the shrapnel in his feet—and his Aussie bush hat. He used to stop by my bunk and accuse me of goldbricking, informing the nurse that he'd spotted me the night before, sneaking out through the fence with 500 piastres in my hand, the going price for a short time downtown.

"Where you going?" I muttered weakly, the first time he used this base canard.

"Oi'm goin' dauntaun to get married!" he said proudly.

"Married?" I replied in amazement.

"Royt!" he replied with utmost aplomb, "for an hour or sao anywye!"

An Australian commando sergeant major once said of Jack, "By God, I don't embarrass easily, but by God, 'e em-

193

barrasses me."

Anyway old Jack looked up from his poker game and demanded, "What're you doin' 'ere?"

"Drinking Scotch."

"'Ow'd you get 'ere?"

"Walked."

"Didn't it hurt?"

I nodded. "Yeah, it hurt!"

Jack Morrison, whom I count as one of the best ever, looked at me for a long time and said, "Boy Gawd, you're an 'ell of a man!"

I don't even know where all those goddamn medals are, but I'll never forget any of those compliments.

That all came later though. Right then I was being wheeled into the operating room. After I was in there a slender, dark-headed doctor with a European accent came in and talked to me. He was a Hungarian refugee named Batsleer. He explained that they would have to take out my left nut, but that would have no effect on my . . . I forget just how he put it, some euphemism or other. Performance, I think. And another doctor was going to work on my shoulder while Batsleer was carving on my scrotum. A big blond major named Richardson, I think, let Batsleer handle the briefing on what to expect.

"Can't save it, huh?" I said, disappointed.

Batsleer nodded, negatively. "We might," he said, "but it would take at least six months to heal, and it won't make any difference at all. This way you'll be out of bed in three weeks."

I thought for a moment and then said, "Sure, okay. Do it!"

The doctors disappeared and a couple of corpsmen came into the room. I was on the table, looking to the side, to keep the light out of my eyes. I felt so awfully scroungy, with my itchy filthy beard and the funky smell from my armpits. I was an offense to everything fine and antiseptic and medical.

"We're going to give you pentothal, sir," one of the medics said.

"Truth serum, huh?" I said. I was beginning to be sort of cheerful. This was new and interesting and I was going to be

194

out during the surgery. There are only two things I can't stand: pain and discomfort.

The kid hung a small bottle filled with clear liquid from a hook stand by the wheeled table I was on and said, "You'll start to feel drowsy in a few minutes, sir."

He wrapped a rubber hose around my upper arm and had me squeeze up a vein, then put in the needle. He was very slick and I barely felt it, at least compared to what I'd expected. Goddamn, how I hate needles.

"Now I'm going to count backwards from one hundred," the kid said. "One hundred, ninety-nine . . ."

"You ever hear the song Johnny Small?" I interrupted. I'd rather shoot the shit with this kid than listen to him count backwards. They weren't launching me into space, after all. "You ever hear it?"

"Huh uh!"

"Goes like this," I said, and I started singing in a voice which has pleased few people. "Oh, my name is Johnny Small, fuck you all. Oh my name is Johnny Small, fuck you all. Oh, my name is Johnny Small, and I only got one ball. Fuck you all, fuck you all, fuck you . . ."

Book Three

"... you must consider that ... instead of
running for your life and taking your chances
you may be going to your doom happily,
filled with your judgments."

— Don Juan
Tales of Power
by Carlos Castaneda

20

That may be the longest flashback in literature. But it brings me back to looking goggle-eyed at Cowboy in Buon Ale A in the fall of 1967.

"Come on in!" said Phillip Drouin, the Cowboy.

We went through the double doors. It was a much more rarefied atmosphere than Kpa Doh's place, with rattan furniture all over the living room, and more flunkies, looking more attentive. We sat down and somebody bustled in with a warm Tiger Beer for each of us. Cowboy turned on his big Akai tape deck. The sound of Herb Alpert's Tijuana Brass filled the room, although one of the speakers was fuzzy sounding. Still, for a Montagnard village, this was a very rarefied atmosphere indeed.

"You still have those records I gave you when I left?" I asked Cowboy.

He nodded. "I keep them at my father-in-law's house in Cheo Reo."

"You don't play them?" I asked, somewhat hurt. I had treasured those records and only given them away out of deep friendship.

He shook his head. "Huh uh. Too jazzy."

He gave me a little bit of a guilty look. To think that he had all that rock 'n' roll locked away in Cheo Reo while I was scuffling for old Cher Bono and Bobby Darin albums at the Pleiku PX. Face it, my friends, we live in a world without justice.

We sat drinking tea, reminiscing about old times and old companions. He told me how things had gone for him. Deserting after he hadn't been paid by the Viets for a year, he went to Nha Trang and was chief interpreter for their Mike

Force for awhile. He got caught organizing the Nha Trang Mike Force into a FULRO unit and was fired the same way Kpa Doh had been. So he came back to Ban Me Thuot, organized his unit and enlarged it so that he now had about three thousand men in the field under his command. They fought without pay, without proper supplies, simply on the charisma and mystique of Phillip Drouin. He was some dude, all right, was my friend the Cowboy.

"How'd you pick the name Dam-Yi Division?" I asked.

He grinned. "Dam-Yi is old time Rhade hero. You want to see my division patch?"

Sure I did. Phillip went and got one; it had been laboriously embroidered. For my taste it had too many colors in it, since the FULRO colors were red, white, blue, and green, and Phillip had yellow and black in his also. It was so encrusted with stars and stripes that it was difficult to make out the central figure, a small insect that looked something like a bee. Above all was the motto HONG-SI. "Hong-Si is a small bug that kills many very quick. I want to have tiger on my patch, but Y Bham, he say everybody has tiger on patch. He say Hong-Si is very quick, very small, can kill tiger." He was grinning.

Phillip grinned a lot, but the quality conveyed by the grin is difficult to describe. It was ingenuous, utterly confident, and deadly.

"Maybe if I could have one of these I could get some made up for you." It seemed like a good idea to do that for Phillip. Also I had a sort of half formed idea in my head about how I might work this FULRO deal into something pretty nice by playing every available end against the middle.

Lest you think this was totally selfish I must point out that what I wanted to do would keep a lot of Montagnards and a lot of Americans from getting killed—probably a lot of Vietnamese, too. If it worked out for the best, I would end up with every Special Forces captain's dream, commanding an "A" team with a real live guerilla warfare unit. It was a sweet thought.

After Phillip told me everything about his previous three years I told him about my little boys, about McCulloch getting out of the army in disgust at both the way the war was being fought and the way the army treated its people in the age of McNamara.

"Do you know where is Captain Swain now?" Phillip asked. His face had a look of happy expectancy. Kpa Doh, who had been cutting in and out of the conversation right along, looked the same.

I suppose my face must have fallen because something of that was mirrored in their own before I spoke. "He's dead!"

"What!" Phillip cried and came half out of his seat.

"Oh, no!" Kpa Doh moaned and buried his head in his hands.

I had not expected such a strong reaction to show, even though I knew they had been the same kind of friends with Walt that I had been. The Montagnard tradition does not involve concealment of feelings as ours does. That is something they have learned from us and it falls away pretty rapidly.

I told them the whole wretched story. They seemed to recover quickly. After all they had been in the same war continuously for as long as they had been alive. They had lost a lot of friends.

After that Phillip showed me his collection of early American 60 and 81 mm mortars, thirty caliber machineguns and automatic carbines, CIA radios and other exotic military stuff. It turned out he was working as an intelligence agent for just about every supersecret military intelligence outfit in Vietnam, none of whom apparently knew about the others. He made enough money that way to run his division and had enough left over for everyone in his outfit to live pretty well.

Apparently he would also rent a battalion of troops out to some of the Special Projects outfits, and thus they would get valuable training and some pay for a while to send home, and he got in solid with the Americans.

"You want to come to my headquarters tomorrow?" Phillip was expansive and bouncing with that controlled dynamic energy that he had when he was really into what he was doing. He was very glad to see me and enjoyed showing off.

I nodded. "Sure. I'd really like that."

The next day I came again in my jeep, without Y Blik this

time. I could have brought goodies for Phillip, but it would have been pointless. His resources were, if anything, more extensive than mine.

He was in uniform the next day. It was the sharpest looking uniform I had seen in Vietnam, tailored, starched and pressed. It was a complete American uniform with a First Cav patch on the left shoulder, jump wings, and a U.S. Army patch. He wore no name tag though. He also wore a big hog leg revolver in a cowboy holster. Except for the pistol he looked exactly like a U.S. trooper. Would have fooled me anytime.

"Why the First Cav patch?" I asked, lurching the jeep over the ruts and out onto the highway.

He sat up straighter in the seat. "When I drive into An Khe," he said, "I drive right into First Cav base camp. Deliver intelligence. Nobody bother me."

I nodded. "Sure. You look just like an American, maybe a Hawaiian or a Puerto Rican."

I asked him how many jumps he had and he allowed as how he had about fifty.

"Okay," I said. "Then you ought to be a senior jumper. When I get back to Pleiku, I'll fix up a certificate and send you a bunch of senior wings to wear on your uniform."

He puffed up a little further in the seat. I had hit him where he lived. It was easy enough to do. It was where I lived too. The wings and the certificate would be easy. I would simply backdate the certificate to a time when he had worked for me and sign it. Then it wouldn't look like I was consorting with illegal characters now.

"You guys seem to operate in the open in Ban Me Thuot," I said.

He nodded. "We have deal with province chief. We don't bother him. He don't bother us. He think maybe FULRO help if VC come to Ban Me Thuot. We have plenty stuff here. Have our own police force. If Montagnard get in trouble word go out quick and guy in Honda Ninety pick him up before Vietnam cops come. We have complete city administration, and fifty Hondas. Use for police and also messages. Run all over mountains, to Nha Trang, Kontum, Da Lat, oh, all over."

If I had the sense to see it then I would have understood that we had already accomplished what we had come to Vietnam to do. The SF troops in the highlands had been sent in to develop the Montagnards so that they could defend themselves against the VC. Of course if they could defend themselves against the VC then they could do it against the South Vietnamese also, which the Viets knew bloody well. From what Phillip told me they had already progressed as far as purely small unit military training like Special Forces could take them.

In that sense our presence was now counterproductive. As long as they leaned on us for leadership they would never develop the capability themselves. But I was still too wrapped up in my Lawrence of Arabia dream to see that.

If they needed advisors now, they were economic and educational advisors. And that effort was so pitifully small compared to the military effort, so sad and puny.

The hell of it was that in my present job I was the economic and educational advisor. I was the Special Forces S-5 for the Central Highlands. I suppose I did as good a job at it as most, but I didn't really give a damn about that. What I wanted to do was get back out in the woods with troops, kill some VC, and get the old adrenalin flowing.

It was getting late too. If I wasn't careful I would be promoted to Major soon, and there is no job in the Army that I was aware of, past the rank of Captain, that is any fun for a guy who likes to run in the woods. I looked forward to that promotion with ambiguous feelings. I wanted an A detachment so badly, before I had too much rank to command one, and yet the thought of being passed over for promotion and embarrassed before my contemporaries was more than my tender ego could bear. I had pretty good efficiency reports, as far as I knew, but having told Kelly I didn't give a shit about his PIO program hadn't helped any, and a few other "frank discussions" I'd had with my superiors might affect it. I was in a paroxysm of dread of that promotion. I wanted out of that headquarters and into the woods. I wanted it more than anything I have ever wanted in my life.

Maybe I haven't made this strong enough. To me commanding an SF A detachment was the pinnacle of ambition.

I would rather command an A detachment in the highlands of Vietnam than be president of the United States or win the Nobel Prize for Literature, or ball each Playmate of the Month for the last five years in alphabetical order. I would have risked my life for that job. I would have even given my life for that job. It was all I had wanted to do since I learned there was such a thing.

Only recently has it occurred to me why I wanted that job so badly. I have rather more than my share of ego, and the reason I was so happy was that for the first time I was involved in something important enough to make me forget myself. For those who haven't tried it I recommend this as the James F. Morris one point formula for perfect happiness. Get involved in something that is more important to you than your own life. I had done it once, and had it taken away from me. Now I wanted to do it again. If I had sufficient sense I would have lost myself in the work I was then doing, which should have been more meaningful than even the command of an A detachment. But I had a fixed idea. I wanted my A team back.

In the meantime, though, I was having a hell of a lot of fun riding out the highway with Phillip.

When we left the city and headed out on the highway toward Tuy Hoa I grinned and jacked a round into the chamber of my M-16. The defects which had got my left nut shot off had been corrected and it was as sweet a little weapon as you'll find anywhere. As Phillip said, "The VC don't like that black rifle."

He grinned at me as though to say, "You won't need that, but I'm glad to see your instincts are still intact." Actually they were more intact than he knew. For one of the reasons I had loaded that round was in case I would have to kill him. Somewhere earlier, I have written that his loyalties were to two things: money and friendship. I didn't think Phillip would have sold out for money, but there was always the chance he had made friends with the VC during the three years I was away. I wouldn't have held it against him, many of the VC are perfectly splendid fellows. But I had to consider the possibility that he was setting me up for an ambush. If he had known what I was thinking I don't think he would have been offended in the slightest. I was an American officer and tied to an ideology, but he was tied only to his own judgment and I knew there were FULRO elements who were allied to the VC and the NVA against the South Vietnamese. Who could blame them? In any case I was prepared for the eventuality that Phillip would try to kill me. My plan was to bail out of the jeep and try to shoot him on the way out. Not too hot an idea, but the best I could do under the circumstances.

I felt kind of smug about the fact that Phillip and I were each sufficiently professional in our outlooks that we could kill each other if it proved necessary, without in any way lessening our mutual regard. It seems a strange existence, but I was at home in it and happy.

But, of course, nothing like that proved necessary. We simply drove out past the rubber plantations and on past the jungle and turned down an ordinary dirt road, just like you find out in the country anywhere, and drove a long way down it past some more rubber orchards and then turned left again and drove a long straight shot to a village.

The road was long, more than a mile, with no shoulder. The trees hung over it and it would probably have been almost invisible from the air. The jungle was so thick that it would have taken two or three days to walk the distance we drove in twenty minutes, and there was no way anyone who wasn't wanted could have got a vehicle down that road without being ambushed. It would have been very nearly impossible to trap someone in that village.

After what seemed an interminable period of driving down the road, every inch of which made me more aware of what a super ambush site it was, we arrived at the gate of a village. It was set up pretty much like a strategic hamlet, bamboo fence and moat, with a belt of punjis outside of the moat, two watchtowers and two gate guards. But there were significant differences.

In every one of the strategic hamlets I had ever seen, the defenses had been allowed to deteriorate almost as fast as they were erected. The watchtowers seemed on the point of collapse and the guards at the gate were doing a little shuck and jive called "The Somnolent Aborigine." In the strategic hamlets the guards would be flaked out just outside the gate, their carbines lying in the dirt, and smoking a banana leaf cigarette or trying to catch a few Z's.

This village was well maintained and the guards, although uniformed only in khaki shorts, black pajama tops and U.S. fatigue caps, were standing in a relaxed, but alert, position in front of the gate. Even from that distance I could tell the carbines they carried were cleaned and oiled. Out in the punji belt there were no empty spaces in the pattern and there were no fallen punjis. The edges of the moat were clean and sharp. It was maintained well.

As we drove up the guards came to attention, not a perfect drill team position of attention, but a salute executed with considerable enthusiasm. The two guards snapped to it, THUD! Their bare feet came together, WHAP! They grabbed the slings on the carbines and BADOINGGGG!! Their right hands came up in a quivering salute. It was done inexpertly, but with a lot of class. I was impressed, very impressed. Nowhere in the Republic of Vietnam had I seen native troops with that kind of *esprit*. Phillip returned their salute with the lazy confidence of a MacArthur as though he were so much in charge that he didn't have to worry about the form of it.

I didn't return their salutes. I had no illusions about who was rating the treatment.

The guards opened the gate and we went on through. Just on the inside of the gate was a bare flagpole.

"You ever fly the FULRO flag on that pole?" I inquired.

Phillip looked at me, and his look filled in all the aspects of the question I had left unasked. How come you don't fly the flag? Are you concealing this from aerial observation? What are your relations with the Vietnamese that they tolerate this village? Phillip had picked up all of this. He grinned. "Just on holidays," he replied.

I nodded.

He pointed me down a well maintained road. The village was very clean for a Yard village and there was none of the wretched detritus of civilization lying about, empty cans, garbage. There was grass growing and everyone appeared healthy and happy. The women wore their breasts bare, but most of the men I saw wore one kind or another of uniform. Everything was well maintained and the people walked with the kind of spring in their step that people have when they have something to do and feel it is important and want to do it.

"Hold it a second," Phillip said and I stopped. There were two young men maybe fifteen and sixteen walking along the road. Phillip snapped a question to them in Rhade that I did not understand. One of them snapped to a not so hot position of attention and popped out the best salute he could manage. The other kid just stood there and looked at Phillip in awe and trembling. Phillip's face became angry and he whipped a string of guttural instructions on this kid. The lad looked as though he had been slapped. His face fell, but his heels came together and he rocked his shoulders back, throwing his chest out. His salute was swift, but imprecise. I thought he was going to poke his eye out.

Phillip proceeded to give the kid what I took to be a five minute block of instruction on military courtesy. The kid's saluting hand straightened out and his stomach went in. He still had a look of pained anxiety, as though he had angered the gods and feared plagues of locusts.

The kid next to him was taking it all in and his salute metamorphosed into something more like the official version.

Finally when he was satisfied Phillip said a few more words. Joy, bliss, ecstasy came into the kids' faces. The Colonel Drouin had said it was all okay.

It did my heart good to see it. I hadn't seen anything like that since I let the Oklahoma Military Academy. No question about it, Phillip had his shit together.

We drove off again, down the same dirt road. Phillip returned the salutes of at least a dozen guerillas as we drove. They all had that same look of earnest dedication.

At last we came to a small bamboo building surrounded by a bamboo fence. The building was almost a cube. A one-room bamboo cube. The fence ran around the small building, set back the same distance all the way around, maybe twenty-five feet away. The way it was set up reminded me of the building where the top secret briefings were given at Fort Benning. Only there, of course, the building was red brick and the fence was a storm fence.

We got out of the jeep and walked to the gate. Another guard opened it and we went inside. There was a small U.S. Army field desk with a Smith-Corona portable on it and a Yard clerk with round, rimless glasses typing out what appeared to be rosters of some sort. The rest of the room was filled with NVA weapons, absolutely jam packed. There were AK's and RPD's and mortars, rocket launchers, the lot. They were all well maintained.

"Where'd ya get all the captured weapons?" I asked in surprise.

Phillip just looked at me and smiled slyly.

I nodded.

"You should have been here last week when we had many."

With allowances for exaggeration it was still a hell of a haul.

I smiled. "What happened to them?"

He gave me another long look, knowing he should say nothing, but finally his natural desire to bullshit overcame security precautions. After all I was his buddy. We were on the same side. "I give to my friend in Saigon, this colonel who is right behind Westmoreland."

I nodded, interpreting this to mean he was on the payroll of someone in military intelligence. He could have been anything, a colonel, a warrant officer, anything. The way it would have worked is that the local spook would have driven out to Phillip's in his civilian clothes with an Army jeep that had been painted blue so people would know he was a spy instead of a regular soldier. The guy claimed to be an agricultural advisor, but all the agricultural advisors drove jeepsters and broncos. Anyhow this person would have introduced himself and Phillip would have refused to have anything to do with him because he was only a captain and Phillip was a FULRO colonel, so the guy would have radioed Saigon or wherever he worked out of, and they would have got an old warrant officer to put on a colonel suit and come down and be Phil's case officer. Or maybe, if he had his shit together and liked to get out, their Colonel would have done it himself. Regardless, I doubt strongly that he was "right behind Westmoreland."

"You want a weapon? Take one home."

I said thanks and looked over the stock. There was some pretty gaudy stuff there, but I was already carrying the M-16, and I had to get it back on a chopper. Besides I wasn't too keen on having to tell everybody I saw where I got it. So I picked out an old French MAT-49 submachine which I calculated would fold up into the attache case I'd brought all my papers to Ban Me Thuot in.

When I picked it up Phillip looked disappointed. "I think maybe you take mortar."

I shook my head. "I don't want to overdo a good thing."

21

Good old long, lanky Bill, the master spy, face as open and boyish as a grilled cheese sandwich looked up as I walked into his office, attache case swinging from my left arm. "Morning Bill," I said.

"Hi, Jim. How was Ban Me Thuot?"

I grinned. "Very interesting," I said. I set the attache case down and snapped the lock. Then I took out the MAT-49, snapped the magazine in place, pulled the wire stock out and tossed it into his lap. "Here's a souvenir for you. A story goes with it. You want it?"

He nodded. I filled him in briefly on what had happened to me in Ban Me Thuot and then sat down and typed out an intelligence spot report on it. I gave all the details I had garnered, mostly the political organization stuff that I hadn't run into anywhere else.

I had read everything on FULRO that had been disseminated through our channels, and it was damned inadequate. The information people were looking for information on the VC and NVA, and they were using FULRO to get it, but the FULRO political situation wasn't being watched at all.

I figured that if I fed enough information into the system it couldn't be ignored if the situation exploded again. The last time that had happened the Viets had tried to trick the Americans into committing American troops against Montagnards.

Wouldn't that have been neat? All of Special Forces would have been hostages to their own Montagnard troops. It would have destroyed the SF program in the highlands, and divided the Yards from their American protectors. They would have been at the mercy of the Viets.

The whole thing stank. Fortunately whatever American General they tried to hustle was either too smart or too lucky to fall for it; but with the existing one year rotation policy the next one might not be that smart, or lucky, again. Anyhow, when I finished typing out my IR I stamped it SECRET NOFORN and gave it to Bill.

I must confess I had another reason for filling out this intelligence report. My tracks were pretty well uncovered in Ban Me Thuot. I had a good association going there and wanted to keep it up. The idea was that if I reported selectively on my activities down there I would be covered when they came to ask me what I was doing. The fact that I had made the reports and had not been ordered to stop my friendship with the FULRO people was enough to serve as permission. And since I didn't expect anybody over the rank of captain to ever see the report until FULRO revolted again there was very little likelihood of my being ordered to stop.

Besides I kind of enjoyed playing spy.

Every time I went to Ban Me Thuot from then on I went out to see Phillip or Kpa Doh. I always brought back a little background information on FULRO. I always wrote a report. It always disappeared into a file somewhere, and I never knew what happened to it.

Little as I enjoyed working in an office in Pleiku I did take the job seriously. The job of Civil Affairs/Psychological Operations officer, S-5 in the military staff numbering system, called for me to advise and report to my commander on CA/Psy Ops activities, and since he didn't give a damn about it one way or the other, that left me free to direct all Special Forces work in this area, in II Corps, which meant that theoretically I was in charge of all work being done in about twenty-four camps.

Actually this was so much bullshit, because I couldn't order anybody to do anything and expect it to be carried out. What I could do was put out a lot of loosely written "guidance directives" in both Vietnamese and English, get both my commander and the Vietnamese "C" team commander to sign them and send them out, hoping that a fair percentage of them would get through our rather spotty distribution system, and, when they got to an "A" detachment, somebody might read them, and further, that if somebody read them, they might be moved to take action.

Somewhere in one of those long rambling directives I made the statement that if a man did not genuinely like and admire the Vietnamese and Montagnard peoples he had no business in Vietnam and should not be permitted to come there. I suppose in a conventional outfit that statement would have been laughable, but in the Forces, which was all volunteer, it made perfect sense, at least to me. There were too many people in Vietnam just because they wanted to see what it felt like to kill somebody with impunity.

Once this document was translated I trotted up to the Vietnamese compound, which was next to ours, and showed it to their colonel. He read it carefully, and said, "I think maybe you understand this country very much."

I tried to look modest and smile at the same time, because that is just the way I felt. I loved Vietnam and her people, but my understanding of the country was far less than it should have been. "I hope so, sir," I muttered and took the document with his signature back down to see if I could get Ludwig to sign it. I almost had tears in my eyes. The Vietnamese are fond of covering their American counterparts with a lot of oily bullshit, but I didn't think the Colonel's remark was that. He had looked genuinely surprised when he said it.

I respected that colonel a lot. He had fought the French with the Viet Minh and changed allegiance after the Indochina war because he was not a communist. He had been offered command of the Vietnamese 22nd Division if he would get up the bribe money for his promotion and he had declined to do the necessary extortion on his troops. His wife had borne six children, three in the jungle when he was fighting the French and three in Saigon, after he joined Diem's army. Even now she was fond of putting on a tiger suit and a bush hat and going out to inspect camps with him. Yeah, I liked that little colonel a lot.

My own commander, Ludwig Faistenhammer, Jr., was another sort of person entirely. Ludwig was a Bavarian who had come to the states when he was about twelve. Robin

Moore called him Fritz Scharne in *The Green Berets* and told his story well and accurately. Ludwig is the guy who set the trap that destroyed an entire VC battalion and their French commander, a guy who was also known as "The Cowbody." In fact Ludwig blew that motherfucker apart with a direct hit from an M-79. I asked him about it later because, although all the stories in *The Green Berets* that I had personal knowledge of were true, that one seemed a little fantastic. "Sure it's true," he said. "I lay awake nights, dreaming about ways to get that son of a bitch." I bet he did, too. And I wouldn't want Ludwig lying awake nights dreaming of ways to get me. He looked sort of like Jeff Chandler, the actor, only shorter, with an incredibly muscular body and Dr. Strangelove glasses. Sometimes on Saturday nights we had parties in the officer's club. Ludwig would put on his lederhosen and lead us in singing German beer hall songs, backed up by a very confused looking rock 'n' roll band of Air Force enlisted men.

He did have certain peculiarities though. He was quite capable of throwing a temper tantrum if there was a fly in the Mess Hall. He fined any man he found without his dogtags $100. In short, he ran his company a little too much on the Prussian model for my route step Asiatic sensibilities.

He did one thing once that really hit me wrong, but it was his right to do it, and it was certainly Ludwig's way of doing things. During the morning briefing we were all sitting around the conference table and the S-3 (Operations) Sergeants were going through the daily sitreps camp by camp, pointing out the progress of patrols on the maps. This was a daily routine at 7:30 every morning. For some reason, the generator malfunctioned or something; the lights kept flickering, which threw the sergeants, reading their briefings, off stride. Also you couldn't see the map.

That got two of the younger staff officers to giggling. I thought it was funny myself, but the sight of those two usually dignified army officers, one of them a West Pointer, giggling like a couple of schoolgirls struck me as funnier.

It didn't amuse Ludwig at all. (I would never have dared call him Ludwig to his face, but for some reason I always thought of him that way. Easier than Colonel Faistenhammer, I suppose.) He started to turn purple and pointed a quivering finger at the West Pointer. "I want lights in this building in three minutes," he bellowed. "If not I want you and all your gear standing out by the chopper pad awaiting reassignment at oh-eight-hundred."

Everything in the room went deadly silent and the young West Pointer snapped out "Yes Sir!" and bounded out of the bunker. He was back in one minute with three high powered flashlights and the briefing continued, without him. The generator was repaired in five minutes.

I guess the point of that little story is that Ludwig could get things done in a hurry if he wanted to. But if he had given me an order like that I wouldn't have bothered with the lights. I'd have been out on the pad as soon as I could get my shit together, because *nobody* talks to me like that, not twice. And Ludwig knew it, and he never talked to me like that. On the other hand, I never gave him cause to.

At the risk of digressing too far there is another story about Ludwig, which I can't verify by personal knowledge. We once arrived to inspect one of his camps in the vicinity of a major battle. There were American dead uncovered and laid out in rows by the airstrip, and the flies were swarming around the bodies. On the other side of the airstrip the division commander, cigar stuffed in his mouth, was going over a map with his staff.

The way the story goes Ludwig stepped up to that General, snapped out a contemptuous salute and told the General that there were American dead being eaten by flies on the other side of the airstrip and that he, Ludwig, was going to inspect his camp, and that when he returned if the bodies were not covered then he, Ludwig, would personally shoot the General with his forty-five. Knowing how Ludwig felt about flies I am sure he meant it, and I am quite certain from the expression on his face when he is angry that the General knew it too.

When he got back the bodies were covered.

If anybody ever wonders why a guy like me becomes a professional soldier, the answer is very simple. It permits me to hang around with guys like Ludwig.

Anyhow he was the guy I was going to have to get to sign

211

this directive, but I wasn't worried about it. I thought he would buy the thinking behind it and certainly he wasn't about to offend our Vietnamese colonel by not signing a document that the colonel had already signed, simply because it said the Americans should genuinely like the Vietnamese.

But he wasn't in, so I wandered back to my own office and settled in to do some work.

Frequently peculiar people came into my office. Once a guy named Fred Battles came in. He was the C.O. at Phu Tuc, the camp that had our old Buon Beng strike force. I asked him how a bunch of the old troops were. Among the names I mentioned were those of Cookie and Minh, Cookie's son who worked in our mess hall. It turned out that Minh had been caught participating in a VC probe of the camp, and the whole family hit the road. I thought that was a shame since I liked both Cookie and Minh. I still like them as a matter of fact, never being one to hold a person's politics against him. I liked almost all the VC I ever met.

Whenever anybody walked in the door it always cut the available light in the place in half, so I looked up to see a short, slender, debonair looking captain saunter in the front door. I stood up and held out my hand. "Jim Morris," I said in my best manly fashion.

"Buck Archer," he replied in the same way, gave my hand two brisk shakes and let go. I fell back in my chair.

He groped for a spare wooden chair behind him and sat down. "Is there any way I can borrow a jeep from you this afternoon?" He was covered from head to toe with red dust. He might have picked some of it up on a chopper pad, but there was just too much of it for that to be all of it. He must have been from somewhere that was the reddest, dustiest place in the Orient. He leaned the M-16 that had dangled from his right arm up against Sergeant Bennett's desk.

I was perfectly willing to lend him my jeep for a while, but I was a little concerned. There are places you can drive with impunity around Pleiku, and there are other places where you can't. "Sure, if you don't keep it too long," I said. "Where you from, Archer?"

"Duc Co."

I nodded. I'd flown over good old red, dusty Duc Co a time or two. It looked like a lousy place to operate from. I also knew from the morning briefings that the name of the Captain from Duc Co wasn't Archer. "What do you do out there?" I asked. This guy looked like the real article, but his story was already beginning to go a little awry.

He smiled drily. "Oh, I'm in charge of Civic Action out there."

I nodded, more drily than he. "That's interesting," I said, "'cause I'm in charge of the guy who's in charge of Civic Action out there, and I never heard of you."

He smiled, cocked his head and waved his hand as though to dismiss the fact that I didn't know who was working for me as the merest trifle. "I work for B-57," he said.

I nodded. "I never heard of B-57 either." From the number I could tell it was a special project B detachment, but all the ones I ever heard of were running recons.

Still smiling, he said, "We're a Civic Action special project."

No way. If there was really such a thing as a Civic Action special project I'd have heard of it. "Bullshit!" I said. "Now if you want my jeep you're going to have to level with me."

He looked at me closely and said, "Okay. We're an intelligence operation and I'm running some cross border agents out of Duc Co. One of them went double, and I want to borrow your jeep to go terminate him."

I thought that over for a moment. "That's interesting," I said. "Look, I been on a lot of ambushes, but I've never participated in an assassination. You mind if I come along?"

He shook his head. "Shit, no! You can cover my back."

"Good!"

We drove out to the guy's house that afternoon, but he wasn't home. I would assume that having two SF captains, both armed, nosing around the house while he was out would have put him on his guard, but Buck didn't seem worried about it.

After we left the guy's house we went out to this little sin city compound the 4th Division maintained outside their base camp. It was a kind of isolated area, with a high storm fence around it, guarded by MP's at the gate. Inside was a

213

sort of Oriental Dodge City with a double row of bar-whorehouses running down the street. People get all upset that such things go on, but nobody is going to stop a GI from getting laid if he can do it, and in Vietnam he most assuredly could. With a setup like that you can at least keep the VD rate down.

We parked in the street and Buck got out and went into the bar where the object of our search was supposedly working, tending bar. He came back alone a few minutes later. "Where's our boy?" I asked.

Buck shrugged. "They say he hasn't been in all week."

"Too bad!" Buck got in the jeep and we started back for the headquarters, got stuck in the mud and had to get a truckload of guys from the 4th Division to help pull us out.

We went out there to grease that bastard three times in all, but we never could catch him at home.

Later that evening I had a couple of drinks with Buck and we wandered back to the transient room where he was staying in our Bachelor Officer's Quarters. Somewhere along the way we had picked up Ludwig's Intelligence Officer and the three of us wound up with a bottle of Scotch in Buck's room.

Buck held his drink up and examined the color through the bare light bulb. "It's just a pile of shit," he said. "I got promoted to major three months ago, but there's no way I can justify being a major out there at Duc Co, so I'm still wearing tracks."

The S-2 and I shook our heads at this injustice.

"Didn't I know you in Germany?" he said to Buck. "You were in civilian clothes and working under the name . . ."

Buck cocked his head at me, the intelligence non-professional, and the S-2 kind of trailed off. Then Buck said to me, kind of embarrassedly, "I'm working under my own name here, of course."

(Of course, only later when he became commander of B-57 and I went down to see him at the B-57 villa in Saigon, I walked in to see a huge poster over the door with a hand-shake symbol on it and a sign that said B-57 CIVIC ACTION. There was a wall of cyclone fencing behind that, with two guards on it, not the doofless types you usually see, but really mean looking motherfuckers, and a Vietnamese receptionist with a visitor's sign-in book.

"I am Captain Morris," I said to him. "I want to see Major Archer."

He gave me a very confused look and snapped something to the guard. The guard went away and returned a few minutes later with a warrant officer of approximately the same age Abraham Lincoln would have been had he lived. "Yes?" he said.

I went through the same routine again.

"Who is Major Archer?" the old warrant officer asked.

I made a disgusted face. "He is the man who gave me to understand that he is the commander of this unit."

He looked blank for a moment. Then something rang a bell and he said, "Oh, you mean Major Clapton. He's out right now. Would you like to come in and wait?"

I shrugged and followed him inside. Sometimes in Vietnam one got the feeling that the earth was shifting out from under his feet. Sometimes, in fact, it was.

Later on that first evening of my friendship with old what's-his-name, the S-2 wandered away and Buck went into an oration about the duplicity of this agent and how he was going to terminate him. "And by God, when I say terminate, I mean terminate." He was fairly blown away by then.

Later, of course, it was determined that General Abrams disapproved of that sort of thing, but Abrams was dead wrong. Any other course of action is disastrous when dealing with a double agent. If you let him go he compromises your net. You have no legal right to keep him. If you turn him over to the Vietnamese your net is then compromised to both the VC and the South Vietnamese. There is no choice but to kill him.

Sometime during one of Buck's subsequent visits when we went out trying to terminate the fellow with the usual extreme prejudice, I got to bragging about my association with FULRO. It was a stupid thing to do, but after all he had leveled with me about B-57 and he was my buddy and so on.

"I advise you to stay away from those people," he said. "You aren't going to get anything out of it but trouble."

I thought about it a lot more. Was it possible that Buck

215

had been sent from Saigon to check me out? Was it possible that his friendly warning was an official one, and that if I didn't keep away from the FULRO people I too would be "terminated with extreme prejudice"? It seemed unlikely that the Americans would have me assassinated when it would be so much easier just to transfer me out, but I didn't even think of that at the time. I just decided that I would be very difficult to assassinate because they didn't have anybody good enough. I got in bed with my rifle for the first time since I had cleaned it improperly at dear old OMA and set my subconscious to jump at the slightest sound. You get to where you can do that.

22

I did manage to get out on one patrol with the Mike Force while I was in Pleiku. I won't describe the operation, because it was one of the most frustrating experiences of my military career, a compendium of tactical errors and blown chances grotesque enough to break the heart of anybody who likes to kill people. The company commander, the Montagnard, not the American, was an old friend from Buon Beng who had since gone airborne. He had been just a little kid at Buon Beng and had started out as a houseboy, graduating to interpreter when he learned enough English. He was a cocky little shit and mean, but neither as bright nor as courageous as was Phillip.

Four days into the operation, after we had fucked up so badly there was no chance whatever of salvaging anything, we were moving through the woods on our way back in and I think we had both just given up playing soldier and were out for a nice stroll back from our camping trip. We were walking along, talking, and he started telling me this story about the time he had been out with his company without any Americans, grinning like a Cheshire cat as he told it.

"We way back in jungle and come into Vietnamese village. We have no Americans with us and we no have Vietnamese. All Vietnamese in village and we hate them very much. I think it okay maybe we kill them. So we do. Every one."

I continued walking along beside him feeling suddenly the weight of my pack and the heat of the day. If I understood right he was announcing, in a lighthearted vein, the massacre of two or three hundred people. "You killed them all?" I asked in amazement. Even Nay Re at his worst would never have pulled a stunt like that. No, that's silly. Nay Re would

217

have killed any or every Vietnamese he could any chance he got. Probably most Montagnards would, and there was no way I could morally blame them after the way the Viets have treated them for centuries, but there was no way I could condone it either.

"Sure," he said, surprised at my disapproval. "Kill them all."

I could feel my face contort in rage and frustration. Those poor schmucks he had killed had never done anything to anybody. Probably none of them had ever fired a gun. Some of them may have been Cong sympathizers, but I doubt if any of them had ever actively done anything to a Montagnard. It was the ARVN and the merchants in town who did that, not the poor farmers the Viets had relocated to the mountains. Try to tell that to a Yard. Well, I tried.

"That's just fine," I said. "They kill the Montagnards and you kill them, and they kill you and you kill them, and there's never any place to get off. Goddamn it. We didn't teach you to kill unarmed civilians. Americans never kill unarmed civilians. Now Goddamnit, I don't want you to ever do that again."

He had expected me to be amused. He simply didn't know how to handle my reaction. His face fell like a kicked puppy's.

"Promise!" I demanded.

He shrugged, still hurt. "Okay, I promise."

"Okay." I'll be willing to bet he never massacred any more villages. Nobody had ever told him not to before. At least I bet he never massacred any more until the news of My Lai came out. I wonder what he thought of my statement that Americans never kill unarmed civilians after that. It was inconceivable to me that an American would do such a thing, but I guess it happened fairly often. Nobody who did such a thing would have let me know about it, because my feelings about the Viets and the Yards were well known.

23

"Morris!" Ludwig fixed me with a gaze eerily reminiscent of a cross between King Kong and Dr. Strangelove. "Can you recruit among those people down there?"

I grinned. He was talking about my FULRO buddies, and sure, I could recruit among them. Phillip was always looking for a chance to get some troops trained at the expense of the United States government, not to mention putting a little bread in the mouths of his troops' children. He had been running what amounted to a Rent-A-Battalion service for months. One of the Special Projects Mike Forces was a battalion of the Dam-Yi division, lock, stock, and barrel. I don't know if their officers knew it, but they were.

I nodded. "Yes, Sir, I can do that." Actually it would be very easy, very easy indeed, but he seemed to think it was a big deal, so I let him go on thinking that it was. Having settled that matter he went on to the rest of the details of the combat jump into Bu Prang to reopen the camp there. We were going in with two companies of Mike Force to provide initial security for the camp. There was no particular reason to jump in, except we were paratroopers, by God, and every paratrooper wants to get that little bronze star on his wings. A combat jump was what we were trained to do and that was what we were going to do.

"We want that champagne iced, and we want proper glasses for it," he was going on to his supply officer, for after all Bu Prang wasn't the Normandy beachhead.

He turned his attention to me again. "And I want press coverage on it."

I nodded, doing my best to look staunch and trustworthy. I wanted that little star on my wings just as badly as anybody. I had been in the airborne for five years and made over sixty-five jumps with no likelihood that I'd ever get to make a combat jump. I wouldn't have missed that opportunity for ten thousand dollars. For that matter there was every possibility we'd get our asses shot off on the drop zone. A movement that large is hard to keep secret and there was no reason not to expect Charles (slang for Viet Cong) to be waiting for us. I assumed that, should we land under fire, the champagne might be allowed to get warm while we defended our position. In the absence of the enemy, however, we would drink it.

No matter, it was still a couple of weeks away.

The conference droned on interminably, and since I wasn't involved in any of it I just let them maunder on about how the companies were to be loaded in the aircraft.

The plan was simple. Ludwig's XO, Major Chumley W. Waldrop of Maude, Oklahoma, would lead in a pathfinder party of one platoon of Mike Force, plus some Americans to run the radio, about half an hour before the main drop. Then the main drop, consisting of two companies of Mike Force and the Mike Force commander and his XO and Ludwig's staff, would drop in out of four C-130's. Then we would organize a perimeter defense, drink the champagne and Ludwig and his staff would get on the helicopter that brought in the A detachment that was going to run the camp and fly back to Pleiku. Nobody mentioned the possibility of letting the A detachment in on the jump. In all fairness, I didn't think of it either. They did, though, and they were plenty pissed off about not getting to go. I was the only officer in Ludwig's staff that got to stay at Bu Prang for any length of time after the jump, because I had a job to do there.

Two weeks away. I looked forward to it with longing. It wasn't a command. It wasn't a chance to run my own patrols, which was what I desired with something approaching desperation. But at least it was a chance to get away from the paper shuffling contest there in the headquarters. At least it was a chance to get in the jungle. At least it was a chance to *operate*.

Meantime I had to be Duty Officer tonight and prepare a

220

report and I was expecting an airplane full of Poland China pigs for the pig breeding program that afternoon. I wasn't looking forward to it. Pigs don't fly well.

It was damp in the little concrete block Tactical Operations Center that night. I had a paperback book, but it was a bore, and there were a couple of *Playboys* down there, but they were a bore too. My technique in reading is total immersion and if I can't do that, which I can't if I have to be ready to react to an emergency, then I'd just as soon not bother.

The radio crackled in the corner, and the duty NCO had his little transistor tuned in to Armed Forces Radio. I got up, wandered outside and watched a flare over on the horizon. There was an occasional CRUMP . . . CRUMP from an artillery battery off somewhere on the other side of Pleiku, firing harassment and interdiction missions.

H and I was such a shuck I must pause and tell you about it. The idea was that the Cong are sneaking around all night on the trails around Pleiku and that all the good folk had to stay in their villages, so it was okay to shoot artillery at unexpected times and places so that the Cong would be in for a nasty surprise if he tried anything sneaky. And just so there was no confusion about this and no chances were taken on shelling one of our own local security patrols the H and I (Harassing and Interdictory) patterns were plotted on the map down at the local Vietnamese Sector Headquarters.

Unfortunately, the room that the map was in, and it was a big map, wasn't airconditioned, so the French windows in the old building were left open and at any hour of the day or night anybody who wanted to could pass by, look in and spot the H and I patterns for the night. Of course, the compound was guarded by Viet troops, no more than fifteen per cent of whom were in the pay of the Viet Cong at any one time, and all the old cleaning ladies were cleared for security, and who would question the validity of a Vietnamese security clearance?

Anyhow I doubt if that H and I ever did anything but keep people awake when they first got into the country and weren't used to it yet.

At one time I thought about mentioning that to

somebody, but then I realized that the advisors in Sector Headquarters didn't have their shit together any better than the morons in I Corps who'd had us send in projections of our patrols a month in advance so that Charlie could either stay out of our way or get together in enough strength to wipe us out. Vietnam had never been noted for its industry, but for sure it was the world's largest producer of stupid bastards.

The night air outside the TOC was heavy and damp and hot, but it was clean and moving slightly, which made it much better than inside the TOC. I like the tropics a lot, which is peculiar since all my ancestors are Nordic. I don't really start to get happy until the temperature and humidity are both over eighty. And in the tropics I like the nights best.

While I was musing bitterly on stupid bastards I thought some more about the situation in the A camps. Each of them had what was called a Tactical Area of Responsibility, or TAOR, which was usually called AO for short. I never could figure out short for what. "Area Of" didn't make any sense. If it was OA it could have stood for Operational Area, but for some reason it was called AO. That's the way it is in the army. To this day nobody has given me a satisfactory answer as to what GI stands for: Government Issue, Galvanized Iron, Gastro Intestinal, nobody knows, but still everybody knows what a GI is.

The only trouble with these AO's was that even where they were contiguous nobody patrolled within a couple of clicks of their border for fear of crossing inadvertently, which made nice little corridors for Charles to run down between the AO's where nobody will bother him. That's how we used to zap those bastards at Buon Beng. We'd go out and sit on the boundary of some little District AO and wait for Charles to come in.

That gave me an idea of something to do to kill time. I went back down in the TOC and got out the big map of II Corps. Then I went in the S-3's office and got out his overlays. The first one I put on showed the AO of every functional and proposed camp in II Corps. In the northern half of the corps they were lined up on the border, neat as little building blocks. Then there was a big notch in it in an area called Tieu Atar, one camp set back about thirty clicks from the border, and then they started running together again. Next I got out the map that showed the main NVA infiltration routes, and slapped that up over the one that showed the camp locations. It seemed a simple enough idea. The main routes ran right down the border, on the other side in Cambodia, until they got to that notch, and then split up and flowed around the camp that was set back.

It was weird. Hadn't anybody ever thought to put those two overlays in juxtaposition before? If not, what criteria were used in picking the camps? I was just standing there scratching my head, trying to figure that out.

The camp that the infiltration routes flowed around was Buon Blech, the one I'd picked for my own. I had been hustling Major Jones, the "B" team commander in Ban Me Thuot, to give me a camp, and he was glad to do it, and glad to give me the one I wanted. The problem was to get Ludwig to release me. If he let me go he had to replace me, and trained S-5's were hard to come by. Besides his philosophy was to keep the experienced officers in his headquarters so that his reports would look pretty and send the younger captains out into the boondocks to "get their feet wet," which in English means get their asses shot off. My own philosophy was exactly the opposite. SF operations were so scattered that each of them was pretty much on his own. Therefore I'd rather have had the experienced guys out running the woods, and let the new captains run the Intelligence and Operations sections in the headquarters, where they could read the reports and see how the big boys did it. In personnel and supply I'd have had good experienced officers in, but those weren't jobs for combat arms officers anyway. That's how I'd have done it if anybody'd asked, but nobody did.

"What you up to, Morris?"

I turned around to see the man himself, Ludwig Faistenhammer, Jr., glaring owlishly from behind his glasses. His face had an open friendly smile. For all his ferociousness there was something boyish about Ludwig. He was one of the real ones, though; in the army to do the work, not just to get his star.

"Hah!" I said. "Sir, take a look at this." I showed him the

223

overlays. "See, they come right in through here. You're committed to Bu Prang now, but my recommendation is that the next camp you put in goes in this notch here."

"Hmmmmmm!" He leaned down and looked closely at the overlay, pulling on his lower lip. He didn't say anything more about it after that though.

I gave him a quick briefing on what was going on that evening. It was quick because there was nothing going on. Then he turned and started to go.

"Sir," I said, "I want an A team." I just blurted it out, with no transition or anything.

He turned and fixed me with those owlish eyes of his. "What's wrong with the job you got?"

I was so stunned I didn't know what to say. Did he really think I had come back on active duty and volunteered for Vietnam again just so I could sit around in a bunkered compound in Pleiku and be somebody else's flunky? His question was so inconceivable, so ludicrous, that I had no idea what to say. Finally I mumbled something lame about "Gettin' stale, runnin' out of ideas." Something like that.

"We'll see!" he said and stomped on out of the TOC.

We'll see! We'll see! We'll see!

I forgot all about Tieu Atar, the camp in the notch.

24

Hot damn, it was just like old times. I leaned back in the shotgun seat of the three quarter, mashed the floppy patrol hat down on my head and jacked a round into the chamber of my M-16. Then I nodded to the driver and the three quarter pulled out of the little village where I'd gone to pick up my recruits for Bu Prang. I was overjoyed that Ludwig had given me this assignment.

Back behind me I heard the kid running the machine gun pull his big heavy bolt and the heavier thud as a thirty caliber round went into the chamber. I looked up and checked out the kid running the gun. He was a happy looking young Montagnard kid in a flak jacket and helmet, with some quarter-inch armor plate in front of him. He had the ballsy look that kids who volunteer to run machine guns in the lead vehicles of convoys have. He would probably unvolunteer out of boredom in a month or so, if he survived. See, the only thing that could happen to break him out of the boredom of the job he had would be for the convoy to get ambushed. And if the convoy were ambushed he'd be the principal target and also just about the most exposed. Probably last about three minutes.

So in a month he'd either be dead or in a new job. For his sake I hoped it would be the latter.

The convoy I was leading was made up of my three-quarter and four two and a half ton trucks. The lead two and a half, just behind my truck, was half full of grinning Montagnards, in loincloths, some of them in shirts, and a few in regular trousers. There were a couple of old experienced guys in faded tiger suits.

It was all very disappointing. The Goddamned Vietnamese

were the cause of it all. After the big jump on Bu Prang, which was a lot like a training jump, except for the champagne, I hung around the new camp for a couple of days and then hopped a chopper for Ban Me Thuot to see Phillip about some troops.

He agreed to furnish me with a battalion.

I shook my head. "Phillip, I don't want a battalion. I want enough men to make a battalion. If you send a battalion out there with their own officers they won't be responsive to the Americans or to the VNSF. They'll respond to their own officers. The Vietnamese will want to appoint officers and NCO's and there might be trouble."

He shook his head and grinned. "Huh uh, no trouble. I'll tell them no trouble."

"Yeah, well, if there's any way to avoid it, I'd rather have untrained troops. Can you do that?"

"Sure!"

So he had agreed to try to produce me four hundred and fifty guys by Thursday, and sent out the word, and come Wednesday they all started walking in to Ban Me Thuot from the village where he told them to gather.

I hadn't bothered to coordinate with the local Vietnamese, mainly because I didn't expect it to affect them. The Yards were just going to show up at the airport; I would put them on airplanes and send them out to Bu Prang. I didn't know they were going to meet somewhere else first.

When the hundred and thirty guys who were going to be the first contingent came walking down the road the province chief went flat out of his mind. Visions of the revolt of '64 flashed through his head and he sent the cops out to break up the riot. All these guys turned around and went back to the village.

"Oh, shit!" I said when I heard the news from Phillip that evening. "Okay, I'll get some trucks from Major Jones and go out there and pick them up."

When I got there most of them had said to hell with it and gone back to the jungle. I got back with fifty men. That was okay, I guess, but we still needed four hundred.

Still, I felt good riding shotgun in a three-quarter. It was a clear, blue, sunshiny day and we were traveling over some pretty country. There was a low range of hills we had to cross with some fairly tight twists and turns that offered a semi-decent ambush site, but I wasn't really very worried about it since we'd just put the convoy together that day and were coming right back. For most of the journey paddies stretched out for quite a way on either side of the road and they didn't offer much in the way of cover for an ambush party.

True, the Cong could have dug in by the side of the road, but that would have taken some time and the local people would have heard about it. They wouldn't have mentioned it to the Viets, or an American convoy, unless asked, but I was traveling with Yards through Yard country. I simply didn't feel as though we were in much danger.

Sure enough the ride back was uneventful. But when I walked into the "B" team's TOC the Operations Officer looked up and grinned at me. "We were kind of worried about you."

I cocked my head. "Oh, yeah, how come?"

"Convoy was ambushed about ten miles down the road from that village today."

I nodded. "Not mine."

I lumbered off, in search of beer, kind of sorry to have missed the fight, but, on the other hand, I didn't want to get wounded again either.

It was a funny thing I had going about combat. I'd discovered it on the first patrol I'd run out of Bu Prang, after the jump.

I was out with one company of Mike Force commanded by an American lieutenant named Bill Jenkins, strap hanging again. I hate strap hanging on patrols, because invariably the guy in charge does something I think is tactically stupid and usually I'm right and we have to fight our way out of it. It's frustrating as hell, but the particularly frustrating thing about it is that since you are a guest of the guy running the patrol you have to keep your mouth shut. Legally, I suppose, I could jump in and just tell the guy what he should do, but I was a staff officer, in a non-tactical staff position, and supposedly only there for the ride, or in this case, there to "assess the area for future civil affairs/psychological operations."

The idea was that we were looking for a way station on the main NVA infiltration route through that area. Bu Prang had been left idle for a long time, since the Montagnard rebellion as a matter of fact, which was why the old camp had been closed. Theoretically it would take the NVA a while to react to the presence of a new force in the area. At any rate this was a reconnaissance operation. We were looking for the way station. I had justified my presence by saying that if we found any villagers I would do some jiffy psychological operations and the medic would treat whatever illnesses they had and, thus loosened up, they would be willing, if not eager, to tell us where the way station was. Maybe.

Anyway, the recruiting job had got me out of Ludwig's headquarters, and this little deal had got me out of Bu Prang, which was not such a bad place until they started putting up tents and stringing wire.

In the meantime I was having a good time running around in the woods with Jenkins' company. Jenkins himself looked like a younger David Niven, tall, slender and with a pencil thin moustache. He was an OCS man, had a tendency to speak somewhat ungrammatically, and was working on it, so that the results were sometimes a little incongruous. I don't mean to put him down. He was a good man and a good officer. He just hadn't got around to going to college yet, and his background hadn't exposed him to the more recondite aspects of English usage.

Jenkins had three NCO's with him, a commo man who was a former juvenile delinquent from Dallas, no name, just initials; R.G. his name was; a long skinny southerner type sergeant who was pissed off because he'd spent six years with the 8th Special Forces in Panama and that's where he wanted to be; and a highly competent fire plug of a man named Murphy, who was the medic.

My kind of people. I enjoyed bullshitting with those guys so much at night I almost forgot my chagrin at not being in command. Jenkins was affecting a pipe and in the evenings before it got too dark to smoke without giving our position away he sat puffing on it and running through about three packs of C-ration matches, trying to keep the damned thing going.

As I recall his principal topic of conversation was how good his company was and how good his NCO's were. Which is exactly how it should have been. The long skinny southerner sergeant, Prescott, who was called the Welder, because with GI shades and his patrol hat bloused down around his ears that's what he looked like, led seminars on the quality of the pussy available in several of our sister republics to the south and Murphy said nothing. Barely grunted as I recall. R.G. was not much more talkative, but he would occasionally make casual reference to an amorous exploit, or with more zest, talk about a car he had rebuilt in high school in 1965.

As for me, I probably told Buon Beng stories, particularly the story of The Ambush, which is something I subject everyone to, or the story of How I Got My Left Nut Shot Off and Gained a Thirty Day Leave.

One of the nice things about being around other soldiers is that they will suffer your bullshit gladly, knowing that sooner or later you will shut up and listen to theirs. Very few categories of people will do you this service. And since I'm putting practically all my stories in this book I will have to shut up about it anyway. Doesn't matter. I don't see soldiers much anymore, and very few of the ones I run into are into revolutionary warfare as The Game. Mostly they're into Heliborne Assaults and how dangerous they are and how horrible it all was. And yes, they are dangerous and that kind of war is horrible, but it is also a bloody bore.

The third day out we made camp on the banks of a little stream and dug in. Jenkins' company had this habit of digging in, which I sort of complied with, although I always thought digging in more of a nuisance than it was worth. If you ran your patrol right you never let the enemy know where you were, but there is no better way to reveal your position than by digging in. They can tell how many of you there were and how long ago you were there. Besides it's hard work.

Anyway we dug in and I put some toothpaste on the end of my brush and went down to the stream to fill my canteen and brush my teeth. I carried my M-16 down there in my right hand. Too many guys had been killed going down for a bath alone not to go armed. So off I went with my toothbrush in my mouth like a pipe, M-16 dangling from my right arm grasped just aft of the front hand guard, the sling long since discarded. The weather was perfect, one of those clear blue days, and since the country around Bu Prang is open we got the full benefit of it. Bu Prang is drier than most of the rest of South Vietnam and the hilltops are flat. The vegetation tends to stay down in the lowlands near the creeks and the hilltops are like flat grassy prairies; they remind me more of golf courses than anything else. You walk along right out in the open for a long way, and then come to what appears to be a grove of trees. You walk along in the grove for awhile and then the ground dives straight down toward a rushing river below, and you are in the same kind of jungle you find elsewhere in Vietnam. You slosh across the river and struggle up the other side, panting and wheezing and pushing yourself up by your rifle, just like any other patrol in the mountains. Then the next thing you come out of the woods and you're walking along the golf course again. It is most peculiar.

Anyway we had camped up on the golf course part, which I suppose is a good reason to dig in, as we had. I wouldn't have run the patrol that way, but I gave Jenkins credit for knowing what he was doing.

Walking down toward the creek I noticed a peculiar thing. There seemed to be smoke hanging in the valley on further up the creek. I put it down to fog and thought no more about it. I suppose it never occurred to me that the NVA would be stupid enough to reveal their position in that way. I'd never seen anything like it before, and I'd spent a lot of time looking for the NVA. Therefore I couldn't be seeing it now. Nothing ever happens for the first time, right?

Many people have observed that the military profession is congenitally stupid, and I must reluctantly grant there is some merit to this position, but have always exempted myself from the rule. Wrongfully so, it might appear.

I trudged down to the creek, brushed my teeth and filled my canteen, and lurched back up the hill. We had walked ten miles that day and my fat, office-softened body was rebelling. Actually, soft as I was, I was doing better than some of the Yards in the comapny. That's where some fat on your body helps, after the first week of a patrol. As somebody at Kham Duc once remarked of the Viets, "These rice-burners don't have much staying power."

I got back to my hole, with a little poncho lean-to over it, made a dinner of Asian patrol ration and sidled over to the other Americans for some conversation.

We kept the same base camp the next day and the platoons split up to look for the NVA way station. I went with Murph, the medic. The idea was that we would run out a trail that was supposed to go to the location of the nearest Yard village.

The way was clear and open as we started off across the golf course part. We passed a couple of bomb craters, which I always hated to see, big eruptions of red dirt around an almost hemispherical raw round hole. They are peculiar looking holes, since the dirt in them is loose, rather than packed hard like a shoveled hole. We'd been seeing these things almost every day since we went out on this one. And we were close enough to the border to see into Cambodia. There were actually houses on the other side with smoke coming out of the chimneys. People over on the next ridge line were leading normal lives while we played war over here.

I nodded. "What kind of voices, Viets or Yards?"

He turned and asked his interpreter. When the answer came back he turned to me and said, "Yards! You wanta check it out?"

I nodded affirmatively.

He consulted his map. "They's a creek down at the foot of this hill, and I'm not sure, but it may be Cambodia on the other side. It's kind of hard to tell. There's a fork here and if we're upstream of it we're in Nam. If we're downstream we're in Cambodia."

I shrugged. "Don't make a shit to me," I said.

He nodded. "Okay. I just wanted to make sure."

We had firm orders, of course, not to go into Cambodia. I don't suppose anybody cared about that, but as a practical consideration we couldn't call in air cover if we got hit there. We'd just have to fight our way out and lie about it later.

I had mixed emotions about that. The only times I'd been in Indochina were to fight the war, so I didn't know which I liked best, the war or Indochina. All I knew was that the place made me happy. On the other hand, most people aren't all that pleased to be shot at. It made me appreciate what a master diplomat Sihanouk was. To be able to steer even a moderately independent course in that part of the world with no more power than he had was a dazzling display of skill.

To be sure he let the Cong run rampant through his countryside, and denied it all the way, but there was absolutely nothing he could do about that, and he certainly didn't want the Vietnamese army or the American army in his country. He could look at Vietnam and see what having the American army in your country could do to it, and the Cambodes had had the Vietnamese army in their country for a couple of hundred years before and hadn't recovered from it yet.

I've heard guys bitch about the Cambodes when they got shot at from across the border, but I can't for the life of me see how we could expect a foreign country to run its foreign policy for our benefit.

Anyway we passed these bomb craters and I looked over and could see the sun gleaming off tin roofed buildings at what I took to be Mondul Kiri Cambodia, which was also where the FULRO headquarters was supposed to be.

Then the trail, a path about a foot wide, turned in under the trees and we walked in the woods for a while. It wasn't jungle there at all. It might as well have been Sherwood Forest. Then Murph held up his hand and the patrol stopped. I started looking around, anticipating the sound of firing momentarily. We hadn't made contact this trip, but that was no reason not to expect it. Then Murph walked back to where I was. Since the purpose of this little patrol was to find a village and do some CA/Psy Ops I had a little more leverage than I usually had as a straphanger.

"They hear some voices on this little trail down to the right," Murph said.

The platoon turned and started off down the fork to the right. We dropped rapidly down into the hill toward the creek. At the bottom of the hill there were two logs laid across the creek. One about six inches in diameter and another about eighteen inches. It was very pretty down there and we could see thatch roofs in the trees on the other side.

We split up and poured across the two logs in two files, about thirty armed men, our rifles dangling in our hands. I walked in, expecting the outlines of longhouses to appear and a Yard village to develop as we crossed the creek. Instead it became deathly still and the Vietnamese Sergeant that went out with Murph turned and looked at me. "VC! VC!" he whispered. I nodded. This was no Yard village. The first building we came upon was just a floor and a thatch roof about six foot square with no walls. I had never seen Montagnards build anything like that before.

We spread out and took up a five yard distance between men, moving into a rough skirmishers formation and advancing rapidly through the woods. I noticed with surprise that my heartbeat and respiration picked up. It had been a long time and I was scared. The outlines of other buildings appeared. They all seemed to have the same type of construction, four poles stuck in the ground and a thatch roof. There were some hammocks strung in one, and a big first aid kit hanging on the wall.

One of the hammocks was heavy. There was a man in it. Four or five of us advanced under the roof and the hammock stirred. The son of a bitch was waking up. I remembered the NVA lying face down and dying the day my nut got shot off and I thought that maybe this guy had a grenade on him. Fear crawled up my back and I started backing toward the edge of the building. For just a second there I was totally consumed by the fear and acting solely on instinct. Once I got over by the edge I felt okay again and looked back.

The guy in the hammock pulled his blanket down for a second and looked out at all those tiger suited Montagnards glaring at him, plus, of course, me and Murph. He pulled the blanket back up over his face again.

One of the Montagnards reached out and pulled the blanket down again and they roughly ordered him to get up. He did, but was shaking so hard he could barely stand up. It wasn't all fear either. The guy had malaria.

There was a low shout from our right and we came out and

went over to another hut. There was another of them in a hammock and one more that was all right. At least he could walk.

The interpreter did some quick questioning and found out that two of them were patients and the other was a medic. They also said there was another in a bunker. Murph told the interpreter to tell him to come out. The interpreter called down again and there was some more muffled conversation from down below.

"He is afraid," the interpreter said.

"Tell him," Murphy said, "that if he comes out he will not be harmed, but that if he doesn't I will throw a grenade down the hole."

The interpreter called down there again. He waited for the reply and then said: "He will not come out."

Murphy nodded, pulled a grenade off his belt and plucked the pin out. Then he dropped it down the hole in the bunker. There was a muffled explosion. Murphy said something to the interpreter, who called down again. There was no reply. Murphy nodded and said, "Wait a minute."

We waited.

After a couple of minutes had gone by he dropped another grenade down there. He nodded. "If he had another little hole in his hole," he said, "I might have got him that time."

Word came in from one of the squads that someone had found a radio. "Let's haul it out," I said.

"Too big," said the Yard who had brought the word.

Murph looked at me and I nodded. "Destroy it!" he said.

There were a lot of Yards milling around, although most of the platoon had taken up security positions in the trees surrounding. We had passed the remains of several camp-fires on the way in. A lot of troops had been in here before this. "Fires still warm," the interpreter said.

I nodded. "How many troops you think use that many fires?"

He thought for a moment. "Maybe battalion."

Good fucking deal. An entire battalion of NVA had pulled out of here about two hours before. That was his assessment at least. Thinking it over later though, I would have reduced that estimate to a company. But by the least reasonable estimate of what had been in here, if we had arrived a little earlier we might have been annihilated.

Probably not though, that's what we had sent the little recon party down for. Our recon party would have got in contact with their outpost and there would have been a little firefight. Then the recon party would have come back and maybe we'd have called air in on them, if they would have flown in, if the way station hadn't been in Cambodia, if-if-if.

It suddenly seemed like an excellent idea to leave, hook up with the rest of the company and get away from here.

I nodded. "Okay, let's get these prisoners and get the fuck out of here."

All three prisoners had been dragged over to where we were, one walking. The other two collapsed immediately.

Murph shook his head. "These guys can't walk."

I nodded. "Okay, make two litters."

The Yards immediately cut two poles and snapped ponchos to them. I must not understand their thinking processes as well as I thought, because when the litters were made I directed them to put the prisoners on them, which they did. Then I said pick them up and let's haul ass.

The interpreter shook his head. "We kill them," he said.

I was amazed. I supposed they figured to kill them and carry them out dead. I know they hated them, but humanitarian principles aside, there was no percentage in killing them when they might have valuable information. "Bullshit!" I said. "Pick them up."

For once my orders were disregarded. The Yards stood in a sullen knot around me, waiting for me to give in and let them kill the prisoners. I was a guest. I was not in command. I had no say. Most of them didn't know me from a load of coal and I wasn't wearing captain's bars. I was just another stupid honky, straphanging on their patrol.

"Aw right, fuck you," I muttered. I picked up one end of one of the litters and started dragging it out. It was slow and there was no way I could have got it over the creek, but it was obvious to one and all now we were going to carry those prisoners out. One of the Yards grabbed the other end of the pole and another moved in and took my place. Two more got on the other litter. By that time the medic prisoner was tied up rather roughly with rope around his arms behind his back and another around his neck. They were treating him severely but not doing anything that would cause permanent damage. I figured I'd pushed them pretty hard for one day and let them have their fun.

We walked up out of the camp, over the creek and up the hill on the other side. For once the Yards didn't burn their way out of an enemy installation. They were not too keen on that battalion or company, or whatever it was, seeing the smoke rising from its former home and coming back to see what was going on.

I guess I estimated too soon though. When we had got a good way out of there Murph called in some fighter aircraft and they laid into the place and burned it to the ground.

While we were waiting for the fighters I saw two of the Yards talking. They were laughing at something and one of them held his arms out like he was holding a rifle. He backed up about three steps, his eyes wide in a pantomime of fear. I thought he was making fun of my moment of fear under the hospital shelter. I burned with embarrassment. It was just a moment of fear, brought back by the experience of having my left nut shot off, but I guess this kid hadn't ever had anything that bad happen to him before. That moment was the most embarrassed one of my life.

That was my first clue. I could still function in combat. I could still do my job as well as I ever had, at least I hoped as well, but I had got over the notion that I was immortal. The thing that had been my chief pleasure in life had turned into something that gave me nothing but a sour burning in the guts.

When I went into this business I was like a little kid with his thumbs in his ears, fingers wiggling, going "Ngyah! Ngyah!" at death. Jumping up and down and seeing how close I could get without getting caught. And that's too close. I almost got caught a couple of times, and I know the bastard is quick and might get me now. I treat him with considerably more respect.

That patrol had been before I'd gone into town to recruit troops. Now my job was much simpler. All I had to do was ask Phillip for the men and have them hauled out to Bu

Prang on huge Chinook helicopters.

Until the Viets screwed us up by sending all those men back home. I went out to Phillip again. "Gotta have those troops, Phil."

He grinned and spread his arms as though there were nothing he could do. "I can give you battalion," he said. "But I cannot get four hundred and fifty untrained men. I would have to go too far away and the Vietnamese would turn them back. If you get me trucks, I can bring in this week."

Mournfully I sipped my Tiger beer. "And there will be no trouble?"

He grinned his devil grin. "No trouble," he said.

Major Jones, the commander of the B team in Ban Me Thuot, was a country kind of a guy, tall and rawboned, old for a Major, sandy headed and laconic. He rode out to the airstrip with me to see how the recruiting was coming along.

We arrived early and sat in my jeep, watching. One entire end of the airstrip had been set up for the Bu Prang airlift. They had four or five big squad tents erected and several fork lifts. The air force flew stuff in from wherever it came from and dropped it off at the Ban Me Thuot airstrip where they could land. Then the army CH-46 (Chinook) helicopters came in and picked up the stuff in huge cargo nets, ammo, food, building materials.

This morning they were set up to haul troops. Their plan was to issue them their gear there at the airport and put them right to work building the camp when they got out to Bu Prang.

Jones and I sat there a long time waiting for the first load to arrive, which was supposed to happen at nine o'clock, only it was already nine-thirty, and the first load hadn't arrived. Jones smoked and I chain smoked. We were both waiting under the shade of the wing of a C-130, sitting in the jeep and waiting.

I had a good feeling with Jones. He had been in and out of Nam since about nineteen sixty and had a vast fund of stories about how it was in those days when, to hear him tell it, the MAAG advisors had been even more stupid than when I arrived. This strains one's credulity to the breaking point. A

237

man has to be of at least average intelligence to become an officer in the first place, and it is difficult to imagine a person with any brains at all doing some of the things he described. But I believed him.

After all, I had witnessed myself the dropping of Vietnamese language propaganda leaflets on the Bahnar, and had myself been present when four thousand Barbie dolls were distributed to the destitute Montagnards of Phu Thien district.

Also Jones wanted to give me the thing I coveted more than anything else in the world, command of the A team at Buon Blech. Gimme that and I'll disappear into the jungle not to reappear until it's time to extend my tour in Vietnam for the same job. Every two weeks they'd have to send me a new company and I'd just keep shucking around in the jungle, hunting Viets, growing meaner, skinnier and shaggier all the time.

Dream on.

"When's these troops gettin' here?" Jones asked with justifiable interest. They were late.

I shrugged. "Beats me, sir," I said. "They're supposed to be here now."

"Where's these men comin' from again?" he asked.

I hadn't said anything about FULRO to him. I didn't think he needed to know about that and I didn't think he would want to know about it. I looked straight ahead across the runway. "Old Montagnard chief named Y Glim Nie," I muttered. "Lives in a village about ten miles west of town."

He looked at me quizzically and sucked on his Pall Mall.

A two and a half ton truck turned the corner down by the control tower, followed by two more. That was all the trucks we had out. They were supposed to make several runs.

"How long you reckon it'll take to train these troops?" Jones asked, sucking meditatively on his cigarette.

I looked at him brightly. "Quite a while," I said. "They're right out of the bush."

The first truck drove straight down the runway and lurched to a stop in front of the tents. We could see the heads of many Montagnards sticking up over the sides. They must have had fifty guys jammed in those trucks. The driver got out and came to the back letting the tailgate down with a squeal and a slam.

Nobody moved.

A minute after the tailgate was dropped one guy jumped down off the back of the truck. He wore a faded tiger suit, but his hair was long. He didn't have any shoes on. He walked to a point about fifty feet from the truck and hacked out a command in Rhade. Immediately the "untrained troops" poured off the back of the truck and ran to a point six paces in front of the first man. They quickly formed themselves into four ranks, the front rank one arm's distance apart, got the ranks straight and came to the position of attention. It was about as professional a formation of troops as I'd ever seen, except that half of them were in loincloths, some were in regular twentieth century civilian clothes and some in faded tiger suits.

The guy in charge barked out another command and they did a fairly neat left face for barefoot soldiers. Then he had them march off single-file to draw their gear. It was obvious that he had told them to be on their best behavior because he didn't want the Americans to think they were a bunch of amateurs.

"Untrained troops." Jones tapped the point of his jaw with his forefinger. "Did you say these were untrained troops?"

I shrugged, grinned sheepishly, and said nothing.

I got back to Bu Prang as soon as I could. There was another Mike Force company going on patrol, and I couldn't justify it as a Ca/Psy Ops action this time, so I just put on a tiger suit and went with them anyway. I had learned to recognize the fear in myself, and hoped I had learned to control it, but I still liked the bush better than the camp, and the camp better than the headquarters. I also invited Phillip Drouin to go with me.

A fine crew of madmen I'd hooked up with this time. Speilman had six purple hearts and looked exactly like Alfred E. Neumann. Siggy Butler was an Austrian whose mother had married a GI. He was easily the most handsome man I'd ever seen in my life, six-three, dark-haired, aquiline features, good physical condition; and the head American was Rodney Flack whom I'd known on Oki. Flack was also a good-looking young man, blond, and serious about the work.

I got good and drunk with Butler and Speilman in Ban Me Thuot the night before we went back out to Bu Prang. I can't remember too much of it. We were with a couple of other guys and I can remember breaking down the door of a whorehouse when another guy we'd hooked up with didn't come out. The girl was kneeling, nude, giving him a blowjob. She looked up in surprise, holding his cock like a microphone, and he looked up in anguish. "Wait a minute, will ya?" We waited, but the girl wouldn't continue, so he got up disgustedly and came along with us.

About on hour later the Mama-San at the Imperial Hotel told me she wanted me, the Captain, to throw one of them out for stirring his drink with his dick, but I refused to do it on the grounds I owed him 2000 piastres.

Phillip and I flew out to Bu Prang with the Mike Force and suited up to go on patrol with them. I had appropriated an M-16 from a Captain in the B Team who had left it unattended while he went to Saigon, and I fully intended to bring it back. But Phillip asked me if he could keep it, since he didn't have one, and I didn't have the heart to refuse him. Later the guy I borrowed it from got very upset about that until I scrounged him another one. Phillip's nostrils glared and he looked critically about the camp as we disembarked at Bu Prang. "First time I go jungle in maybe three years," he said, which surprised me very much. I had just assumed he ran in the woods all the time.

We left out with the Mike Force; I was halfway back in the column, with Phillip right behind me, as befits a guest. I tried to pretend that it was just like the old days, but it wasn't. In the old days we were both always right up behind the point, functioning smoothly together. Now he had become a demigod and a legend, and I had become a fat staff officer. Neither one of us had any business being where we were, an he didn't even want to be. He was just showing me he hadn't lost his guts. God knows what I was doing, pretending I was still Lawrence of the Jungle, I guess.

This time our mission was to find a main enemy base camp in the Bu Prang area. We expected it to be hard, but we had reckoned without the fact that they had run unobstructed for three years there. The second day we were sauntering along, fat, dumb and happy, and walked right into it.

It was a beautiful place, concealed from aerial observation by the heavy tree cover, a wide flat area down by a river bottom. The hills around it were steep and high, and down in the bottom the trees were widely spread apart.

The way down put me right back at Kham Duc. We struggled down that trail for a half hour; it was so steep and the brush was so thick. But down in the bottom it was like a well-kept picnic area in a public park.

One of the Yards found a wicker NVA helmet and took a crap in it.

My dream rose up in me. This was the place. We could take the company back up the sides of the mountain and simply wait there for the next NVA infiltration to come in and, Jesus, it would be like shooting fish in a barrel. I went up to Flack and laid the plan out for him.

He pushed his bush hat back on his head and scratched his jaw. "I dunno, sir. That's not the plan we were sent out here to follow." He held his map out for me to see. "We're supposed to follow this trail here until we link up with the other company and continue the search for the base camp."

I was so excited I was almost hopping up and down. "But goddamnit, Rodney," I said. "We're supposed to be looking for the base camp, and this is it. We're standing in it."

He nodded. "Yessir, I know, but the plan calls for us to follow this route here and link up with the other company. There wasn't anything in the plan about any ambush."

I was close to tears with frustration. I simply didn't believe in usurping another man's command. If the plan succeeded he would get the credit, and if it failed I would take the rap. I didn't have enough faith in their company's training to do that. They might fuck up the ambush and fire early, get us in a big firefight with an NVA battalion and that would be too bad for sure. A recon team would have a better chance than we would. They could hide up there and call in an air strike and lay waste to a battalion. In fact, that's what they did a lot of the time.

But I just couldn't understand how he could fail to see it.

"For Christ's sake," I said. "Call Bu Prang on the radio and get permission to do it."

"But, sir," he said, and I could see he didn't want to. I don't know why, but he didn't want to, and it was his company. If he ordered them to do something in which he had no faith, they would fuck it up and get a lot of people killed, but Goddamn it, rage and frustration still filled me as I walked off muttering to myself. If it were my company. If only I had a company. If only I had anything . . . aw shit!

Phillip looked at me very carefully as I retook my place in the column. His face was almost totally blank, but I read all kinds of things in it. Contempt, incredulity, plain bafflement. "You are captain. I think he must do as you order," he said evenly.

"It doesn't always work like that," I muttered. In addition to being outraged by Rodney's intransigence, I was now just plain embarrassed. I had brought the best guerilla leader I ever saw or heard of out to see this simple fuckup. He expected better of me.

I wish I could have put on a better show. It was the last time I ever saw him.

We finished our break and the Yards in the company left their magic hero sign on a tree trunk so the NVA would know we had been there and we started on up out of the bottom.

It was a long haul out of that place and we stopped for a break almost as soon as we got to the top of the hill. I threw off my patrol harness, leaned my rifle up against a tree and lay down for a smoke. I'd no sooner hit the ground than firing broke out up ahead and I was up, crouching and groping for my weapon. By the time I was squared away it was all over. We had two wounded and they had two wounded and the battalion I had wanted to ambush was long gone. Oh, yeah, and we had captured two. Big deal.

I was pretty sullen for the rest of the patrol.

I laughed, though, when the CBS camera crew jumped out of the chopper that came out to pick up the prisoners. I guess somebody somewhere did think it was a big deal.

A few weeks after I got back to Pleiku I went looking for Ludwig on some matter of relative importance and was informed that he had gone to Bu Prang.

Since I had an interest in the place I leaned on the adjutant's desk and asked, "What's going on at Bu Prang?"

He gave me a kind of breathless look, as though we were in the presence of larger political issues such as soldiers are seldom called on to handle and said, "The strike force is in revolt. They want to name their own officers and they surrounded the team headquarters and threatened to kill one of the Vietnamese sergeants."

I nodded, still not overly concerned. I had expected something like this to happen, but, of course, I had assumed that the American detachment commander would order the Yards to get the hell away from his teamhouse and go back to work, and then sweettalk the Viets into keeping off everybody's ass until some new crisis built up. Fending off a revolt in your camp is no big deal if you've got any idea who you're working with at all.

The techniques vary though. Some guys have genuinely good relations with their counterparts and they hassle it out like normal people. Or you can keep the bastards drunk and out of your hair, like we did Khue at Buon Beng. I can't verify this story, but one team procured a silenced .22 cal. pistol and let the Vietnamese commander find out about it. He became very cooperative.

Another bunch simply hired a Cambodian to kill the son of a bitch, which was the best fifteen dollar investment they ever made.

But the guy at Bu Prang hadn't done any of those things. He clutched and called Ludwig.

I nodded at the adjutant and talked a few minutes about something else. Then I went back to my office to nurse my wounded feelings. The least Ludwig could have done was asked me to go along. After all I had recruited those guys and knew something about them. I took the fact that he didn't ask me to go with him as a lack of confidence, as though I had performed poorly down there. If you think a mutiny is a big deal then you might be moved to make such a conclusion.

Apparently Ludwig thought it was a big enough deal because he got the Darlac Province Chief, who was a full colonel in the ARVN and Phillip and a whole bunch of other extraneous people and went out there to "negotiate" with the Yards. Blew a fifteen minute hassle into an international incident. But they got it smoothed over.

When Ludwig got back I went in and asked him what had happened. That's how I found out about the Darlac Province Chief and all that. I didn't want to criticize him for taking all those people with him. So I just shut up and went on back to work.

25

I had been to Nha Trang a couple of times on business and made good friends in the Group S-5 Section. Somehow or other they got involved in a question concerning FULRO and Carl McCarden, who was the Group S-5 officer, had me called down there to write a staff study of the subject. I did and had to hang around for two weeks while I waited for the Group Commander to read it. My final recommendation was that an A detachment be infiltrated to work with FULRO in Cambodia, just as we're supposed to in a hot war situation. I then went on to describe in detail the kind of men who should make up the detachment. I made sure that I fitted all the requirements recommended for the commander. I didn't go quite so far as to recommend that he have red hair and glasses, but the rest of it was there.

Then a terrible thing happened. Woody Garrett showed up. Colonel Garrett had been my commanding officer on Okinawa, before Kelly. He was the man who hijacked me into the PIO job in the first place. Worse, he thought I was the best PIO in the army. It was true, but I didn't want it to get around. Most people thought the PIO was a wimp job. I didn't care so much what people thought, except that I thought so too. I was put in that job because I had a journalism degree, and it was my considered professional opinion both as a soldier and as a journalist that the job should be done away with.

Garrett told Colonel Ladd, the 5th Group commander, what an outstanding PIO I was and Ladd wanted a PIO. Guess who was elected.

The Group Adjutant smiled impassively at me as I towered over him, glowering. He was a short, fat man with a bland, impassive face who had once run a loan office in Omaha. He was an asshole.

I leaned on his desk and lowered my face close to his. "I won't have it!" I grated. "This is a crock of shit. I want out of this chickenshit outfit. I'll terminate my goddamned jump status before I'll serve as a PIO again." I was close to tears. I was in a fury. The bastards.

"I don't understand what you're so upset about," he said, spreading his hands. "Working in this headquarters will further your career. If you do a good job you'll almost certainly get an outstanding efficiency report and there you are."

Pounding on his desk to emphasize every syllable I said slowly and carefully: "I-don't-want-an-out-standing-eff-ic-iency-report. I-want-to-command-an-A-Detach-ment."

He shook his head as though swishing away a fly. "The A detachment really isn't so important anymore."

I sputtered, turned and walked off. It was no use to talk to the bastard. He thought the only reason any officer was in the army was to become a general. Why, shit, if anybody gave twenty minutes thought to what it is a general actually *does* he wouldn't have the job on a bet. The A detachment wasn't important to whom? It was fucking well important to me. I knew how to win this Goddamned war and I could demonstrate it if given half a chance.

Ah, that's all only part of it. I guess I was still trying to prove I was one of the boys, and really, way down deep I didn't believe it myself. Really, way down deep I felt like the four-eyed, fat, new kid and I really believed that they kept putting me in these screwy jobs that nobody else could do because I wasn't one of the boys. I had been a damned good A detachment XO and a damned good A detachment CO, but still they thought of me as the PIO. I had to get out to the woods and be, not just good, but the best goddamned A detachment CO in the business. I had to show the rest of them how. And the way to do that was simply by practicing what they taught us at Fort Bragg. They all said, "Yeah, but that was when we were learning to be the guerillas; we're the counterinsurgents now." And to that McCulloch and I would say, "Bullshit!" There is only one way to fight a guerilla and that is to outguerilla the guerilla. You have to steal his political issues and his social issues and his tactics, and if you do that he has nothing left to sell and the war is won.

It was so easy. Why couldn't the bastards see it? Maybe that was what made me not one of the boys. The fact that I had moved around so much as a kid that I was highly sensitive to new social situations. That was what made me not one of the boys. Maybe I knew what I was doing and "The Boys" didn't.

But I wasn't that confident. Maybe deep down somewhere I was afraid that I wasn't really that good. I don't know. Anyway I stormed off down to the S-5 office and stormed up to their sergeant's desk. "Gimme a fucking 1049," I said; "I'm going to get out of this fucking outfit."

He reached into his desk and produced it.

I hurled myself into a seat behind an empty desk and whirled it into the typewriter.

SUBJECT: Transfer

TO: Group Commander

Wait a minute. The bastards really had me by the balls. If I transferred out of the Forces my chance to do something useful would be gone forever. I'd be stuck in some little office somewhere wearing a goddamned olive green baseball cap and writing horseshit directives. The fact was that I always hated everything about the army until I got in the Forces. If Special Forces had been part of the Coast and Geodesic Survey that's what I'd have been in. Or the Border Patrol, or the Girl Scouts of America. I would rather be a demo man in a ricky-tick A detachment advising the Igluks in East Jesus than be Chief of Staff of the fucking Army. Everything that was wrong with the Forces was something that was enforced generally throughout the army. Everything that was right about it was something that Creighton Abrams never heard of.

They had me. I tore the 1049 out of the typewriter and wadded it into a ball, throwing it in the nearest wastebasket. "Motherfuckers!" I muttered and stomped out of the office.

But there might be another way. Disobeying orders is not my style. I didn't think I belonged in the PIO job and I

247

wanted out of it, but I had been trained as a soldier too long, growing up in World War II and going to military schools since I was eleven, being a cadet in the Civil Air Patrol. I was too well trained not to believe in the Chain of Command and all that. Any plan, no matter how lousy, is better than no plan, and for any plan to be successful it has to be carried out.

But the 5th Special Forces Group (Airborne), 1st Special Forces, for shit sure didn't need no Goddamned PIO. The purpose of the PIO was to raise the morale of the troops by telling them how good they were. If anything would improve the Forces it would be telling all those smug jerks that a Green Beret didn't make a Special Forces man and that most of them had a long way to go.

The ideal of the Forces is that every man be a volunteer for the Army, for jump training, and for the Forces. Then after he got in he was supposed to be highly trained in one of the five SF specialties, and cross-trained in two others. Also he was supposed to be fluent in one foreign language and adequate in two others. We were so far from that in Nam it was pathetic. At one time I was cross-trained in commo and demo, but I couldn't even sit down and write out the morse code now, and I'd really have to cram for a while to blow something up. And as for language, I had "survival" French, and that was it. I'd been in the Forces for four years and was a hell of a lot better trained than most of those kids.

I didn't think the Forces needed anybody to tell them how good they were. They needed somebody to kick their asses. Somebody they could respect, though, not some leg general.

And as for convincing the rest of the world, the rest of the world outside the army was already convinced, and the best thing to do in the army was to maintain a low profile. They were jealous enough already. We didn't need publicity. We needed the exact opposite of publicity. That was what I wanted to believe.

I stomped across the compound and stormed up the stairs to the Information Office.

I threw open the door and stormed past the office that was to be mine. Scowling, leaning forward, mad as hell, I came out into a room with about six desks. Two or three kids and a

Vietnamese girl were typing. A skinny guy in a T-shirt with SSG SCENA stenciled on the front of it leaped to attention and said, "May I help you, sir?"

I put my hands on my hips and glared at him. "I'm your new boss," I said. "And my plan is to fuck up so bad that I'll get sent down to an A camp."

He gave me a look of absolute horror. "Oh, okay," he said and sat back down.

I sat down in a chair and glared around the room at the two or three spec fours who had stopped typing to look at me in wonderment. "Fucking candy-assed PIO job," I muttered.

My eye was caught by the seven or eight copies of the magazine, called *The Green Beret*, naturally, framed and hanging from the wall. I hadn't paid any attention to it all the time I was in Pleiku, I had just thought of it as some more of Kelly's bullshit. He had started the magazine when he was the 5th Group commander. The cover was the worst make-up job I had ever seen. The masthead was in four colors. It had a little representation of a green beret that looked like a green turd with one end hanging over the edge, the unit crest, the unit flash, the shoulder patch, the flag of South Vietnam running diagonally up the masthead, with the letters *The Green Beret*, in olde Englishe, yet, in the shape of an arch. All this over a black and white photo. The goddamned printer prints four pages at a time, and they were paying for four press runs to get those colors, and the rest of the front page and the three inside pages were in black and white. What a waste.

I had intended to just fuck off in the new job until I finally goaded the group into deciding they needed a new PIO. But I couldn't stand that masthead. It was a disgrace. I shot out my arm, pointing at it. "That goes!"

The kids all leaned back in their chairs and grinned. They hated it to.

From then on it was a brief slide to oblivion. I couldn't just stay at the club and drink; and the job of PIO, however useless, was too much fun and too easy not to do. Besides, if I covered stories I could get out in the woods. As a straphanger.

It was too bad I couldn't take a more objective view at the

time. I should have counted my blessings. I got to spend a whole year without winter, and I have always hated being cold.

Working in Nha Trang had its moments, though. Comparatively speaking we were living in the lap of luxury, with the beach nearby, and a club, and you could get pizza at the Playboy Club, which was now the club for the lower ranking enlisted men, and there was a theater, The Green Beret Theater, naturally, with movies every night. Ever since Robin Moore wrote that book we'd just been green bereting up a storm. There were little paintings of green berets all over the compound. It was enough to make you sick.

In all the time I was in Pleiku the camp never got attacked or mortared. We got mortared quite a bit while I was in the "rear" in Nha Trang though. In fact we got mortared the first night I was there. It was a bloody nuisance. We had to get our weapons and patrol harnesses, and wear a damned steel pot on our heads. Usually we would only get four hours sleep when we got mortared. Besides that every so often somebody got wounded. That first night I was there my assistant PIO, First Lieutenant Frank Orians, got his nose broken in a mortar attack. It had been broken before, but this time it got broken back the other way, so that he looked like a mirror image of himself.

One night I was watching the Flim-Flam Man at the movie. When the part came, early in the movie, where the MPs were coming down the road looking for Michael Sarrazin, a siren went off. I thought it was the MP siren in the movie until the theater started to clear out. Then I realized it was the camp alert siren. Everybody else was going out the side doors, but I went back out into the lobby. Sure enough the guys at the refreshment counter had left it unattended, so I went back behind the counter and helped myself to a big bag of popcorn. It would help to pass the hours in the bunker. I strolled casually back to my BOQ to get my rifle and steel hat for the alert. The mortars were falling behind me somewhere and they didn't seem to be moving my way.

I felt pretty silly in the bunker in a pair of blue corduroy jeans, sneaks and a white knit T-shirt with a patrol harness and a steel hat. The popcorn was fresh though, and that was something.

Once, just before Tet, we were mortared while I was in the club with a young lady who was a provincial nurse in Da Lat. She was a very nice young lady, much nicer than I deserved, or wanted for that matter, and her name was Rosemary. We were with a couple of other officers from the Group S-5 office, and they were with a couple of nurses from the Nha Trang province hospital, American nurses.

What could we do with all these mortars falling around? Well, I had my little portable record player, and Scott ran a line from his BOQ, which was adjacent to the bunker. Roy had some wine, a red Algerian as I recall, and the bunker had a smooth flat concrete floor. It was very pleasant, dancing the night away under the full moon which we could glimpse through the slits in the bunker. The mortars hardly bothered us at all.

There was another advantage to my tenure in Nha Trang. Soon after I got there I ran over to the Group S-2 and convinced him I was the world's foremost authority on FULRO and that I was just the boy to keep him informed of what they were doing so we couldn't get into the mess we got into in '64. He bought it. Then I typed out a letter to my immediate boss, the Deputy Commander for Administration and Logistics. The gist of the letter was that I had talked with the 2 and he wanted me to keep up on matters FULRO and keep the group informed. Immediately after that I was called over to this officer's office.

"Come in, Captain."

I walked in and saluted.

"Take a chair."

I sat down and looked at him. The army was full of older officers who had been around since World War II that I either loved or hated. This man was one of the ones I loved. He was wizened and wore a gray crew cut, was obviously brilliant, though relatively unlettered and so cool in a crisis he could freeze your fingers. You had only to see him from the back, one hand on his hip, weight on one hip, beret mashed down over his nose, to see the cocky eighteen year old paratrooper he had been at Normandy, and to see that kid was still in him. Fact of the matter is he was just swell. His name was Beck.

251

He didn't look swell right then though. He held the letter out in front of him as though it were some sort of fecal matter. "You shouldn't have written this letter, Captain Morris," he said. He struck a match to it and threw it into his empty wastebasket. "This organization has no official interest in FULRO, and, in fact, we have been ordered not to have any."

I nodded. He had read my staff study. He knew that ninety percent of our troopers in II Corps were FULRO. He knew everything I had told him. Yet he was telling me to leave it alone. My heart sank. I could just see myself cooped up in this wretched headquarters, getting fatter and banging my typewriter, while the war raged around me.

He glared at me hard. "There is no way I can order you to go forth and spy on FULRO. In fact I have to forbid it."

I nodded sadly, already trying to think up some scheme that would get me to Ban Me Thuot on PIO business.

He smiled and cocked his head. "On the other hand," he went on, eyes twinkling, palms up, "if, in the course of your travels, you come across any information on any subject that you think we might need to know, you would be remiss in your duty not to tell us." He looked at me levelly. "If you get what I mean?"

I grinned. "I think I do, sir." Sure I did. It was a license to steal. He wouldn't stop me and he wouldn't get in my way. But if I got caught I took the rap myself. No big deal. That was the usual spy hassle.

"Good," he said. "Have fun."

26

I left feeling happy for the first time since I left Pleiku. It wasn't the ideal, but it was something.

So I settled into the PIO job, which wasn't too bad. In fact I loved the work. I just felt it was a waste of time when there were more important things to be done. Also I was afraid I'd be promoted to Major before I ever got back to an A ' detachment. I might be able to avoid it if I extended my tour in Nam for six months. Shit, if the opportunity was there I'd extend my tour in Nam as long as I'd be alive. But for some reason the Department of the Army would not let officers extend for longer than two years. Enlisted men could extend longer than that. In fact, there was a guy in Saigon who had been there six years. But he had a good deal, a desk job, a beautiful mistress, and so on. I guess that's what they were afraid of. That a guy would latch on to a good deal and just drink and ball his life away. It was incomprehensible to them that a man would stay in Nam for as long as he cold just because he loved to run combat patrols. Some army!

Anyway, I was stuck there in Nha Trang, running a magazine and getting out press releases. But for a lone operator it was a good deal. Once a month I ran down to Saigon to get the magazine cleared, got a little drunk and took in the sights of the big city. I wasn't exactly thrilled by it but it was something to do. I got up to Ban Me Thuot once more and got to visit Kpa Doh but Phillip was gone somewhere.

And I discovered there was something to ESP after all. See, my office was on the second story and I had my little typing desk shoved over into a corner so that I looked out a window while I typed and there were sidewalks running every which way within sight. Nha Trang was the headquarters for all Special Forces in Vietnam and everybody checked in there again before he went home, plus a lot of people came in with some frequency on business.

So I sat up there at this world crossroads for Green Berets and looked down, running my little typewriter. And when I saw somebody I knew, naturally I looked at him. The way my window was screened and shaded there was no way I could be seen by anybody even if they were looking directly at me. And they did just that. As my eyes would lock on them they would stomp boldly on, as though they expected to be opposed but not stopped, then stop, look around. Sometimes they would look directly at my window, then shrug and walk on.

That was something to think about, as were the amazing number of people who predicted their own combat deaths, apparently with complete equanimity, as though it were the most natural thing in the world.

I had always had that feeling about Nam anyway, as though there were demons loose there, and this only confirmed it. Spirits, magic is afoot, God is alive. Vietnam is a sort of morbid Oz.

Sometimes when the recipient of these gazes was somebody I wanted to see I would call down to them.

Larry Dring, though, I met as he walked into the club.

I couldn't believe it. For one thing he was a Captain. The first time I'd seen Larry Dring I'd been a first lieutenant.

Our first meeting had been somewhat embarrassing. There is a long stretch of soft sand that parallels the Han river just outside of Seoul, Korea. It is the softest, most easy spot to land on I have ever seen or heard of. The 1st Special Forces Group (Abn) S-3, in his infinite wisdom, used to wait until it was frozen solid in the wintertime and then schedule us for night infiltration problems there. I made two jumps there when I was adjutant of a B team on Okinawa.

Tom Kiernan and I had been walking up the sidewalk and I was picking my teeth after lunch and wondering what the hell we were going to do to kill the afternoon. There was absolutely nothing going on. I heard a car squeal to a stop behind me and the C team adjutant yelled at me, "Hey, Morris, Kiernan! Get your hats. You're jumpin' into Korea tonight."

That was the nice thing about the Forces. You never knew what was going to happen next. Seems our Colonel wanted somebody to make the jump and evaluate it for a later problem for D company.

It was so cold we wore all our winter gear and overshoes, the whole thing. And we also carried rucksacks and weapons. Parachutes and all, each man probably weighed 260 pounds and we were packed in there like sardines. That wouldn't have been so bad, but they dropped down to jump altitude and opened the doors twenty minutes out. We had been sitting there sweating under the heaters and then the temperature dropped to what must have been below zero in the aircraft. I was so cold and it was so dark and I had the usual pre-jump flutters, aggravated by making a night equipment drop. More dangerous. And I wondered if I'd ever get to see anything of Korea. So the doors went open and the red light came on by the door and we sat huddled and miserable in over a hundred pounds of gear while the adrenalin roared through our bodies, through my body anyway. Until all I wanted, more than anything else in the world, was to get out that door. But how would we ever stand up in all that shit?

As I recall, we did it by reaching across the aisle and pulling each other upright. The jumpmaster was Major Irving C. Hudlin, who was one of my classmates from Bragg. One of the ones who survived. Major Hudlin was a tall, skinny, light skinned black man who always seemed to have a cigar in his mouth. He had one now, unlighted in the wind, as he stood by the open paratroop door. He was unrecognizable except for the cigar there in the dark in all that gear. We couldn't hear the commands, but we could follow the hand and arm signals. We groped to our feet at stand up. I didn't hear or see the signal, but when they stood up I stood up.

The adrenalin was up so high I opened my mouth and sucked air into my lungs in great gasps. All in the world I wanted was to get out that door. If someone had told me my backpack was filled with orange peels it would have made no difference. I wanted out of that airplane.

Blood roaring, I didn't bother to wait for the jump commands. I don't think anybody else in there did either. We just hooked up and put the safety wire through the snap link. Without command, I checked my equipment in front and the equipment on the back of the guy in front of me. I heard a muffled shout over the roar of the aircraft and saw the jump-master cup his hand over his ear.

A few seconds later I heard another shout from behind and felt a padded slap on my rump. I yelled "Okay!", not having the foggiest idea what my number in the stick was and slapped the guy in front, hard. Then I hung on the static line like a communter on the five o'clock subway and waited for the light to flash green. Supposedly we were six minutes out when we started hooking up, but it seemed like a half hour we were hanging there in that subway strap. The equipment got heavier and heavier and my blood roared higher and, oh, for Christ's sweet sake, how I wanted out of that mother-fucking airplane.

Finally the guy ahead of me took a step, then another. Then it started to go like a freight train as I strode rapidly toward the rear of the aircraft. Then I was by the door. I slammed the static line toward the tailgate and turned to face all the enormity of black starry space before me and felt the wind sucking. I snapped briefly into a sloppy door position and then I was gone.

Wham! How fast my status was changed. I had been jammed in like a sardine, the wind had swirled around and I had been so scared. The equipment had been so heavy. Zip! I was weightless, swept breathlessly toward the tail of the air-craft. Then I felt the four little pops at my back as the break cord snapped and I was hanging under the great dark globe of my parachute. I looked around and saw not a goddamned thing. There were some stars above me and that was all. Then over in the distance I saw the oscillating red dot of what I took to be Hudlin's cigar.

That was it. I had no idea how far I was from the ground, no idea how fast I was falling. The parachute seemed all right and in the normal course of events I would be on the ground in a minute.

Then I caught a glimpse of ground moving by toward my rear and got ready for a front parachute landing fall. I put my fat gloved hands on the risers, got my feet as close as they'd go together in all that gear and stared at where the horizon should have been if I'd been able to see it.

I sat flat down on my behind and felt something break in there. "OH MY ASS!" I bellowed, and listened to the sound of it reverberate all over the Han river basin. You weren't supposed to do that sort of thing on a clandestine infiltration. Oh, but it hurt so bad. I moaned again, "Oh, my ass!"

I lay stunned on the ground, trying to get the belly band loose. Finally I did that and tried to roll over to get up. Before I'd had a chance to get to my feet four Korean Special Forces men came over and stood me on my feet. I muttered "Thanks" and they said "De Nada," or whatever "You're Welcome" is in Korean and helped me out of my gear. They took my parachutes and kit bag and I slung my rucksack and carbine. Then they led me over to where a jeep was parked. There was a grinning American Special Forces sergeant behind the wheel.

"Bust your ass, huh?" he said, grinning as though that was the funniest joke in the world. There was nothing disrespectful about the smile, it was just as though that was the sort of joke we could all expect to have played on us from time to time.

"Think I broke it," I said and introduced myself.

"Sergeant Dring," he said. "Larry Dring. I'll run you over to the hospital and we'll see if you're gonna live or not."

I eased myself gingerly into the right hand front seat, and he started the jeep and drove off.

"You gonna die right away?" he asked. "Or do you think you might survive awhile, sir?"

"It's nothin' disastrous," I replied. "Why?"

"I was thinkin' we might stop for a cup of coffee on the way."

I nodded. "Yeah! I could go for a cup of anything hot."

"Coffee it is then," he said.

We drove for awhile, then went through a gate guarded

by a Korean and an American guard, both of them sharp. Inside it looked like your standard military base, and if you don't know what that looks like then you don't want to. He pulled up in front of a low, boxy building, obviously a big consolidated mess hall.

Inside it was all squares and rectangles, under the pale fluorescent glow of the lights, and miles up ahead the stainless steel of the serving tables. We went all the way forward and got two of the tan plastic cups that the army serves coffee in all over the world and then filled them from the urns that seemed like fifty-five gallon stainless steel drums. My butt hurt and I was limping, but I eased down into a chair at one of the tables and found an awkward but fairly painless position.

The steam rose from the cups and I looked over at my companion. He seemed a perfectly respectable young man, sort of a cross between Audie Murphy and Mickey Rooney as Andy Hardy. He held his cup in both hands and looked at me over the rim as he sucked some out.

I fished around in my pocket for a cigarette and offered him one. He shook his head. "You stationed here?" I asked.

He shook his head negatively. "No sir, I'm here on leave to see some of my Korean friends."

I nodded. "Reckon you used to be stationed here?" A logical conclusion. Otherwise he wouldn't have had any Korean friends.

His mouth took on a bitter quirk. Then he nodded and said, "Yep! I was until they threw me out of the country."

I started to lean back on the two legs of my chair, then thought better of it as pain shot up my spine. "Oh, how come?" I asked, sensing a Special Forces story in the offing. My version of a Special Forces story is like nothing you read in *The Green Berets*. Robby stressed the hard, competent aspects of the Forces. But the stories I loved were illustrations of the difficulties encountered by the cockeyed freebooters who wind up in that kind of outfit. Like the time Mad Jack Shannon jumped five teams into Korea on an exercise, neglecting to notify the Koreans or 8th Army. That caused something of a stir. Or the guy in Nam who got busted for coming in off patrol and going into this MACV

258

bar for a beer. The guy behind the bar, a Vietnamese, very deliberately turned and snapped a padlock on the refrigerator and then turned, smiled, held his palms up and said, "So sorry, bar closed."

The SF guy, whoever he was, whipped out his forty-five, blew the lock off the refrigerator and growled, "Gimme a fuckin' beer."

Larry, Sergeant Dring as I thought of him then, smiled and said, "Well, I used to be the Minister of Agriculture for the Republic of Korea, and that didn't set too well with the 8th Army, so they threw me out of the country."

I pursed my lips. There was obviously more to come. I cocked my head and coaxed a little. "Er-uh, how did you happen to become Minister of Agriculture for the Republic of Korea?"

Dring leaned forward, still smiling. "Well, I was walkin' down the street one day, mindin' my own business, so to speak, nothin' to do and this black Mercedes Benz sedan whizzed up to the curb and a Korean Special Forces captain, friend of mine, stuck his head out the window and says in Korean, 'Hey Dring, where ya goin'?' "

"So naturally I turn and say, 'No place special.' He says to hop in. I get in and ask him what's goin' on. He tells me that they are havin' a little *coup d'etat* there and the distinguished looking joker in the back seat with the homberg hat is Mr. John Chang, who is the president of the Republic of Korea and he is my friend's prisoner and they are takin' him to the Hotel Bando, where he is to be held incommunicado, and since I'm not doin' anything, how would I like to go along?

"I said, sure, why not? So off we go to the Bando to hold this guy prisoner. This turns out to be something of a drag, as there is nothing to do up there but play double sol and shoot the breeze and my friend waves his forty-five at this Chang if he makes any sudden moves.

"We'd been there all day and maybe the next afternoon my friend said, 'You know, legally Mr. Chang is still the president of the Republic with powers to appoint and disappoint and so on. How would you like to be Minister for Agriculture?'

"I say, sure, why not, and my friend jacks a round into the

chamber, waves his pistol at Mr. Chang and says, 'He's the Minister for Agriculture, right?'

"Chang agreed with vigor, but 8th Army has no sense of humor so right after the coup I was sent to Oki."

That was my introduction to Larry Dring. It was about typical. He and I played leapfrog in and out of Nam for the next three years, so I didn't see him too much. He bought a salvage jeep on Oki which was okay except for the engine. I later heard he went down to the airport at Da Nang when a load of new jeep engines came in, painted the natural wooden box olive drab, stenciled it with some official looking stencils that said it was to be sent to him care of his wife on Oki, put it on a fork lift and ran it over to the weekly Marine flight home.

Worked like a charm.

That's just a rumor, of course.

After we finished our coffee, he took me to the hospital at Ascom City, where my x-rays were examined by a sleepy physician named Golub, fat, balding in green hospital suit, alternately scratching his ass and his belly. "You've got a fractured coccyx there, my man," he informed me and gave me a bottle of darvon and a chemical heating pad.

"That all?" I inquired.

"Young man," he said, "contrary to popular opinion we cannot put your ass in a sling."

When I got back to Nam and heard people talking about Lieutenant Dring and his Mike Force company I had difficulty in believing it was the same guy. I couldn't visualize him in a regular uniform long enough to get through OCS. That just wasn't his style.

My feelings about OCS were that it was a kind of school for spitshines with side courses in harassment and duckspeak. I just couldn't see Larry in that sort of environment. Years later I met a guy who was one of his classmates, who told me I was right. Larry spent most of his time in OCS giving weapons demonstrations of one sort or another, usually in a French camouflage bush jacket and a red Vietnamese paratrooper beret.

I had been told that he had left Nam a month or so before I arrived. The turnaround time for infantry officers was running about two years then. That is, a guy would spend a year in Nam and come home for a couple of years and then go back again. For helicopter pilots the turnaround time was about a year.

So I was doubly surprised to look up as I was leaving the club one evening to see Captain Larry Dring come strolling into the dining room.

We were glad to see each other and went through the what are you doing here routine, and the manly handshake routine. I turned around and went back inside, got another glass of tea and sat down while he started his dinner. He had been an Instructor at the Ranger mountain camp while he was Stateside. Came back to Nam at his own request.

"Where you goin'?" I asked him.

He smiled. "Goin' back to the 25th Mike Force Company," he replied.

I sensed a coming disappointment for him, after the way I had been jacked around on getting the assignment I wanted. "No telling where they're going to send you when you get to Pleiku," I said.

He gave me a sly, determined smile.

"Ya know when I got off the airplane in Saigon they sent me to someplace called the 9th Replacement Battalion. There was a spade captain there who told me I was going to the 9th Division. I told him, no, I was going up to Nha Trang and report in to Special Forces. He gave me a line of guff to the effect that no matter what my orders read, MACV made the assignments here and they were going to send me to the 9th Division."

He leaned back and grinned. "I cited this regulation I made up on the spot that if a guy had three Purple Hearts he could go wherever he wanted to, and told him that I had six, which is true, and if he didn't cut orders sending me to Special Forces I was going to get back on the airplane and go back to Benning."

I rolled my eyes and went "Whew! Did he do it?"

Larry nodded. "Then I got up here and went through the same routine with that wonderful adjutant. He wanted to send me to the Delta. I told him I was going back to the 25th Company and they knew I was coming and were ready for me and had some patrols planned. He pointed out that he cut the orders and not me."

"Yeah?"

"And I pointed out that he could cut orders to wherever he wanted to but that I was getting on the airplane for Pleiku in the morning and if he wanted me and the orders to coincide then he'd cut orders sending me to Pleiku."

By now I had the idea. "And he did it?"

He shrugged. "Sure!"

It was a kind of shattering blow for me. I felt as though I had cheated myself. If I had pulled that kind of stuff I'd probably be running in the woods at Buon Blech right now. But it had never in my life occurred to me to simply refuse to obey an order. I would have expected to be struck dead by lightning. The military just wouldn't work if everybody disobeyed orders and I wantd to be part of something that worked. I was glad for Larry and jealous as hell, but it wouldn't have worked for me. For one thing I had been tabbed for my job by the group commander and nobody, repeat nobody, runs a bluff on Colonel Ladd.

But I was glad to see him, and glad for him and glad for the 25th company.

In some ways Carl McCarden was a typical Special Forces officer and in others he was not. For instance, he never wore underwear. That was pretty typical. I don't wear underwear. And when I'm in the woods in boots I don't wear socks either. Ludwig taught me that. Socks just roll up in your boots and wear blisters on your feet. But on the other hand Carl didn't believe in killing people, which was rather atypical for a Special Forces officer.

It was the belief in not killing people that got Carl in the S-5 business. He had been leader of a platoon of door gunners for a while and hated that because he had to kill people all over Vietnam. So somehow he wrangled a transfer to the forces and then got in the S-5 business.

I don't think Carl could have prospered in any other organization in the army but the Forces because in his own way he was almost a classic Forces freebooter. Other than this curious prejudice against killing people that is.

For awhile there he went with Mme. Thieu's secretary, which was the source of a lot of good background information on what the Viets thought. No hard intelligence, just normal gossip. Fascinating though. I have seen Carl spend hours trying to find a job for a pretty Vietnamese lady with a baby to take care of, and so on. I suppose most of us would have tried to help, but they all came to Carl. Gallant, Carl was gallant.

Anyway Carl and I were friends and he was the guy who had got me to come to Nha Trang and write the FULRO staff study that got me caught in the PIO job.

As it turned out it was just as well. I went back up to Pleiku about a month later to pick up the rest of my stuff. Had a talk with Ludwig. He had decided to give me an A camp, but one away from the Montagnards. It was in the Bong Son valley, as a matter of fact. Same general area where Swain was killed. I was supposed to build the camp with 450 Viet strikers. I was lucky to get out of this job, because I have never built anything in my life and don't believe in camps. Besides that, I have no more ability to get Viets to fight than anybody else. I suspect, actually, that had I got that job I would have been dead now. I'm pretty sure of it. It would have been Kham Duc all over again, only this time I wouldn't have been so lucky.

So I guess being the PIO was a fairly good fate for me. Not what I wanted, but okay.

Anyway they had a conference on Montagnards scheduled in Saigon. Carl asked me to go along. After all I was the Special Forces Montagnard expert. So I went along.

We flew into Saigon. I had a rucksack with a shaving kit in it and an M-16 slung over my shoulder. I had an extra suit of fatigues, some ammo, and that was it. Carl had his M-16, an attache case and a Samsonite suitcase with a beautifully tailored vested suit in it and some miscellaneous haberdashery. Miscellaneous to me, anyhow. I'm sure he picked it out with care.

We checked into Camp Goodman, which was a Special Forces installation in Saigon, and Carl put on his suit and went out for an evening with the embassy people or whoever it was he ran around with. I went over to the Camp Goodman bar and started drinking beer. It was crowded with low-life enlisted swine and quite a few of them were friends of mine. It was also crowded with some low-life commissioned swine and the music was okay and the company was great and shortly I was drunk and got into a ferocious discussion about the use of silencers on recon patrols with an Australian SAS sergeant, a rawboned, redheaded degenerate whose name I never got, but whose face I'll never forget. His contention was that there was no point having one guy with a silencer if everybody didn't have one. My contention was that a silencer was a special purpose weapon and if everybody was going to fire there was no use trying to hide it because people would know. But if you had to take out a sniper or a guard you only needed one weapon for that.

There was a continuous roar of conversation around us as everybody yelled to be heard. None of us could hear worth a damn anyway because our ears were all blasted out from aircraft engines and artillery. And me, I'd been a range officer for a year at Fort Dix and nobody could tell me you needed to wear earplugs. They were too much of a hassle.

The most common word in my vocabulary these days is "Huh?"

So there was this continuous roar of talk and Annie the Chinese bargirl's giggle as she passed out beers like cocktail peanuts. A group of madmen sat in a circle, barechested, on the floor, swilling beer and writing the usual obscene words in red grease pencil on each other's foreheads, making obeisances with pressed palms against their foreheads chanting: *BUDDHA SUCKS!*
BUDDHA SUCKS!
BUDDHA SUCKS!

I immediately put these clowns down as recon men. I like recon people a lot because I have found them to be uniformly crazy. I had wanted to run a story on recon for a long time, and the way I wanted to do it was to go on one. Nothing much to it. You and five other guys just drop down at dusk in the middle of an enemy troop concentration and tiptoe around for a week or two, not talking, or breathing too loud. Fun!

So I hinted around to this kid sergeant who looked about twelve that anytime he wanted a fat clumsy captain I was happy to join him. He said, sure, come on down some time and we'll go out. Then we proceeded to hoist a few more. Somewhere along the way there he wrapped an arm around me and said, "Ya know, motherfucker, I like you." I was flattered, but nowhere in any course I ever took on military courtesy was it pronounced okay to call your superior officer motherfucker. I don't mind. I just mention it.

Anyway I figured these guys chanting "BUDDHA SUCKS!" were recon. I was beginning to feel that the war was getting crazy. But I really like these guys. I liked them better than anybody I'd ever known before. And the people

265

I've liked since are people who would have been like that in that kind of situation.

I got very drunk and went to bed and woke up hung over.

The next morning Carl got me up and we went over for breakfast. He, as usual, was gorgeous in spanking clean, starched tailored jungle fatigues. I wore the same old rumpled cruddies I'd worn to Saigon. I didn't want anybody to think I was from there. Saigon could be a beautiful city. It has been, and the streets are lined with wonderful buildings that the French designed for the tropics. There was a lot of tropic vegetation and big city hustle, but the streets were choked with military vehicles and noxious fumes, lousy noises and choky gases, ill-natured taxi drivers in little Renaults that the Smithsonian would love to get its hands on.

I slouched in the back of the jeep, nursing my hangover and wishing I had hopped a chopper for Ban Me Thuot to see Phillip or hooked up with a patrol going somewhere. Saigon had been to beautiful to see this way now. It was sort of like visiting the girl you love in the hospital where she's recuperating from being gang raped by a band of marauding outlaw motorcyclists.

We oozed through the traffic down the Rue Pasteur, on downtown, past the square where the Continental Palace, the National Assembly, and the Caravelle Hotel were. The Caravelle I had never liked particularly. It was a junior grade Hilton sort of place. Once I had been to the bar there, got a drink and gone up to the roof to watch artillery flashes on the horizon, which had given me a deliciously decadent, fiddling while Rome burns, feeling. I liked the music in the bar, which was French, and there were autographed pictures of Juliette Greco on the walls. Beautiful photos, not like the scroungy framed jobs you usually see in bars of the owner with his arm around Knute Rockne's shoulders, but beautifully shot, elegantly framed photos of this beautiful woman.

But mainly I liked to stay at the Continental Palace when I was staying somewhere downtown in Saigon, something I hadn't done since Camp Goodman was built. The Continental had this beautiful old bird cage elevator, obsequious waiters who had been there serving the French when Victor

Hugo was studying penmanship, and spacious old rooms with French doors leading out to the balcony and yards and yards of gauze mosquito net over the beds.

I always had the feeling I would find Humphrey Bogart, Sidney Greenstreet and Peter Lorre hatching a plot at the bar. There were a lot of those kinds of characters hanging around there, as a matter of fact. Scroungy old civilians who had been in the Far East for decades, picking up a buck and hustling for more.

Foody and I had gone there to change money the second week we were at Buon Beng, changed all the bread the whole team had at almost double the official rate of exchange. We went down to open the commissary account and change the money, and I can still see Foody sitting at a table on the verandah, sipping *cafe au lait*, the waiter handling the whole thing very cool while Bill sat there with a cigar box with three or four thousand dollars in it and his Browning 9mm pistol, just in case.

Later I had to come up to Saigon because of some business. It was when we were running *beaucoup* patrols out of Buon Beng, and I went to the bookstore across the way, bought *Say, Darling* by Richard Bissell, *The Diamond as Big as the Ritz* by Scott Fitzgerald and Faulkner's *The Wild Palms* and lay in one of those big old rooms for three days, reading. That's all I did, read, and rolled over periodically so my muscles wouldn't freeze in one position. I wallowed all over that bed, and read on my back, on my stomach, with the book on the floor and my head hanging over.

Maybe once a day I'd get up and go downstairs and have a good meal, maybe sit on the veranda and watch the girls glide by in the Ao Dai's and look at all the strange characters you see in the street in Saigon. Then I'd go back upstairs for a read. I didn't want to see anybody or talk to anybody.

Once I went down to a joint that catered to Americans and had a hamburger and a malt. But that was it. I didn't look up anybody I knew in Saigon and I didn't get drunk. I didn't go down on Tu Do for a steambath and a blowjob. I just lay up in that hotel and read my books. I look back on it as one of the most delicious experiences of my life.

We drove past there and past some other places and

around some. I didn't really know my way around Saigon that well, and finally we wound up at the embassy. It was a tall, gray, wretched office building with sandbags and concertina wire outside it and Marine guards standing out front.

Inside it was like any other American office building built in the past twenty years, which was to say it was like a brick mausoleum. It made the hair on the back of my neck prickle, and the muscles in my stomach started forming a knot.

I expected that any second someone would give me a form to fill out.

Fortunately this did not happen and we stepped into a carpeted, self-service Otis elevator which whisked us to whatever floor we were going to. We went down a long hall and through another door which led us into what appeared to be an anteroom. And there within the larger room was a smaller room. It stood about eight inches off the floor held up by thin metal rods. It did not quite reach the ceiling and the little room itself was made entirely of plexiglass.

In fact, I did have to fill out a form in that room. I had to promise on pain of death or maybe a nasty talking-to never to tell anybody about this "secure" room, the idea of which was that it was bug proof and we could all go in there and talk our heads off and the nasty Cong wouldn't be able to hear a thing.

It put me in mind immediately of a bad James Bond movie. I, of course, deduced that nothing whatever could be gained by talking to anybody whose mind worked like that. But I determined to see the charade through, and if these people wanted to play secret agent it was all right with me. I gave Carl a lopsided grin and he answered me back with an expression which indicated that I shouldn't be too hasty. Maybe something would come of this after all.

We were the only ones there in uniform. All the others were gentlemen in civilian clothes ranging in age from about twenty-six to maybe forty-five. They all looked very serious. We milled around awhile, shaking hands and exchanging pleasantries and then started trooping into the bug-proof room the door of which was then closed, locked and hermetically sealed. We all looked at each other for a moment.

The chair I sat in was upholstered in some sort of green

nubby material and looked and felt expensive. So did the table before which we sat. The gentlemen around it ranged from civil service time servers to ardent young strivers. They all appeared well manicured and well fed. For a moment I was self conscious about my scroungy fatigues and then I felt good about them. Here we were planning important strategy in the middle of a revolutionary war and there wasn't a revolutionary or a warrior in the room with the possible exception of myself and Carl. We had at least, as Woody Garrett called it, "smelled smoke in combat." Carl wasn't really raunchy enough for the role though. I slumped in my seat, regarded them all with narrowed eyes and two-fingered a cigarette out of my shirt pocket.

These fellows were all looking around at each other and smiling a lot. They seemed like decent enough chaps, and I wondered whatever brought them out from Harvard or wherever the hell that kind of people came from.

Perhaps I'm being unfair. I knew only one of the civilians in the room personally, Dr. Gerald C. Hickey, an anthropologist working for Rand Corporation. He too was a well-fed smooth civilian, but he turned up at the strangest times, almost got his ass shot off in whatever crisis it was that was happening, and then split. He was always quiet, always amiable, always friendly and he knew what the score was in Vietnam more than any other American I have ever met, far more than I. I gave him a nod. He returned it.

Before each of us was a little printed agenda for the meeting which was entirely concerned with refugee affairs. I forget what the itinerary was, but Montagnard affairs was part of it and something about a Vietnamese parliamentary act giving the Montagnards title to at least some of the land they had been occupying for the last 900 years before the Viets came in and ripped it off.

And right in the middle of this agenda was this item.

PHILLIPPE DROUIN

I looked again just to make sure. But that's what it was all right. It started an apprehensive feeling in my stomach to think that these clowns were going to discuss Phillip. I couldn't imagine what I'd hear them say about him, but I was really curious to know what it was. Phillip was my friend, the best guerrilla leader I'd ever known, except for maybe Luette—no, Luette was more political. Phillip was the best guerrilla leader I'd ever known, period. Che Guevara wouldn't have made a pimple on Phillip's ass. Most of these men had never seen Phil. Didn't know about the whacky smile that consumed his entire face when the prospect of a fight came up. Didn't know anything about him. What would they say? Would they consider him a menace to be done away with? By God, I'd set them straight on that score soon enough.

No, wait a minute, Morris. Just keep it cool. These idiots aren't going to listen to you. Haven't you learned yet that the U.S. Government isn't interested in information that comes from the bottom up? All they want to know is what the President wants to hear so they can tell it to him. Just bide your peace and if anything comes up here that would put Phillip or FULRO in any danger, get it to them quickly and they can get themselves out of the way.

Hickey looked up and smiled. It was kind of interesting. Before I'd only seen the friendly disinterested scholar side of his nature. But this time he smiled like a shark. He was an okay guy, all right, but he worked indirectly for the United States government and therefore was not to be trusted.

He smiled and shook his head, sweeping the room with his eyes, which were intelligent and saw far more than the eyes of anyone else in the room.

"I think, gentlemen, we can cross one item off the agenda. My information is that Phillippe Drouin was assassinated yesterday by political opponents within the FULRO organization. He will trouble us no more."

It always hits me that way. When one of my friends is killed I simply note it quite calmly and file it away for further consideration. I took a black ball point marked U.S. GOVERNMENT out of my pocket and coolly crossed his name off the list. My grief was private and I would trot it out later and examine it. If it in fact did turn out that this intelligence was correct. Phillip had been reported dead before, and so, for that matter, had I. I had to get to Ban Me Thuot to check this out. I had to see what the current situation in FULRO was and I had to . . . had to . . . had to, what? I didn't have to anything. If Phillip was dead because of some little ratshit

270

intramural squabble, what was I to do? Offer to help his wife and kids, sure. Which side of the intramural squabble was Kpa Doh on? What was the fucking story? First thing was to get to Ban Me Thuot; after that things would start to come clear.

I slid down further in my chair. There was nothing more going to be said here today to interest me. I looked at Carl, who knew how I felt about Phillip. He looked at me closely, sadly, then away. The rest of this thing was his meat. I don't remember anything that was said during the conference. All I remember is that after we left the secret room we went downstairs to the little cafe in the basement of the embassy and ate. I had a bacon, tomato and lettuce sandwich and a chocolate malt and we finished our discussion of the same stuff we'd been talking about in the secret room while the little Vietnamese waitresses took it all down in shorthand on their order pads.

It took me about two weeks to come up with a convincing enough reason to go to Ban Me Thuot. As soon as I got there I headed out for Buon Ale A to piece together as much as I could of what had happened to Phillip.

It was a very complicated situation. Phillip was one of the youngest of the high-ranking FULRO people at twenty-six. As commanding officer of the Dam-Yi division he was also one of the most powerful, and as an intelligence agent for the Americans he was one of the most wealthy. For that reason he was regarded with jealousy by a lot of the other leaders. When you put his monumental ego on top of that, it wasn't hard to deduce that he was also widely hated.

But Phillip was a power in Ban Me Thuot. Nobody touched him. The Province Chief left him alone. Since I had been down there the last time, FULRO had gotten so open in Ban Me Thuot that FULRO officers in full uniform were seen in the street.

Phillip was also very proud of his new wealth and influence, and on occasion he was known to dally with the ladies. He was even known to dally with Vietnamese ladies, which did nothing to endear him to anybody at all, I gather. To some he was arrogant to the point of being unbearable. It was easy enough for me to see that all this was caused by the

271

same inferiority complex that had turned him into a wild man. I had plenty of the same in my own personality, and for that matter, so does almost anybody I ever knew who has accomplished anything.

At any rate one evening Phillip and some members of his staff had gone out to hit the bars in Ban Me Thuot. Apparently he made a pass at one of the young ladies in attendance at the Imperial, and she didn't go for it. Neither did the Vietnamese Special Forces sergeant she was with. There was the usual heated exchange of words and the Viet asked Phillip outside, or Phillip asked him outside, one or the other. Accounts vary.

Once they got outside they squared off. Phillip's bodyguard, consisting of several ex–Mike Force soldiers, lounged against his jeep outside, armed with M-2 carbines. The Mike Force has no great love for the VNSF and when they saw their colonel in an altercation with one they took the next logical step and shot the son of a bitch.

He died.

I ran across some speculation that the Viets went to rather elaborate lengths to insure that he did die, so they would have an excuse to go after Phillip, but I couldn't know about that for sure.

In any case the Province Chief got in touch with the other FULRO leaders in Ban Me Thuot and said something had to be done about Phillip. His enemies, which by that time appeared to be in the majority, threw him up for grabs.

Phillip was not one to surrender lightly though. He got to one of his American Air Force buddies and flew to Saigon. There he got in touch with whoever it was he did intelligence work for and got a wad of money that would choke a horse. Then he flew back to Ban Me Thuot and got all the people who were loyal to him, plus all the people whom he could buy, and started going around the city assassinating his political enemies.

At the same time his political enemies were getting together and forming their forces to chase Phillip around the city and try to assassinate him.

Unfortunately, his guys were on bicycles and their guys were on the famous FULRO gray Honda 90's. So they caught him first.

All these details I was able to confirm.

But I never talked to anybody who had seen the body.

28

It would probably fit one's normal expectations better if I said that I was so desolated by the news of Phillip's probable demise that I became despondent, but I was working too hard, and really too busy to let it affect me that much. At this point I had more dead than living friends anyway.

The PIO job, worthless as it was, was really a lot of fun. I got to travel around Vietnam and meet a lot of interesting people, writers and TV correspondents and so on. The best writer I met was Mike Herr, who was doing what later turned out to be the best magazine series on Vietnam that I ever read, bar none. Somewhere in his series Mike said: "Vietnam was what we had instead of happy childhoods." That statement, I believe, is at the core of the whole Vietnamese experience.

We were able to improve *The Green Beret* magazine, which means that it climbed from absolute wretchedness to mediocrity. In the process I managed to offend almost every senior officer and NCO in the Group. They had liked it better the way it was. My feeling was that I had been put in the job because I was the guy who was supposed to know how to do it. I didn't want the job, and if they didn't like the way I ran it they could bloody well send me to the field. Unfortunately, the only one who did like it was Colonel Ladd.

Rick Scena, my sergeant, was a good PIO man and a good man generally. Rick a happy-go-lucky little Italian dude with a great sense of humor and a good brain. Like me, he was proud as hell of his beret, but not totally immune to how ridiculous the role looked when it was played to the hilt.

One day we were going to the big headquarters building across the street. As we stepped out on the little porch that led to the steps, I glanced down and saw all the guys in their green berets moving around the compound. Some strutted, some stomped, some sauntered, but they all had the cocky elegance that indicated they expected to be opposed but not stopped. The champ was a sergeant, scowling horrendously as he stomped down the street, a sheaf of papers and several manila envelopes under his arm, cigar jammed manfully into his teeth.

As we walked down the steps I adjusted my beret to the improbable angle I always wore it, sort of the way Veronica Lake wore her hair, and thought about the way all those guys were walking. At the bottom of the steps I looked at Rick and he looked at me and I knew he was thinking the same thing. His own beret was down on his nose in the Beetle Bailey manner. I grinned and he grinned and we held hands and skipped, giggling, across the street to the big head-quarters building.

We got some funny looks.

So I hung around and worked on the PIO stuff and did a little running at noon and lifted weights a little and tried not to let the office job turn me into a complete marshmallow. I was still overweight and slow. It was just too easy to sit on my ass by the typewriter all day every day and hit the mess for a couple of beers after work and then go back and clean up what work there was or go downtown and see the USAID nurses or hang around the club, or any number of things there were to do that did nothing for your mind or body.

For so long I had been chafing in the headquarters. But with Phillip gone I had no hope of organizing an intel net at Buon Blech. Might as well try another outfit. C and C needed people.

C and C, I came to learn, meant Command and Control detachment. Command and Control of what? I had first become aware of the existence of C and C when I reported into the country. I had been in the adjutant's office awaiting orders when a Lieutenant Colonel I had known on Oki came in. I had known him when he was a captain. He was a nice fellow, bald, aggressive and stupid. Now he was a Lieutenant Colonel and he carried a Browning 9 mm pistol. It was the kind the Agency usually issued their people. Therefore I was to assume he worked for them. It was probably true, since

275

personal weapons were now forbidden in Vietnam. They had been since Westmoreland. He didn't like all those cowboy rigs that the chopper pilots and SF guys affected.

So there he stood, in stupendous physical condition for someone of his age, which was probably around thirty-eight. At thirty I considered thirty-eight pretty old. Most sergeants retired when they were thirty-eight. We exchanged the usual pleasantries, and I asked him what his outfit was.

"C and C," he said with a condescending smirk..

"What's C and C?" I asked.

He tilted his head and smirked some more. "If you don't know," he said, "you're not supposed to."

Later when I was at Pleiku a sergeant had come in wearing a uniform I had never seen before. It looked kind of halfway between a U.S. uniform and an NVA uniform. It was a very strange uniform. This sergeant was rugged looking, although a little on the chubby side, and he was carrying a Swedish "K" instead of an M-16. He had a bad tic in his right eye. We fell to talking. "What outfit you with?"

"C and C."

"How you like it?" That seemed like an unclassified question.

"Oh, it's okay," he said, his right eye jerking like a jack-hammer.

Of course, as I went along I learned a lot more about C and C. It was a secret outfit and they carried the war to the enemy wherever he might be. That was kind of dangerous since you never had any artillery support and no troops on the ground to support you. They worked with "indigenous" troops, Viets or Yards or Nungs. But they were mercenaries, for sure.

C and C performed exactly the same mission as Project Delta, and the other Recon projects, except that they didn't do it in the same place. C and C had started out as a volunteer outfit, but it wasn't volunteer anymore. The reason for that was that they had two hundred percent casualties a year.

That was my means to escape the headquarters. I would volunteer for C and C. I mulled it over for a long time and gathered all the information I could about C and C.

I went down to Project Delta and talked with my friends down there. I couldn't get a job with Delta, because it had all the personnel it could use, and guys were stacked up trying to get in.

"Why is that?" I asked my friend, the Delta S-3. "You have essentially the same mission as C and C, but they need people and you have too many."

He leaned back and pulled on his cigarette. We were sitting in the bar at the Project Delta Officers Club; I was in uniform and he was in very collegiate looking bermuda shorts and a banlon T-shirt. It was nice in the Delta bar with the Vietnamese paintings on the walls and the little rock fountain bubbling in the corner, with the rock garden and the padded bar, the indirect lighting and the piped music. I hung around down there quite a lot and felt glad to be welcome. Not everyone was. Not even in the Forces. Chuck Allen, the Delta commander, was an old friend, since I had been in his company at Fort Dix as a second lieutenant, and later when he was an old captain about to make major and I was a young one with my first team we had gone through predeployment training together and played war against each other in the mountains of northern Okinawa. It was a lot of fun, but his team whipped our ass.

Old Chuck was a mountain of a man, from the back as trim as a track star. But from the front he appeared to have a bushel basket tucked up under his shirt. He wasn't just fat. He was big, and very strong. He was, in fact, just about the strongest man I ever knew. And at two hundred and fifty pounds he could run me into the ground the best day I ever saw.

Chuck looked like a football player, and could have been except he didn't want to play. He wanted to fight.

Rumor has it that his career had been seriously impeded by an incident at Fort Campbell which had kept him a captain for over ten years. He had declined to play on the Post football team, pointing out to everyone who would listen to him that football was a volunteer project and he wanted to soldier. "There's no MOS for a football player," was the way he put it.

He kept saying this to people of progressively higher and higher rank until finally he uttered the same phrase to the

277

commanding general in his office. The general was a football nut.

Chuck was tired of saying this same phrase over and over again, but he thought it so succinct and apt that he never amended it. But he was so tired that rather than listen to the general go into the usual spiel about the honor of the unit and his duty and all that he turned and started to walk out. Chuck had the same hassle with football that I had with being PIO. But I could never have done what he did. Larry Dring would have, and Chuck did, but it kept him a captain for over ten years.

When he had started to walk out, the chief of staff of the division, a full colonel, had put his hand on Chuck's chest and said, "Now just a minute, Captain . . ."

This was a mistake, because anyone who knows Chuck knows not to attempt to physically restrain him. Of course the colonel didn't know him very well, and that was why it was such a surprise when Chuck, quite without thinking about it, knocked him flat on his ass.

That sort of thing isn't done, you know.

Yes, I liked all the guys I knew with Project Delta quite a lot. I had a sort of tentative agreement to go out on an operation with them the first chance I could get away that long.

Bill Larrabee, that was the Delta Operations Officer's name, a young captain, maybe twenty-five or twenty-six. For a time Westmoreland had suspected that he was not getting the straight scoop from Delta's reconnaissance patrols, which consisted of two American SF men, both NCO's, and four VNSF. So they put an American lieutenant in charge of each patrol. This caused the quality of the intelligence to fall off somewhat and so the policy was discontinued. Bill had been one of these patrol leaders, and he was one of the few who had been successful. He had been with the project ever since. To me he looked like someone you'd expect to find president of the Sigma Chi chapter at a small social school. Except, of course, that his eyes were large and soft and if you looked deeply into them they came to sharp diamond points, somewhere in their depths. Bill was a quiet, friendly young fellow who would do that which was necessary to achieve that which he set out to achieve.

278

He hoisted a drink and I listened to the ice tinkle and to the piped music. "Bill, what's the difference between Delta and C and C? You perform essentially the same mission, in different places. Why the big spread in friendly casualties?"

Bill shook his head sadly. "The big difference," he said, "is that we work for the Forces while C and C works directly for MACV. We have our own choppers assigned to us, and we have three choppers, two guns and a slick, manned at all times. The crews sleep on them. That means if one of our patrol is in trouble he breathes one word into his radio and the choppers are in the air to get him out, day or night."

I nodded. "Sure," I said. "That's the only way to do it."

"Not according to C and C," he went on. "MACV hasn't given them permission to extract a team in trouble on their own authority. If one of their teams gets in trouble they have to call back to the FOB with a lengthy explanation of why they want to get out. The guy at the FOB has to put in a call to Saigon, and if it's after duty hours they have to chase down the duty officer, who is, like as not, a second lieutenant in intelligence who has never been shot at before. He is only on call, so he has to be found and come back and get on the radio and then he has to be convinced that the team needs to come out."

I put my head in my hands. "Oh shit!" I muttered. Two hundred per cent casualties a year. The U.S. Army does it again. For the umpteenth thousandth time I wished the Forces was a separate service and had nothing to do with the army.

By contrast Delta had been around so long, and was so professional, that almost everybody assigned to it, and they were all volunteers, extended. Usually, unless a guy had some sort of family trouble he stayed in Delta until he was wounded badly enough to be sent home, or killed.

That was one of the reasons they had the fancy clubs and bars. They made good money, what with jump pay and combat pay. And the guys in Delta put a lot of that money into their compound. When they were in the field they lived like rats. When they were in garison they lived like kings. My first choice would have been Buon Blech, my second would have been an outfit like Delta. But it looked like C and C was my only way out of the headquarters.

One night when I was feeling horrible about working there while other people with less experience and skill at combat operations in Vietnam were running the woods, I went to the club alone, went to the bar upstairs and got myself quietly drunk. I sat there and thought about C and C for a long time.

I remember reading about World War I aviators, who had a low life expectancy, and how some of them seemed to shift into a sort of supercharged existence. Somehow that's what happened to me while I was thinking about those two hundred per cent casualties a year. I have taken some gaudy and ridiculous chances in my life, even sought them, but they have only been taken when I was sure I could count on myself and the people I was with. That wasn't true with C and C. Not at all.

This is a very peculiar thing to describe, but my vision altered. All the colors in that dim bar became very vivid, even though the lights were subdued. I can recall it with extraordinary clarity now, the whole scene. I sat at my table alone with a scotch and water in front of me and I was present in all those vivid extraordinary colors, and my depth perception was extremely pronounced. I was looking down the hall which led to the little alcove where the slot machines and the manager's office were. And the little Viet girl who sat in her booth and made change. You gave her military pay certificates and she gave you tokens for the slots. And that little short hall I was looking down seemed about a block long, and I knew that at the end of it was death.

I had this certain feeling that if I volunteered for C and C I would not be merely taking a chance, I would be committing suicide. I knew it didn't happen to everybody in C and C, but I was certain that if *I* did it *I* would die, and for no reason. C and C was a pure combat outfit, and my feeling was that the decisive work in Vietnam had to be with the people. I was a volunteer, not a suicide. I finished my drink and walked back to my little room to lie on the bunk and smoke a cigarette and think about it. As long as I was alive there was a chance I might get back to my true work, and C and C wasn't it.

29

"Larry Dring! What are you doing here?" I had looked up from my salad at lunch and there was Mad Larry striding into the dining room. He had his usual Peck's Bad Boy humor written on his face. He saw me and strode over. I was eating with a couple of other staff officers and was eager to show off my lunatic to them. I don't know if the rest of them longed to be in the field as passionately as I did. It's not something we talked about a great deal. But old Dring . . .

He came over and sat down, picking up the menu. A little Vietnamese waitress hustled over and took his order. Then he looked up. "Got a few grenade fragments in my back a couple of weeks ago, and in the press of events I forgot about them and they festered. I came in to get them sewed up. Figure I'll scrounge up some chow from the Seabees while I'm here. They're always eager for VC weapons for souvenirs, and I got plenty of those." He unbottoned his jungle fatigue jacket. "Looka here. They sewed these things up with wire. Uncomfortable as all get out." He leaned forward and lifted his undershirt to show off the wire. I could barely see a couple of lumps on his back. But I was interested in the undershirt. It was olive drab like ours, but it was different somehow. I couldn't put my finger on the difference. "Where'd you get that shirt?" I asked.

He grinned. "Oh, that's NVA underwear. I get it free." I noticed he was also wearing an NVA belt.

"Where'd you get hit?" one of the others at the table asked.

Larry was grinning a little. He knew he was performing for the rear echelon. We were in the Forces and we had been shot at, so he wasn't laying complete bullshit on us like he would have a bunch of leg commissary officers, but he was playing

281

the role just a little. We didn't mind. In his place we'd do the same. In fact, we had all done the same at one time or another. "Tieu Atar," he said. "It's a new camp we just opened up."

I thought back to that night I had been duty officer at Pleiku and I wondered if my taking the map out and showing it to Ludwig had anything to do with that camp being opened. I hoped so. It would be the first tangible thing I had done in this entire tour that I could point to and say, "Look, that was worthwhile and I had a hand in it."

Larry looked at me and his grin broadened. "Boy you talk about Psy Ops. Lemme try this on you for Psy Ops. I took my Mike Force company in there when we opened the place up and we started operating. Man, they'd been in there for years with nobody to bother them and first thing we found this enormous trail. Big, everything but a yellow line down the middle and stop and go lights." He held his hands about three feet apart. No doubt about it, that was a big trail. You could run two bicycles abreast down such a trail. I had been right. I could feel a simultaneous welling of pride that I had examined the intelligence information that was available to everyone and had made that recommendation, as well as chagrin that I had not been there myself. If I had got Buon Blech like I wanted I would have operated in that notch. I wouldn't have been supposed to, but there would have been no way to stop me. I would have found that mother sure.

"Anyway we set up beside the trail, the whole company, and waited there a night and a day. Finally we ambushed a whole NVA company. Got nineteen kills."

I was in a near ecstasy of jealousy. This kid had taken my suggestion, my estimate of the intelligence and carried off my operation. I was proud of him. At that moment I loved him like a brother. Still, I wished I'd been there—for selfish reasons, to demonstrate that I was more than a capable staff officer, that I was a combat commander.

It was only later, years later, in fact, that I came to accept that it made no difference who did it, that we had all played an indispensable part in this event, and that who played what part was only our own ego trip. It is a valuable knowledge to have. But then I could only follow Larry's narrative with interest, wishing I could have been a part of his adventure, never thinking that in a sense I had been.

"Anyway, we buried all these cats beside the trail with their right arms sticking up out of the ground and a note on each that said: 'Surrender or die.' Now, my friends, that's Psy Ops."

We all laughed heartily. He was right too. It was damn fine Psy Ops. It would scare the shit out of all the Viets who passed by there.

Larry was around for a day or so and I helped him scrounge some chow and we also had dinner with some missionary friends of his. I've never heard Larry curse, or known him to whore around. When he got to town he headed for the missionaries and helped paint churches and scrounge rice and clothes for them. Their kids all called him Uncle Larry.

30

There was a rumor circulating that the VC had something planned for Tet, but I didn't take a lot of stock in it. I figured that the Tet holiday was so sacred to the majority of Vietnamese that it would be psychologically bad for them to try anything then. Maybe they'd hit a couple of towns, but I didn't figure it would be anything much.

Everybody was looking forward to Tet that year. The Viets put half the ARVN on leave. They figured about the same as I did, that it would be bad for the Cong to try something at that time.

It was really a great holiday while it lasted. Sergeant Bat, our Vietnamese photographer, had Frank and me and some other guys from the PIO section to his house for a sumptuous lunch a couple of days before it started. It was delightful. The PIO of the Vietnamese Special Forces was there, too, and he and I kidded around. It was a kind of funny place for me to be, because I really like the Vietnamese a hell of a lot, although I owe my allegiance to the Montagnards. It's too bad that they hate each other as they do.

Anyway the thing I remember most about that lunch at Sergeant Bat's was his kids. They were so pretty and shy, just as all Vietnamese kids seem to be. I teased around with them a little bit, like you can kids in the States, and they liked it, but they just couldn't get into it. Too shy. But they were nice kids. He knew it too. So did Mrs. Bat.

Lots of meals and lots of celebrations. The night before Tet officially started Scott Gantt came and asked me if I'd like to join him and Sally Maxwell, the USAID nurse, for dinner at the prison. I, of course, immediately accepted.

Most American ideas about Vietnamese prisons are predicated on the disclosures of the cages at Con Son, but the prison at Nha Trang wasn't like that at all. As far as I know no American press person has ever picked up the story of the prison at Nha Trang, so I will tell it here. I tried for months, without success, to interest some TV or newspaper people in this story, but by that time there was no way you could get anybody to print anything good at all about Vietnam or the Vietnamese.

This is something you should know about the press. The journalistic fraternity arrives at a kind of consensus by osmosis about what The Story is on a particular subject and you can bet your sweet ass that nothing that contradicts The Story will ever see the light of day.

As a PR man and magazine writer I have been on the fringes of journalism for most of my adult life, and I am very proud of the profession and the service it performs. But journalism is no better than any other profession, and many of the people in it are venal, and many are stupid, and more are lazy. Just as bankers misuse cash, and clerics misuse God and politicians misuse trust, journalists misuse the truth, too often.

In truth most Vietnamese prisons were wretched, but that is because the people in charge of them were bad people and on top of that had limited resources. There were two thousand prisoners in the Nha Trang prison, ten people on the staff, and less than ten cents a day per prisoner to run it on. As it happens, though, the prison at Nha Trang was put under the command of a compassionate genius, and he organized it in the following manner.

The prisoners, who consisted of NVA, VC, ARVN military prisoners, civil offenders, men and women, were divided into eleven compounds. The first compound was an orientation compound in which the prisoners were placed for two weeks while it was explained to them how the place ran. The other ten compounds were administered by the prisoners. They were permitted maximum freedom and helped to organize shops and schools. The prisoners ran a barber shop and school, a furniture factory, a shoe factory, photo shop and tailor shop. Everybody in the prison was gainfully employed. Forty per cent of the money was given to the compound fund. They were allowed to keep sixty per cent. They were allowed to send a large percentage of that home. The North Vietnamese prisoners were sending home more money than their total salaries had been before they were drafted.

In fact, the prison was run by a major in the NVA, a psychological operations officer.

Now the forty per cent that was donated to the compound fund was devoted to prison improvement. There was an inspection every Saturday morning and the compound which was chosen as the most beautiful, clean and happy was permitted twenty per cent overnight passes for that week. That meant that every prisoner was given a night out on the town.

That was where the orientation compound came into it. The prisoners knew that if there were any escapes the prison would go back to the conventional system. The new prisoners had it explained to them that no matter how dedicated to the communist cause they were, if they escaped they better make it good. If they screwed up this deal and were brought back to the prison they would have the other prisoners to deal with. Once the NVA actually ran a raid and breached the wall. They finally herded six people out at gunpoint. Nobody else would go.

This area beautification business had gone to fantastic extremes. Scott had become interested in the prison when he helped one of the compounds import an especially beautiful kind of grass from Taiwan. The palms, I believe, were from the Philippines.

I hadn't ever been out there before, but Scott had described it to me several times. He was very proud of the place. The night before the Tet offensive started I put on clean starched fatigues and a pair of spitshined jungle boots and checked out the jeep to go downtown. Scotty and I went down to the nurses villa across the street from the MP compound and picked up Sally.

Sally was a doll. She was dressed to the hilt, in a blue silk dress, high heels and pearls. Sally and Scott were close friends and I liked her very much too.

She had been a Peace Corps volunteer in Nigeria or someplace like that and had been threatened with being returned home. The hospital where she worked was supposed to be free, but the native doctors took kickbacks from the patients and all of the staff including Sally had signed a complaint against the practice. As a troublemaker she was threatened with expulsion and being sent back to Washington in disgrace.

"Washington," she exclaimed, "sure, send me back. I'd like a chance to tell the home office how this place is run."

"What, you want to go home?" and that was the last she heard of that.

Anyway, there she was, a brownhaired, truly wonderful girl, in blue silk and pearls, being picked up by two SF captains, one tall and stocky and the other tall and emaciated. Scotty was driving so I hopped in the back and she got in front. We drove to the prison and woke up the guard to let us in. It was grim and foreboding on the outside, but the inside of the prison had to be seen to be believed.

Scotty proudly showed us around the place. The grass was like the most carefully kept park you ever saw. The prisoners had their own zoo and deer roamed freely throughout the grounds. The prisoners seemed to be happy people, well groomed and dressed in clean, pressed civilian clothes. Scotty proudly showed us through the non-denominational chapel that the prisoners had built by hand. Buddhist, Cao Dai, and Catholic services were held in it. It was a wonder of light and color and rich detail, somewhat crudely constructed, but beautiful in a gaudy way. It would have delighted, say, Timothy Leary. It certainly delighted me.

The banquet was set up outdoors for a good many visiting dignitaries, before a stage for the review, with skits and musical numbers by the prison band afterwards. As I recall the first course was asparagus and crab soup and the skits were done with great good humor by people who had formerly been enemies. There was a Vietnamese Ranger sergeant in one of them, and a lot of NVA. They all seemed to be having a wonderful time.

We left about ten-thirty, full and happy at having seen something work right in Vietnam.

We dropped Sally off at her villa and drove on back to the compound only to find we were on fifty per cent alert. There was supposed to be a fight of some sort downtown. I went and got my harness, rifle and steel hat and went out to the bunker to sit around until two o'clock in the morning when the second shift came on. There was nothing at all to do except sit there and smoke cigarettes and watch the flares cast their weird flickering yellow light and the shadows creep across the paddies as the flares drifted down under their parachutes. Then it was time for the second shift.

I undressed and slept the sleep of the just.

For about four hours. At six I was awakened by Frank Orians in green fatigues and beret, but with rifle and patrol harness. He looked eager and happy. "Say, there's a little fight going on downtown. I heard there was a company of Mike Force down there against maybe two companies of NVA. What say we get some cameras and go down and see if there's a story in it?"

I sat up, really still too tired to think well. "Yeah, yeah," I muttered. "Okay, but there better be some war down there if you're going to get me up this early." By the time I had my fatigues on Frank was back with the jeep. I had a half-frame 35mm camera in one pocket of my BAR belt, something I had carried ever since becoming PIO. The half-frame was plenty good enough for me; I am one of the world's worst photographers. I stomped out of my hooch feeling crabby, sure we were off on a wild goose chase.

Two extremely mean looking sergeants from C and C came up and asked expectantly if they could go too, and I began to think there might be something to it. We said sure and they got in the jeep with us. As we drove out the compound gate I heard them jack back their bolts, just like you would on a combat patrol. The air was very still and it was too quiet for a great national holiday. A little trickle of apprehension slid up my back and I jacked my bolt back too. Frank turned the jeep toward downtown and it all seemed very strange to me to be heading for a fight down the same road I had returned on the night before after a gourmet dinner and theatrical review.

The drive downtown was uneventful except that halfway there a little kid threw a string of firecrackers and the sergeant sitting beside me whirled to fire.

"Steady!" I muttered and he didn't shoot. The kid had been an ace from being shattered by M-16 fire.

It was about four blocks past where the kid had thrown the firecrackers to the prison. It looked different in the daytime, more grim with concertina wire on top of the red stone wall. The guard out front was a little more alert. He drew down on us with his carbine, then looked sheepish and put it away.

I grinned and waved at him as we parked the jeep. There were four of us, Frank and myself and the two sergeants we had picked up.

That's one of the nice things about working with professionals. There was no talking. We simply spread out ten yards between men, on both sides of the road, took our weapons off safety and started moving slowly down the road in a manner infantrymen have always adopted when moving into a fight. Slow.

We didn't have to talk about who went where, either. The junior sergeant automatically took the point, and I slid in behind him, with Frank on the other side of the street to my left. If a situation came where an order had to be given I would give it. I did not anticipate such an eventuality. If we were fired upon we would take cover and return fire. If we could take them we would and, if not, we would withdraw. When you work with professionals you don't have to choose up sides and argue about who's in charge.

We moved soundlessly down the street with our rifles at the ready, on full auto. There was the sporadic sound of automatic weapons fire up ahead and the occasional crump—crump of a 60 mm mortar. Two blocks down the street there was an American two and a half ton truck stopped with a number of regularly spaced bullet holes in it, neat little indentations with ragged edges, exposing a bit of gray metal. There was also a corpse in the middle of the street, with civilian clothes on and an NVA haircut.

Looking around I could see we had come into a small ARVN compound. There were a couple of guard gates around us and the buildings were set up for offices, rather than dwellings. Also there were some scared looking uniformed Vietnamese crouched against the walls. I caught a few glimpses of Mike Force tiger suits on guys tucked into the firing position here and there and the air was deadly still. I began to feel as though we were not in the right place, there in the road.

There was a burst from a machine gun somewhere and then the dirt did its little John Wayne number, just like in *Sands of Iwo Jima*, where it kicks up in a regularly spaced and timed series of spurts. We ran for the safety of the buildings, like stripe-assed gazelles.

I slid to a stop beside Captain Larry O'Neal, the commander of the Nha Trang Mike Force, who looked exactly like what you'd expect somebody in that job, with that name, to look like, except he wore glasses.

He grinned. "Ah, *Turistas!*"

I popped out my camera, took his picture, and said, "What's the story, Larry?"

The situation, as he explained it to me, was that a sizable enemy force had hit this compound about two in the morning and when the little ARVN Signal Compound couldn't handle it they called for reinforcements. He had been sent down to help out and had been here ever since. He was pinned down and couldn't move against the enemy, which he estimated to be at least two companies. The enemy hadn't been able to budge him either.

He pointed up over a fence to a two story house on the other side, across a brief space of rice paddy. "See that house over there?"

I nodded.

"Got two machine guns in it. We been trying to knock them out all morning without any success!"

As he spoke one of his Mike Force strikers bobbed up from behind a Renault sedan which someone had made the error of parking in the line of fire of the machine guns. It had been carefully covered over with a canvas tonneau cover. It was, of course, riddled with bullet holes and all four tires were flat. The kid, who had turned his helmet around backwards to aim better, bobbed up and ponked out an M-79 round and then ducked back down. It seemed like a good hit to me, just below the window where one of the machine guns was. But it was answered by a burst of fire from the window.

They must have sandbagged the guns in. That had taken a lot of time to prepare.

The firing picked up now and all of us straphangers, easily identifiable because we wore starched fatigues and berets, got in on it. None of us had been involved in city fighting before and we soon found that there were a lot of tricks to it. For instance, if you were behind certain walls you were absolutely safe, but if you took one step around the corner you were absolutely exposed.

Only you had to go around the corners to change position, and you had to go around the corners to fire back at the enemy. So you adopted a kind of slow-fast way of doing things. I sat in a doorway on the front side of the Signal Compound for quite a while, smoking a cigarette. I had given up smoking, then decided, what the fuck. In Vietnam I wasn't particularly worried about lung cancer. So I sat there and listened to the firing and took some pictures, but after a few minutes I exhausted the picture taking possibilities of that particular little nook and got up to move around.

There was a little alley between two buildings and it was under observation. Every time anybody moved in that alley he got shot at. So you had to do it fast. I blasted across it and took some more pictures. I got a good one of Larry O'Neal firing around the corner. I kind of dug it because the heat from the muzzle blast from his CAR-15 caused the paint to blister off the side of the building, so that he was firing through a little snowstorm.

We were pouring a lot of fire out into the houses surrounding the signal compound, so occasionally some Vietnamese civilians would come out and get caught in the cross-fire.

This is the kind of thing that pisses me off about the press. Every time a civilian showed up, everybody in the compound stopped firing. And when we quit all the NVA popped up and opened up on us, and, of course, on the civilians we had stopped firing to protect. I got one shot of Sammy Coutts, a sergeant from the Mike Force, running square out in the middle of the street to scoop up a little Vietnamese girl who was standing there in fright and confusion. Sam scooped her up and ran with her to safety through the literal hail of bullets you read so much about.

Most people in the States believe that the American Army went through Vietnam in a storm of atrocities. Maybe some did, but I never personally saw any of it, other than some pretty intense POW interrogations. And I heard the view advanced that Special Forces were the worst of any at atrocities. Actually the reverse is true. We lived with the Viets and the Yards and certainly we didn't think of them as ciphers. Amateurs are the ones who, frightened by a little gunfire, turn to atrocities. These kinds of assholes shouldn't be allowed in a war anyway. They give it a bad name.

Sammy Coutts wasn't the only American I saw risk his life to save a civilian that day either. It was a common occurrence. One of my own sergeants, not Scena, did it repeatedly. I won't name this sergeant, because he was the lousiest PIO man I ever came across, but that day he turned to and did damned fine as a line sergeant. If I ever die and go to heaven and they give me an "A" team, he could be my team sergeant any time. But to turn him loose with a magazine layout, no way!

Frank and I hung around for a couple of hours shooting pictures and people and then I sprinted across the alley again and tapped him on the shoulder. "You know, Frank," I said, "this is a lot of fun and all that, but we do have to get back and get a story out on this. They pay us too much to function as grunts."

He gave me a look that said, "Spoilsport," and muttered assent.

O'Neal was crouching and moving and so I called to him and said, "Hate to shoot and run, Larry, but we gotta get back to work." I kept doing the flip dialog, feeling loose and happy in the fight.

He waved. "Sure, I understand."

I checked with the sergeants, but it was Saturday, as I recall, and none of them had to be anyplace special so they elected to stay and fight.

Frank and I sort of d-d-dodged out of the area where the gunfire was and went back to the jeep. It took us a few minutes to return to the shop. We gave our film to Fred Fawcett, the lab man, to develop and I went into my office to work on a story. It didn't take long to write and the pictures came out fast so we sent Fawcett on an airplane to Saigon to get clearance so we could get the stuff out. I figured it would be a really good story.

Unfortunately, by the time he got to Saigon, the Tet offensive had started there too, so he was bottled up in town for five days and never did get out to Long Binh to get it cleared. If I had known that, I would have had him give the stuff to a reporter to send out under a wire service by-line, but Fred didn't call and so it never appeared anywhere but in our little magazine.

I had just about finished writing the story when the phone rang. I snatched it off the hook and said, "Captain Morris," in my best authoritative manner.

A dim voice was on the other end, bellowing, but I could barely hear it. "Jim?"

"Yeah!"

"Jim, this is Sy Wohlen, of CBS. I understand you guys got a fight there."

"That's right!"

"I'm gonna have a camera crew in to Nha Trang in half an hour. Can you pick them up?"

"Sure, Sy, no problem."

"Good! Good!"

I hung the phone up smiling. "Hey, Frank!"

Old broken-nosed Orians poked his head around the door. "We got to go back to the war, Frank. Sy Wohlen's sending a camera crew in. Send Dusty down to pick them up and we'll meet them at the compound. Then we'll get a little lunch and go on down."

He was off and running.

I stepped down the stairs and strolled over toward the headquarters to fill in my colonel on what was going on down there. Just as I was going in the door, Lieutenant Gordon, the assistant adjutant, came out. Gordon was a very good man, having been an admin clerk in George Dunaway's empire on Okinawa. He had gone to OCS, got shot at enough to get his CIB and then been scooped back up into the headquarters. They're gonna keep doing that to Gordon for the rest of his life. He's a good combat man, but there are a lot of those and not very many good adminstrators.

"Colonel in?" I asked.

He shook his head. "Nope! There's too much going on. Where you guys been?"

I told him about the fight at the Signal Compound and he nodded sadly, unhappy to have to be watching the store.

"You hear what happened downtown?"

I said, "Huh uh," and he told me.

"Bastards came up on the beach last night and hit the province headquarters. A bunch of them marched in a column of twos right past the MP compound. The MP's thought they were a bunch of drunk ARVN's until they started lobbing grenades over the wall."

I was, for just a second, afraid for Sally and her roommates. But then I realized that if the USAID nurses had been killed or injured that would have been the first thing Gordon told me. Anyway the thing was still going on downtown and the Province headquarters was still under seige. We stood there chatting for a second more and then he had to hurry on.

Having the war nearby seemed to have changed the very air. It felt thinner, and the compound seemed almost empty. But the air was so still, quiet, exactly like the calm before a storm. It's funny how one sometimes falls back on cliches, but then certain expressions become cliches because they are so apt.

As Gordon left I wandered over to the club for lunch. The air in there was very silent too. The Vietnamese waitresses were in a state of near panic and they jabbered to themselves incessantly, serving food and cleaning tables, quickly but not very efficiently. Somebody had put the most grotesquely inappropriate country and western tape on the Musak and some adenoidal fellow backed up by a weepy pedal steel guitar was droning senselessly about how his baby fucked around on him and hung out in bars all the time. The dining room was about half empty, and the men who were there sat beefily under their crewcuts, slipping into a pre-combat glower.

I had a very small appetite. I was getting a solid adrenalin rush prior to going back downtown and wasn't hungry at all. I figured that I should eat somethng though and got down half my meat and salad. Then I picked my teeth as I strolled back to the office. Frank was all set to go when I got there and so we got into the jeep and went.

When we got back downtown the situation had changed. Everything seemed quiet. Scotty was standing in the middle of the street talking to Carl McCarden. "What's going on?" I asked.

"We went around to the left through the paddies with those two Mike Force companies twice," he said. "But we couldn't make any headway either time. Had to go through too much of an open area."

I nodded. "Seems pretty quiet now though."

He nodded again.

"Whatcha gonna do now?"

"We're gonna soften them up a little bit. The idea is that we'll call in gunships to make one pass. Then I'll get on the loudspeaker. This is a signal compound and we can use their equipment and we'll tell the civilians to come out. Then we'll make another pass and this time the civilians will believe us and come out. Then we'll level the fucking place."

I thought for a moment about the fact that this was a residential area and there were a lot of people in it. Some of them were going to be killed, and there is nothing you or I or anybody else in the world can do about it. I nodded.

A couple of Viets ran up and handed Scotty the hand mike to do the announcing on. Scotty never claimed his Vietnamese was the best, but it was serviceable for what he intended. He called out to the Vietnamese to come out of the area where they lived. Then there was a long pause in all shooting and there was a thin trickle of civilians who tried to come through our lines. I supposed a good many others got out the other three sides of the box they were in. We waited for about five minutes. Then the trickle stopped. Their eagerness was restrained by the fact that as they departed the NVA shot at them, hitting quite a few. There were a lot of bloody civilians when they came through to us.

Frank tapped me on the shoulder. "You need me?"

"Huh uh!" He nodded and went over to the medics. Frank had been a medic before he went to OCS and there were plenty of officers around, but not nearly enough medics to handle the number of wounded civilians.

There were several Hueys whopping around in the sky above us, and I could see rocket pods under some of them. Gunships. Scotty spoke into the radio that the little signal corps major who was advisor to this ARVN unit had loaned him. The major was a chubby little fellow who was scared as hell. Since he knew nothing about combat operations he left the whole thing to Scotty, who had assumed command earlier when Larry O'Neal and some of the Mike Force had pulled out. Carl and I both outranked him, but he had assumed command when he was the ranking man and date of rank was far too petty a thing to worry about at a time like this. Besides, I had a PIO job to do and Carl was going back to the SF compound. I really thought about usurping command for a couple of minutes there, because I figured that whoever it was that saved this place was going to get a Distinguished Service Cross and I wanted one. Then I realized that the kind of asshole who would cause turmoil by changing commanders every five minutes wouldn't be able to hold the place anyway and I didn't want to be such a person.

The gunships in the air whirled and came down at an angle, much flatter than a conventional ship. They looked like dragonflies in line, or like old WW I fighters except for the whirling blades above them going *whocka whocka whocka* as they dived and one after another released their rockets which crashed into the houses on the other side of the line that the edge of the signal compound had become. crack-*whooooooooosh*-Blam! crack-*whooooooooosh*-Blam! crack-*whooooooooosh*-Blam! Then they lifted back up and flew away.

Scotty handed the mike back to a Vietnamese lieutenant who spoke into it again. A few minutes later twice as many civilians as before poured out of the housing area. Again the NVA shot them as they came.

It was a funny thing, all day the firing had been going north and south and over to the west was a rice paddy. But I could look down between the rows of houses on our east. A large crowd of Vietnamese civilians had collected to watch the battle. They had started gathering that morning and now

I could see soup vendors pushing their little carts through the crowd, and I surmised they were waiting to see which side won before making up their minds who they supported. There were no pennants.

Then Scotty got back on the radio and the gunships made another pass.

About that time Dusty Hobbs arrived in a three-quarter with the CBS crew in the back. They were Don Webster, a heavy, black-haired man, and a little skinny guy named John Smith on camera. The sound man was a Vietnamese and I never did catch his name. He seemed damned efficient though.

They bounced off the truck and Don came up and asked me what was going on. Smith started to shoot and Webster stuck the mike in my face.

"Hold it," I said. "You want somebody more photogenic and better spoken than me to do this. Hey Carl."

McCarden came over and I introduced him to Webster, "Carl's been here all day," I said. "He can explain it fine." Carl didn't have on a patrol harness. He had on clean starched fatigues with maybe a couple of magazines shoved in the side pockets. He did have his rifle, though. I took off my patrol harness and draped it over his shoulders. "Put this on and look fierce," I said.

While they were doing that I went over and zinged a few more rounds in on those two machine guns that were still active in the house across the paddy.

The CBS camera crew hung around for about an hour, taking pictures of Mike Force machinegun crews shooting off into the air at nonexistent targets and recording rat-a-tats for the sound track. Then they went away. I was kind of disappointed that they weren't there for any of the real action.

A couple of weeks later I was up in Da Nang to set up a press conference for the survivors of Lang Vei and I ran into Don and John Smith at the airport. He said the Nha Trang footage was some of the best stuff to come out of Tet, but it didn't make the Cronkite show because of a bad plane connection in Tokyo. It made the eleven o'clock news that night, though, and the CBS morning news.

The last of the Mike Force was pulled out shortly after the CBS crew left. We were going to leave too, except the little signal corps major pointed out that with the Mike Force gone he only had about twenty guys to hold the compound against whatever it was we were facing.

So we elected to stay. By that time "we" consisted of almost my entire PIO section, and the goddamnedest collection of clerks, cooks, and guys who were just passing through Nha Trang you ever saw. They were all Special Forces guys, of course. Not a leg in the bunch. There were about thirty of us in all. The clerks were all guys who had volunteered for the army, volunteered for jump training, volunteered for the Forces, and volunteered for Nam. Then somebody found out they could type or something and they had got trapped in Nha Trang. This was probably going to be the only fight they got into their entire year in Nam and they were just like a bunch of junkies waiting around for a connection.

There was sporadic sniping going on and we were still pouring it out. I suddenly realized I was down to about two magazines. "Hey, Scotty," I called. "Where's the M-16 ammo?"

"We're about out," he called back.

"You got any radio contact with the headquarters?"

He shook his head. "See if you can get somebody on the phone."

I went into the office of the Vietnamese signal unit and picked up the phone. Miraculously I got a dial tone. They didn't have a phone book and the only number I could think of was the adjutant's office. I called that and got another assistant adjutant on the line, not Gordon. This one was a captain and just as officious as the asshole he worked for.

"Where are you?" he demanded.

"I'm at the Vietnamese signal compound. We're almost out of ammo. Can you call the ammo dump for me and have some sent down?"

"Who authorized you to go down there?" he demanded.

"Nobody authorized it. I came down here to cover a story, and if we leave now these guys are going to be overrun."

"We've got a compound of our own to defend," he said.

"You better get your men and come back here, before you get into trouble."

I thought about pointing out that they had to go through us to get to him, but decided it wasn't worth the trouble. "We can't leave now," I said, "and we need that ammo bad. Will you call the ammo dump for us?"

"No," he replied, "I can't condone this unauthorized . . ."

"Listen, you howling, fucking idiot . . ."

There was another crack *whooooooooooosh* BLAM and the phone went dead.

I went outside to tell Scotty what the story was.

"That's just swell," he said.

Frank was bandaging the leg of an old Vietnamese lady nearby. He looked up as we talked. "Listen," he said, "I've got a bunch of wounded that I need to take to the province hospital. What say I take a deuce and a half and swing by the ammo dump after I drop them off?"

"Sounds okay to me," I agreed and looked at Scotty. He was in charge and the decision would be up to him.

"Do it!" he said and went to worry about something else.

I worked pretty much as a grunt all night long. There was nothing for me to be in charge of, and I was having the time of my life. We didn't seem to be in any spectacular danger of being overrun and it didn't seem possible to counterattack, so I studiously avoided doing anything rash. A lot of guys who were getting in on their first fight in a long time, or their first and only one ever, though, did wonderful gaudy deeds of derring-do. About two in the morning I was lying behind a pile of sandbags with two other guys. The chaplain's assistant and another kid, who was passing through from Charlie Company, came running down the street just ahead of a long machine gun burst and slid down behind the sandbag wall. "Sir," the chaplain's assistant said, a beefy Italian kid from the Bronx or New Jersey or some other place north or east of Little Rock, "Sir, me and whatsisname here are going to go down that street and knock out a sniper or two. You want to cover us?"

"Well, if you're going to do that," I said, "I reckon I better."

The kid grinned happily and I poked my head up and sent

a long burst across the street as they ducked around to the right and dived across the street and down the alley between the two-story houses. I saw one of them fire an M-79 as they ran. The other was pulling the pins out of grenades as fast as he could and throwing them into open windows.

I kept changing magazines and firing at moving shadows all the time they were gone, the other two guys and I behind our little wall of sandbags. The roar of gunfire as constant all through the night. Two or three minutes after they left I saw the chaplain's assistant and the other kid come bursting back around the corner and I fired over their heads as they charged back across the street and grabbed a gatepost to slide in beside me. "How far did you go?" I asked.

"Maybe two-three blocks down the street," said the chaplain's assistant. I whistled. I wouldn't have taken such a chance for anything. If anyone had been looking down from one of those windows they'd have been sitting ducks. I'd done all sorts of equally stupid things at Buon Beng and got away with them, but that was when I was young and thought I was immortal. I suppose that belief is the best armor a young soldier has, as long as it lasts. If an old soldier tried a stunt like that he'd be so paralyzed with fear that the vibrations themselves would draw fire. Anyway I was glad they'd got away with it.

"Thanks for the covering fire, sir."

I smiled. "Oh, my pleasure."

They were gone, bursting for the cover of the buildings behind, running the fully exposed half block down the street that you had to cover to get there.

I made that same run ten or fifteen times during the night, not of necessity, but just because when I got bored with one thing I'd go do something else. My thigh muscles were sore for four days afterward. I hadn't tried to sprint like that since high school.

That was later, though. It was only about seven o'clock when Frank Orians left for the ammo. Actually that was the worst time. We were almost totally out of ammunition, and appeared to be surrounded on two sides by the enemy. If they penetrated the housing area to our right we'd be encircled on three sides and have only the paddies to take to for escape. It was a bad position to be in. Also our defenses inside the compound were pathetic. We had only the buildings and one little sandbagged enclosure around an eighty-one mm mortar, and that was only one sandbag thick. If you leaned against it, it would topple over.

Charlie had a mortar set up, as near as I could figure, on the same hill as the wonderful old huge white Buddha that sits benignly on the crest overlooking the city. From wherever it was they could walk mortar bursts down the main street leading up to the sand bag wall. The mortar walked bursts down the street until it reached the end of its range, and that was close enough to send fragments into the sandbag wall. But no closer. If they'd had enough sense to displace it forward they could have decimated the defenders of the little signal compound.

It was quite bad then, and at that point things could have gone either way. But then we started to get some breaks. Frank arrived with all the ammo in the world. We unloaded it gratefully. "Have any trouble?" I asked.

Frank grinned. "Not really. An MP stopped us on our way to the hospital and asked for a pass, so I showed it to him." He held up his M-16. "Called him a lot of dirty names. Also I almost ran over two Air Force guys out walking their Vietnamese girlfriends."

"How about the ammo dump?"

He shrugged. "Well, it wasn't really any trouble. They didn't want to give me the ammo, but I just drew down on the fucker and they gave me all I wanted."

I clapped him on the shoulder. "Frank," I said, "I like your attitude."

"Any more patients?" he asked.

Since we had plenty of mortar ammo now we could start putting out flares and a little return fire. I helped unload some of the ammo and sat down behind the sandbags to open up the cans. They were just like great big cans of Spam, only painted olive drab. It was sort of relaxing to sit behind that semi-circular wall of sandbags and pull the big key off the bottom of the can and then roll up the strip around them then take out the black cardboard cylinders that held the mortar rounds and pull out the shell and then take the

301

charges off the end. It's been a long time, but as I recall they had eight charges crimped onto the bottom. They were one and a half inches across, square, with a small hole in the middle, like oiled paper, only thicker. We were firing the mortar at such a short range that we weren't using the charges, only the propellant in the shell.

It was such a simple, mechanical task that I thoroughly enjoyed it. It didn't require any alertness at all, and I was tired of the constant scanning of the street for flickering shadows or muzzle flashes, which I never saw.

The sergeant who was acting as gunner was a burly fellow, and quite loquacious. I found out he was from B-50, which was one of the Special Project B detachments, and had been newly installed at Ban Me Thuot. We chatted between blasts from the mortar as I stacked the shells up beside him. I hadn't been up to Ban Me Thuot since Phillip's death, but quite a few of the guys from B-50 knew him. The B-50 Mike Force was one of the battalions of the Dam-Yi Division, and I think all of the Americans knew that, though none of them would admit it, certainly not to another American that they didn't know.

"That was really too bad about Phillip Drouin," I said, in kind of an exploratory way. Because, as I said before, there was no corpus delicti, and Phillip had been reported dead a time or two before.

"What?" he said, and looked at me wonderingly. I was not a particularly knowledgeable looking fellow stuck off in Nha Trang, and therefore not considered privy to anything approaching inside information, but I had caught him off guard.

"You know Phillip?" I asked.

He shrugged. "Sure."

"We usta be pretty good friends," I said offhandedly. "I was sorry to hear he got greased."

The guy looked at me for a long time, as though determining whether I could be trusted or not. "He ain't dead," he said. "He got away from them people on a bicycle."

I don't know how to describe the feeling that came over me. It was such a feeling of relief and happiness as I've seldom had before or since I was almost . . . I started to write

302

"in tears," but that is not it. There was no question of my crying over it, but the emotion was just as intense. It wasn't even so much that it was a happy feeling, although it was certainly that, but Phillip, Jesus I could just see him, pedaling quickly along some jungle trail on a bicycle. How the hell had he done it? How had he got them to leave him alone? Had he feigned sleep? Had he set them to arguing until they forgot about him, or had his chance just come and he seized it? Old fucking Phillip . . . on a bicycle. Undoubtedly he would have preferred something with more style.

I started to laugh. Not a chuckle or a ripple, but a huge rolling guffaw. I couldn't stop. I collapsed against the sandbags and just let it roll, my belly surging to it, HAW!HAW! HAW!HAW!HAW! I couldn't stop. It came and came for four or five minutes. It's a reaction I've had a number of times to close calls, but every time before it was to my own close calls.

Scotty said later that just at that time, at the worst part of the evening, it was the greatest morale boost the poor little Vietnamese defenders of that wretched post could have had. They figured if anybody could laugh like that at a time like that then the situation wasn't as bad as it seemed.

I felt so good after that that I didn't worry at all about the Tet Offensive, which was, after all, nothing but a welcome break in a boring routine.

When I read the reports of Tet in the papers and the news magazines later it was with plain shock and amazement and finally fury, a cold sinking rage that hasn't subsided yet. The stupid bastards didn't know a victory from a defeat.

So what if they attacked in the cities? Anybody that knows anything at all about the military knows anybody can attack anywhere anytime they want to. Attacking is one thing and winning is something else again. Tet was a kamikaze attack. Later, more than a year later, most of the journalistic fraternity were prepared to admit that Tet was a military defeat for the Viet Cong, but still insisted that it was a psychological victory for them. What they wouldn't admit as that it was a psychological victory only because journalists didn't do their job, which was to find out what was really going on and report it.

These are the facts about Tet. The ARVN found itself during Tet. Units that had never fought well before, or thought about fighting at all, did a creditable job. Public opinion was mobilized against the VC for daring to profane the Tet holiday, and the cities were alienated, when before they had been entirely indifferent to the war except as a profit making venture.

Just in our own little area there, when the Mike Force, which was Montagnard, came through to mop up and check the place out, Vietnamese housewives who, two days before, wouldn't have walked across the street to spit on a Yard came out of their houses with tea and cakes for them and hailed them as liberators. Vietnamese actually *feeding* Montagnards. Tet was such a bad fuckup for the VC that it is scarcely describable, but the press reported it the other way, and people believed it.

American journalists, pah!

But at the time I could hardly wait for the stories to come out, because it was such a beautiful story. We had waited for years for the VC to come out and fight, the U.S. Army being too stupid to go down to the villages and ask where they were, and then they finally came, and right on schedule the U.S. and ARVN armies waxed their ass. And then nobody believed it.

So much for believing what you read in the newspapers, or what you see on television.

But, of course, such a bizarre development as the press turning our great victory into a "psychological defeat" didn't occur to me then. I was just happy to hear that Phillip was alive, and eager to get to Ban Me Thuot to chase him down. That was assuming that what the sergeant told me was correct. I had no more way of knowing for sure Phil was alive, just because that sergeant told me so, then I was sure he was dead just because I heard it in a secret briefing.

Anyway, I finished unwrapping mortar rounds and picked up my rifle and went back up to the sandbagged gate. I sat there by the wall most of the night and fired at flickering shadows, which were either NVA running across the street or shadows from falling flares moving through the smoke that drifted across the street.

Oh, those poor suffering bastards, the NVA. They were so stoned, though, that they probably enjoyed the experience as much as I did. The body of one of them lay about twenty feet from me. He was on his back, with a tremendous hard-on, which is something that happens to corpses. Sometime during the day somebody told me that early that morning when the NVA first hit the place, he was accosted by five Mike Force guys and he just grinned and turned and ran straight down the street. Naturally they cut him in half.

When Scotty and I went down to see Sally and the other nurses a couple of days later, she said that the NVA who were brought into the province hospital were totally fucked up on opium and had more to take when they came down off that. They also had notes pinned to their collars, like little kids when they're put on the bus, to the effect that they had volunteered to die for their brothers in the South. The notes didn't say whether they had volunteered before or after they were doped.

It was a very hectic morning for Sally and the girls too. A company of NVA came out of the house in the next lot, diagonally, from theirs. Little old ladies had been coming in with bundles and walking out clean for weeks. The girls thought nothing of it, but when they thought about it later those bundles were the right size and shape for an AK-47. The soldiers had been smuggled in one at a time too, apparently, and come up out of a tunnel in the yard and assaulted the compound next door.

At one point during the night the girls were under the bed on the second floor, the MP's held the roof, and the NVA held the first floor. One of the speakers on Sally's big Akai tapecorder had a bullet hole through it and the living room wall, which was on the second floor, had a nice line of evenly spaced machinegun holes in it. The landlord fixed the wall, but the speaker worked fine, and Sally left the bullet hole in the speaker cloth as a souvenir of the Tet offensive.

The poor bastards we were up against. When the Mike Force moved through the next day they found over two hundred bodies and enough documents to indicate that we had fought off two battalions that night. They had sand tables set up and their assault plan meticulously worked out and rehearsed as usual.

On the sand table layout for the signal compound they had each of the guard posts carefully plotted and the number of defenders and the kind of weapons they expected to find there. They didn't take any chances. They threw entire platoons up against little two-man guard posts where one guard had a BAR and the other had an M-1 carbine.

Only what they found when they came was the same two guys who were supposed to be there backed up by a couple of Mike Force (we got one platoon of them sometime during the night), and five or six totally insane Special Forces clerks, out for that one big fight, with an inexhaustible supply of ammunition. One of those guys was a kid who went AWOL off guard to get in on the fight. He was put in for a Bronze Star and a court-martial on the same day. I think they finally decided to cancel both actions and let it go at that.

So these NVA would come skidding around the corner to take this little easy guard post with one automatic weapon, and eight M-16's opened up on them, plus the BAR and the carbine, because those guards caught the spirit too. The NVA just crumpled and fell back and regrouped and tried it again, only to run up against the same wall of lead.

We had quite a few LAW's that Frank had got for us too. A LAW is a little rocket. LAW stands for Light Anti-tank Weapon, and is fired from the container it comes in. Pretty neat, comes wrapped in a little cardboard tube with a plastic sight on it and an electrical trigger. You sight, fire the rocket, and discard the tube. Beats a bazooka all hollow. At one point during the night one of those NVA platoons went up against this one post to our immediate right. In amazement I watched an American break and run over a little wall behind their post. I couldn't figure what he was running for, because he was protected in the post and out there he was fully exposed and they were firing all around him. I guessed he was just a nervous clerk who had cracked under fire. Then I heard him yell, "DON'T LET 'EM GET AWAY. I'M GOING FOR ANOTHER LAW!"

That was pretty much the tone for the whole evening. It was the happiest time I had spent in almost a year in

Vietnam.

At one point, about two o'clock in the morning, they set fire to all the houses around the compound, the idea, I guess, being to catch the signal outfit's fuel dump on fire and burn us out. It looked like the burning of Atlanta all around us. But the fuel dump itself never did catch fire and we never did get burned out. We just sat there all night and shot at everything that moved.

The next morning another Mike Force company showed up to relieve us. By that time I was sitting on an old ammo box among all the olive drab debris and eating cold C-rations, just like a real combat soldier, boy.

We hadn't had a man shot all evening, and they were glad to hear it, but their news wasn't so good. Larry O'Neal had been wounded and would have to be evacuated. Ducky Millard, the Colonel's driver, had gone along downtown with the Mike Force and they had been shot at and somebody said get down, and he looked up to see what they wanted him to get down for, and got shot in the head. The kid should have known better because he had his left nut shot off, same as I had, when he was a door gunner on a chopper. We used to kid about it. I heard of four or five guys who got their left nuts shot off, but none who ever got the right one shot off. Isn't that strange?

And Joe Zamara got killed. He had been a captain about three weeks, and was due to go home the next day on an extension leave. But he had to get in on that one last fight. He would have been back in a month anyway.

When I first published the story about the Tet Offensive in *The Green Beret* I said he was going home at the end of his tour, which is what I thought. Some guys from the Mike Force, highly indignant, came over to set me straight that by God Joe Zamara wasn't the kind of candy ass who would go home just because his tour was up. He meant to come back.

31

It was about the time of the Tet Offensive that I started hanging around with the officers from Project Delta. Chuck Allen had been down there all the time I was in the country, but he was in an important command position, and I was kind of embarrassed to go down there and hang around with all those real soldiers when I was flying my desk up there in the headquarters. But sometime during Tet I had to go there on business and Chuck or somebody asked me back socially, and I started going to their club every now and again.

I was starting to get a little short. "Short" in army terms means I was getting close to going home. I suppose if I'd been in a combat job it might have been different, but being behind the desk for most of the year, and having such a senior date of rank I knew I didn't stand a chance of coming back to Vietnam as a captain. And I had no place to extend for. I had no openings into a combat job that was tailormade for my specifications like the "A" team at Buon Blech. Ludwig had gone home, extended for Vietnam, and been transferred to the Delta. His replacement didn't know me from Adam and I had never yet been able to make anybody understand my hunger to command a specific camp. They were just so many interchangeable parts to them. I was starting to thirst after combat. I wanted to get in as much time in the field as I could before going home.

So when Lang Vei was overrun, and Chuck Allen called and told me Project Delta was going to jump in and take the place back, I grabbed my field gear and a volunteer photographer and away we went.

When we got to Da Nang, which was to have been the staging area for the jump, we found that the NVA had

308

withdrawn and the survivors were being brought in by chopper. It had been a hell of a fight, the NVA using tanks for the first time in the war, and they had overrun the place finally with just a few Americans and Viets holding them off at the command bunker.

I Corps was run by the Marines at that time, and I got to a Marine PIO Colonel and suggested that we hold a press conference for those Lang Vei survivors who wanted to appear. Four of the Lang Vei survivors came over to the press camp and were interviewed on all three TV networks and all the wire services and news magazines. I wasn't too happy about their being scrubbed and put into baggy fatigues with the supply room smell still on them. I'd have been happier to have them in tiger suits and bandages.

There was no question about it. We had the shit kicked out of us at Lang Vei, but those guys were so cool at their press conference, and it was obvious they had fought so bravely when outnumbered so badly that I like to think we turned our military defeat into a psychological victory. My own little Tet Offensive within a Tet Offensive.

After the press conference the guys from Lang Vei were whisked back to the SF headquarters in Da Nang and my sergeant photographer and I went and got good and drunk with the correspondents. It was a good time and somebody played the guitar and I croaked out the Viet Cong Blues and the Jungle Rot Blues in my wretched baritone and some other songs were sung and some jokes were told and we all agreed that nobody in any position of authority knew what the fuck was coming off.

My good sergeant got a great deal drunker than I did, since all he was doing was getting drunk, while I was cleverly cementing relations with my journalistic colleagues. As we drove away from the Marine compound way after the curfew he fired a two round burst from his M-16, which I then took away from him, and not seeing anybody around, drove off.

It seems, though, that the sergeant of the guard ran up to the gate and apparently my good sergeant shot him in the bird. Colonel Ladd got a somewhat exaggerated account of the incident, through channels, which he then asked me to explain. My reply was about the best creative writing I have ever done.

And I had established a precedent for hanging out with Project Delta, so that when they set up an FOB at Phu Bai to run a recon of a valley about five kilometers from A Shau, I went down there to cover it for my little magazine.

If Delta lived plush in garrison, they lived Spartan in the field. They had a number of squad tents set up and a chopper pad beside their headquarters bunker and a defensive perimeter with some wire and that was it.

I sat around up there for a couple of days waiting for an operation I could go out on. Chuck wouldn't let me go out with a recon team, which was probably a good idea. I wasn't in as good shape as his recon people were and I wasn't trained for that kind of work, at least not to Delta's specifications. I had run recons before, of course, but the recon projects had their own tricks to the trade and although I knew *about* most of them, that knowledge was not the same as experience.

But they had brought a couple of companies of the Nha Trang Mike Force with them and they put these guys in for five days. I went with them.

Delta's choppers had knocked out a bunch of Russian trucks running through the A Shau valley and Chuck wanted pictures of them. His Intelligence Officer and I went in with one of the Mike Force companies. We made a couple of contacts, got shot up fairly well, got a few pictures of the trucks, got chased, set fire to a bunch of NVA ammo caches and finally lost our pursuers when they got in a firefight with their own exploding ammunition. The Intel Officer's shots didn't develop and Delta commandeered the ones I'd got for my magazine.

Then we walked down two kilometers of road from the trucks to our LZ. We looked like a company coming from a training exercise, walking in a column of twos right down that road, and I could hear NVA talking to each other in the trees on either side of the road. They didn't bother us though. I guess they thought we were NVA too.

"How'd you like your first trip out with the Project?" Bill Larrabee asked me when we got back to the FOB.

I shrugged. "Okay!"

We sat and I sipped a beer while he drank a cold Coke. "How'd you like the Mike Force?"

I looked at him closely. "The troops worked good," I said. "But I don't think I would have handled them exactly the way they were handled. Why?"

He cocked his head at me a little and said, "Major Allen needs a larger reaction force, and one that's more responsive to American control than the Vietnamese Ranger Battalion. We were thinking of a couple of companies of Montagnards. You think you could recruit them?"

I nodded. "No problem. You think maybe he'd like an American captain to run the two companies?"

Bill grinned. "Who knows what's in Allen's mind?"

Not me, but certainly it looked as though there might be some place for me to light in Vietnam and extend for six months, and I'd be working with Yards. This might develop into something good. I didn't even pause. I whipped up to a typewriter and started working out my proposed organization of the companies. That was the easy part. I wanted to impress Chuck that I was thorough and knew what I was doing. I figured if I wanted to do that I had better type my plan perfectly. And I am the worst typist in the world.

I had spent nine and a half months in Vietnam looking for a home, and now finally I might have found it.

I had come out of the woods as filthy, or more filthy, than usual, so I took my time under the shower. It was a fifty-five gallon drum on a platform with a turn valve and a soap dish, not near as fancy as the one McCulloch had devised for Buon Beng, but adequate for the occasion. After I got out of there I went and put on a clean tiger suit, smoked a leisurely cigarette and went to shave and brush my teeth. I do indeed savor a bath and shave after an operation. This one was especially fine because it was outside. They had built a wooden rack, which held the kind of old tin wash pans your Aunt Tillie used to use down on the farm, with a couple of old five-gallon gas cans full of water beside them. I shaved very carefully while admiring the scenery around the FOB. We were on a low hill, ringed with a fine set of misty mountains on either side and the sky was just starting to go misty pink and sea green as it does sometimes when there is no wind and the clouds are all strung out across the sky, not going anywhere. I admired the view while scraping what felt

311

like green fungus off my teeth. It's bad enough to have a clammy crotch and armpits like the breath of Beelzebub, but a foul tasting mouth is too much.

I heard a kind of high shrieking whistle, and then an explosion about five hundred yards away, not too far outside the perimeter. I assumed from the explosion that Charlie was off in the hills rocketing the place. I couldn't tell from the first one whether he was aiming for the Delta FOB or for one of the nearby Marine installations.

The second one was about half as far away as the first and I began to be a little apprehensive since they were obviously creeping toward the FOB. It was very annoying to have my toilet interrupted in this fashion. I finished brushing my teeth and rinsed them out as another round came crashing inside the perimeter. Rather more rapidly than I normally do I rinsed out the pan and gathered my toilet articles together. Accompanied by the sound of another high whistling shriek, I took off like a striped-assed gazelle, diving into a slit trench just as the last round hit too close for comfort.

I suppose I should have taken off for the trench at the sound of the first round, but I was enjoying my tooth brushing and I wasn't about to let the fuckers interrupt it. Besides, I'm not especially afraid of indirect fire weapons, never having been hit by one.

I guess they had expended all their ammo. They didn't fire any more and they hadn't done any particular damage, just blown up a lot of bare dirt.

The next day Chuck was going out on a team extraction and I asked to go along. He said sure.

It was interesting to go with him. He had the business of aerial reconnaissance down to a science. He and Bill and their two Vietnamese counterparts sat in the door, the Viets on one side and Bill and Chuck on the other. Bill and Chuck both had chopper pilot's helmets so that they could hook in with their patrol on the ground and all the choppers in the air at the same time. Major Huan, the Vietnamese commander, had a similar setup on another frequency with the Viets on the ground. He didn't have contact with the choppers, but his English wasn't too hot anyway.

Bill and Chuck both had their radio call signs lettered in

312

script on the backs of their helmets. It was an amusing conceit, since the signs were supposed to be secret. As a lot of guys with distinguishing characteristics do, they had their nicknames as call signs. Chuck's was BRUISER and Bill's was JOKER. Ludwig's had been BLUE MAX and he had it made up on a sign as a wheel cover on his jeep. Some secret.

All the choppers were from the 281st Assault Helicopter Company, which for my money was the best chopper outfit in Nam. They were very proud of their association with the Project, wore camouflage fatigues and put their lives on the line continuously. They had a tradition of disregarding any regulation which interfered with the performance of their mission. They were mostly young guys, and almost all of them were warrant officers.

The Marine chopper pilots in I Corps, by way of contrast, went strictly by the book. They were mostly older officers and career people. They also had shitty equipment, while the 281st had the newest and best, so you can't blame the Marines too much. They didn't have much and they had a hard time replacing what they had, so they couldn't afford to abuse it.

The Marines would only carry as much ammunition as they were supposed to. The 281st put so many rockets on their choppers that they would barely lift off. They would lift a little, go forward some and thud against the ground, gaining more momentum from the thud than from the rotors. After two or three repeats of this they would finally limp airborne and gather enough speed to gain altitude.

Since Chuck and Bill and the Viets were in the door seats I had to crouch behind them with my little camera. Bill sat with his helmet on, cradling a scope sighted CAR-15. Chuck had a new toy, a scope sighted M-60 machine gun hanging from a heavy bungee cord by his seat. I had known Chuck for a hell of a long time and had ceased to think of him as what you might call precisely a human being. He was more of a natural force with none of the distracting fears and hungers of people. Away from battle he was a bit of a sports car type of dandy, with a huge guffawing laugh, but in combat he was a commander, a computer, and a killer. He had a ludicrous number of Air Medals, something like twenty-five, and that murderous M-60.

I wanted very badly to listen in on the radio communications, but couldn't.

We lifted off and soon we were flying over the jungle. Flying in a command and control chopper like that turns the war into something of a chess game. You can see the battlefield from this godlike eminence and follow everything at every turn, with a little plastic covered map in your lap and your radio in your ear.

I gather from conversations with friends who served in conventional units that some of the battalion commanders made their lives an absolute hell by constantly hovering over them and overseeing each move. It all looks so easy from the air. I can imagine how somebody would have seen it from the air around Kham Duc, going and hovering over almost the same spot every day, bellowing over the radio. "Why aren't you people on the ground making progress?" Those guys said they had to make a radio report every hour on the hour.

Looking back on the war, I thank God every time I think about it that I never had to serve with an American unit.

But Chuck wasn't the kind of commander who rode his subordinates from the air. He just used his C and C ship as it should have been used. He knew how it was on the ground. He had chased North Korean guerillas all over behind the lines in Korea.

The extraction process was a fascinating thing to watch from the air. We were on top, way over the canopy of jungle, and the entire performance unwound beneath us like a tableau of little models.

We flew for maybe twenty minutes over the lush green mountained jungle, looking down on rivers, rapids and waterfalls. As always Vietnam was beautiful from the air. I loved to fly over Vietnam almost as much as I loved to walk over it. God, I remember how I felt when my plane landed at Travis Air Force Base the last time I came home and I saw all those bare brown hills rolling away, unbroken by rice paddies or rivers or jungle; just a heartbreaking sinking feeling, like, oh shit, here we are back in Dull City.

Finally we picked up the flash of a signaling mirror, a high intensity dot of light coming out of the green. It wavered as

314

the guy on the ground flasned it at the aircraft. Amazing. Just a small mirror, exactly like the one they'd used since World War II. I had one in my ammo pouch, but had never used it. We were at about 3,500 feet and it was bright as hell.

Down below us the three gunships whirled in trail and set up an orbit around the men on the ground. They ran in a tight circle around the patrol, and I saw white puffs of smoke coming off the orbiting choppers as they fired their rockets into the hills surrounding the men on the ground. I couldn't see them, of course, just the nubby green of the trees as the choppers whirled around like toys.

Then the extraction ship started easing down between the orbiting gunships. Down, down, slowly, into the trees. There was no LZ, just jungle. The patrol had been intercepted and had run and kept on running, with one man wounded, maybe dead. They hadn't been going for an LZ, they had just kept running until the choppers got there. The extraction chopper had to lower itself down through the trees as far as it could, then drop a McGuire rig.

The rig, named after Sergeant Major McGuire, who had been with the Project when he invented it, consisted of three weighted ropes with heavy canvas slings to sit in and a small strap to hook your right wrist to in case you were hit and couldn't hang on. The ropes were weighted with sandbags and dropped down through the trees.

The idea was to sit in the sling, hook your wrist into the cuff and all three guys link arms. Then the chopper lifts them right through the tree canopy. For a six man patrol, which this was, you had to use two choppers. I rode one once in training and enjoyed it tremendously, but then no one was shooting at me at the time. I imagine it's a tremendous relief to see one come crashing down through the trees.

They tell a story about a guy in C and C who was a dead shot with an M-79. He got so involved in ponking rounds out at a pursuing machine gun that he didn't hook up his wrist and got shot again and fell out of the sling from about a hundred and fifty feet up. Fired his last M-79 round in mid air. Hit the fucker too.

The first extraction chopper eased down between the gunships and lifted out with two guys in it. This had been an all

Viet patrol and had only had five men. One was wounded and they had his gear strapped to the extra seat. So they didn't hang together. The extraction chopper lifted straight up and climbed for altitude with all the power it had while the two guys and the gear whirled around underneath. It must have been an uncomfortable ride for them because the reason for linking arms is so that everyone will hang in a clump and not be whirled around under the chopper. Those two must have been spinning like tops.

The next chopper settled in the slot and picked up the remaining three guys. Then lifted out again. It seemed to take an incredible length of time, and all the time the gunships were circling and firing rockets. Then all the choppers lifted and climbed for altitude and soon we were all scooting for home in formation, the guys in the McGuire rigs streaming out behind at a forty-five degree angle, enjoying the breeze.

It took about ten minutes for us to get away from Indian Country and set down at a Firebase of the 101st Airborne Division. The idea was to let the guys in the McGuire rigs get out of the rigs and into the choppers. The McGuire rig, after all, is an emergency measure and something less than comfortable.

As soon as we landed, a couple of gunjeeps from the Firebase roared up, the sergeant in charge throwing out his bare belly through his flak jacket and doing an Up Front number, swinging his M-16 at the end of his arms. There were maybe six or seven troopers with him and they looked gross in their shaggy crewcuts, coated with the red dirt of their bulldozed firebase, white under the goggles which they shoved up on their foreheads when they arrived.

I wasn't highly impressed with their appearance. The Forces guys break a lot of regulations and wear some unconventional uniforms, but they don't look sloppy. In our tiger suits we looked positively spiffy next to these guys. Their appearance, to me, did not denote that they were being loose because they were in constant danger, just that they lacked professionalism.

The sergeant in charge got out of his jeep and started to walk around real slow.

Chuck gave him a brief glance, disdain implicit, but not expressed since it was beneath him, and we jumped back in the choppers and lifted off without a word.

It must have made an interesting story when they got back to the Firebase. Three helicopters land and five Vietnamese in NVA uniforms get out and get in the choppers. The choppers are manned and flown by Americans in tiger suits and carrying .38 revolvers instead of .45 automatics and then they were gone and no one had ever heard of anything like that before and they never would again.

That night Chuck asked me if I wanted to go back into the valley with his reaction force, the 91st Airborne Ranger Battalion, the next day. The idea was to blow up a bunch of the caches and get some further identification on the Russian made trucks that we'd found the week before. I said sure.

The headquarters usually operated until some time between ten-thirty and midnight, every day in the field, and then knocked off until seven the next morning, except for the duty officer and NCO. There was a movie outside for the off duty recon teams and chopper crews, though. If enough of the headquarters people wanted to see it they showed it again in the briefing room after everybody knocked off work. It meant staying up too late to get enough sleep, but a little diversion was welcome.

They decided to show the movie in the briefing room that night and I thought that it might be a good idea to do something like that before going into the field again. I had seen it before, but it was a good flick, *Up the Down Staircase*. I thought a movie about the trials and tribulations of a high school teacher might be a welcome relief from all that machinegun fire. Particularly with a lady like Sandy Dennis, who was the antithesis of everything my life was right then.

I sat there enjoying it thoroughly, but after five minutes I started watching Chuck instead. As usual he sat leaning forward in his seat, jaw thrust forward literally draining the images from the screen. As the show progressed he became more and more restive. "What is this shit?" he muttered. He took it for twelve minutes, then stood, jaw more outthrust than usual, and muttered something that sounded like, "Buncha goddamned shit," and rolled out of the briefing

317

room.

They had shown *A Fistful of Dollars* the night before, and he'd liked that fine.

I stayed for another half hour and then went to get some sleep. Big day tomorrow.

32

Our ship flared out about thirty feet up and settled slowly to earth. When she was about five feet off the ground, Ken Nauman hitched the seat of his pants and dropped out of sight. I barrelled out after him, jumping off the skids; landing bent over, running for the edge of the LZ where a perimeter was starting to form. I hit the ground behind a dirt bank covered with dry reeds and looked around.

The choppers lifted off, whipping rotors pulling them upward. Vietnamese Rangers ran in 360 degrees to fill in a good defensive perimeter. Rotors blasted dust into the air, into our hair, teeth and eyes and down the backs of our necks. The gunships went around again; rockets whooshed and cracked, machine guns chattered, miniguns bu-u-urped out their streams of fire.

When the dust settled everything was still. There was no firing. I got up and looked closely at the gentle hills, the lush green jungle. There was no movement.

Ken sat about ten feet away, looking bored, next to the Vietnamese carrying his radio. He took the handset and said, "Crusade Zero-five, this is Zero-six. Over." There was a pause and he said "This is Zero-six. You in position? Over." Another pause. "Roger, out."

Ken was of medium height, and generally looked bored. He had big, soft, baggy eyes. He was twenty-nine but looked far older. Three tours in Nam had aged him.

He got up and started to stroll off, head down talking into the handset, radioman trotting along behind.

We walked over a dugout dirt bank and came up on a Vietnamese lieutenant kneeling, talking into his own radio. He was getting positions from the Vietnamese commanders.

Ken explained he was Lieutenant Linh, commander of the first lift.

The lieutenant wore his helmet cocked back, chinstraps dangling on either side of his chubby cheeks. He looked like a younger version of Prince Norodom Sihanouk of Cambodia. Ken went over and knelt beside him for a moment, checking to see if they were getting the same information over the radio. Then he nodded and walked away.

I stayed and shot some pictures of the lieutenant talking into his radio.

A three man sixty millimeter mortar crew hustled around under Linh's direction, trying to keep their tube out from under the trees. They fired handheld, the skinny mortarman moving his little knee high olive drab pipe proudly, with great precision. When he was satisfied, they'd drop two or three rounds down the tube and then shift again.

After a few minutes I wandered off to find Ken.

He stood on the edge of the LZ looking out across it. There was a huge B-52 bomb crater to our right front and another one further to the left front. And to our immediate left front, about thirty meters away sat a UHID, a Huey helicopter.

I nodded toward it. "What's that doing there?"

He shrugged. "Shot down," he said.

No bullet holes were visible, but it sat still and empty. It looked dead.

"Everybody get out all right?"

He nodded. "Uh huh."

"When's the next lift coming in?"

He pushed his hat back on his head and said, "It's overdue now. I hope to hell it gets here soon. We're just sittin' here waiting for Charles to get his stuff together. We're not making any money here," he said, jerking his head toward the trees. "Let's go get in the shade."

We walked off together, Ken, the radioman and I, automatically keeping five yards between.

In Lieutenant Linh's shady nook we crashed under the trees. There was a little bit of breeze and the shade. Everything was quiet. The mortarmen were flaked out around their tube, eating rice and fish. I opened my pack and got out a long range patrol ration. Chili. Slitting the heavy OD envelope, I took out the plastic bag inside, filled it half full of lukewarm canteen water, then stirred the dry crumbly red mess with a plastic spoon. Five minutes later it looked like real chili, complete with beans. It was a little bland but not bad.

"Hey, Ken," I said, waving the bag, "you want half of this chili? I can't eat it all."

He lay under a tree, head on his pack, hat over his eyes, smoking a cigarette. "No thanks, Babe," he said, not moving, "not hungry."

I finished the chili, lay down, lit a cigarette and mashed my own hat down over my nose. Bright sunlight turned all the tree leaves around us to pale translucent green.

Lieutenant Linh sat crosslegged under a tree, one arm propped up on his radio, eating sausage. He held out a slice to me, smiling.

"Da Khong, cam on Chung 'Uy," I said.

He ate that slice and cut himself another. Breezes blew, tree limbs waved, shivering the translucent leaves. We sucked down cigarette smoke and the day grew hotter. We waited. The sun burned through the trees and the shade drifted away with the sun. I took off my hat to wipe the sweat from my forehead and the inside of my eyelids turned red.

"Hey!" Ken said.

I pushed my hat back a little and looked at his inert form. "Huh, what?"

"How'd you like to have one of those cold cokes we were drinking before we left?"

I smiled cruelly. "How'd you like to have a big orange drink in a tall waxed paper cup, so full of ice you crunch on it for half an hour after you finish your drink?"

"Why you rotten son of a bitch," he muttered, without moving.

I glanced at my watch. "We've been here almost four hours now," I said. "The longer we wait, the more trouble we're going to be in when we move."

Ken stirred uneasily. "What I'm afraid of is that we'll get moving late and get in a firefight about six-thirty, just when we don't want it."

I pushed my hat lower, dimly hearing some sounds in the distance.

"Incoming!" Ken said.

Without consciously moving I found myself face first in the dirt, M-16 in the firing position. Four B-40 rockets exploded out on the LZ and there was the sound of four more being fired.

When Ken saw they didn't have the range on us he sat back up and got on the radio, talking intently into the microphone. "Falcon, this is Crusade Zero-six, Zero-six. Over. Falcon . . . Roger Falcon Two-two . . . Oh! Hi John. Good to have you out. What've you got? Over."

A little Air Force 02B aircraft buzzed around, front and rear propellers outlined against the sky. It was Falcon, the Delta Forward Air Controller.

Ken looked up and said, "Keep low. We're gonna have some F-105's in here in a minute." He looked at Linh. "*Chung 'Uy*, you get adjustments from the companies over your radio and feed them to me. I'll keep adjusting the aircraft." Then back into the microphone, "Hey John! You see the high ground about a hundred meters north of the LZ. Put your marking round in there."

Two flights of F-105's appeared over the horizon. They roared in low over the LZ and swung, clean, sweptback and beautiful into the sky. The little FAC dropped over in a tight 180 and buzzed the hill mass Ken had indicated.

Crack-whoosh-WHOMP! went the marking round, leaving a plume of white smoke hanging over the target.

"Very good!" Ken said. "Bring your first round in right there."

It was very quiet after the marking round. The B-40's quit falling.

The fighters came around and the first one came in on the target.

"Hit it!" Ken said and fell to earth.

I sat up and watched. They hit. The entire landscape jumped and I picked a jagged piece of hot steel off my lap. I decided after that to do what the man said.

"That was pretty good, John," Ken said. "Put 'em in on that ridge line right there."

322

The jets peeled off one after the other and came in. The arc of the falling high-drag bombs was slow. We hit the ground a fraction of a second before they struck and were all right. Ken put in napalm too. We didn't need to crouch for the huge orange and black blossoms ballooning across the horizon.

When the aircraft dumped their loads and headed for home it was quiet again. The FAC kept buzzing around, and for that or other reasons Charles left us alone.

A few minutes later we heard the whop-whop-whop of returning helicopters. I cradled the rifle under my arm and got out my camera, walking down to the edge of the LZ.

Two gunships circled the LZ. Apparently the other had been hit that morning. A cloud of slicks whirled in to dump their troops, UHID's from the 281st and Marine CH-46's.

Two and three at a time the slicks landed. Tailgates on the big CH-46's dropped, troops poured off the ramp and the choppers clawed back into the sky. One limped in smoking and the crew barrelled out with the troops.

A Huey lifted off, shuddered, started to go down, shuddered, straightened up and limped over the horizon. Another went through the same drill and crashed in the trees about two hundred meters past the LZ. Right where Charles was. It began to occur to me that all the firing wasn't coming from our perimeter.

When all the ships were gone it was quiet again. There were three ships down on the LZ and I had seen one more go down. That was four. I didn't know if there were others or not. One thing for sure, everybody wasn't here yet. I didn't know if Ken was going to try to bring in another lift or not. He wasn't there to ask.

Some guys were out on the LZ poking around the first Huey that went down. There was no firing so I went over to see if there might be any pictures. Two guys from the Project sat in the door on the shady side, smoking. A couple of others looked in the pilot's compartment. The machine guns had been taken out.

I sat down in the doorway, got a cigarette out and gave the interior of the chopper a quick once-over to see if maybe there was any ice water inside. There wasn't.

"You guys just get here?" I asked, taking a drag on the cigarette.

There was a burst of automatic weapons fire and the dirt kicked up around us. Other weapons joined in and the LZ became a field of little dirt geysers. The guy I was talking to started running.

We ran full tilt toward the bomb crater. I charged over the side and dropped into the slanted dirt on the inside about halfway down, sliding half the rest of the way to the bottom. There were already eight men there, but there was plenty of room for more.

One of them was a big darkheaded wooly bear of a man who worked for me as a photographer, Sp4 Bob Christiansen.

"Hello, Chris," I said.

He smiled. "Morning, sir."

I dusted myself off and flicked some dirt off my weapon. B-40's were coming in on the LZ and it seemed like a hell of a racket had been going on since that first burst. "How come you didn't make it on that first lift?" I asked Christiansen.

"Chopper got hit and we had a bunch of wounded. Had to go back," he replied. He shook his head. "I thought it over quite a while before I came back out."

I laughed. "You shoulda thought longer."

A Marine sergeant from one of the helicopters stood a little further up the dirt bank looking nervously over the rim He wore a forty-five in a cowboy rig and a flak vest. "Look," he said, "we better get out of here. This old chopper's going to blow any minute now."

I crawled up beside him. The CH-46 was still smoking badly. The idea of its blowing up didn't bother me any more than the B-40's and automatic weapons fire upstairs. Still, we had to leave sometime.

"Okay! Do it!" I said.

Everybody took a couple of deep breaths and looked at each other and then they were over the edge.

I don't know if dirt kicked at our heels in neat straight bursts as it does in the movies. I don't know if B-40's burst around us or not. I did not feel the weight of the 300 rounds of ammunition on my belt, or the knife, or the camera, or the

324

grenades. I do not remember running. I have a memory of red dirt moving beneath my feet and another of the next crater as I blasted over the side and slid down. This one already had about five guys in it.

Somebody yelled, "Medic!" from the other side of the crater. I poked my head up just as Meder, the little dark-headed medic with the Bronx accent, started over the rim. He didn't have to go out. A skinny figure in a tiger suit and bush hat rolled into the crater, rounds kicking up dirt all around him.

"Got hit in the chest!" he said as he crashed into the crater, M-16 in hand. It was First Lieutenant Tom Humphus, one of the company advisors.

Meder tore his shirt open, looked closely at it and said, "In and out pec. Didn't go in the chest cavity. He's gonna be all right."

"What the hell were you doing up there?" I asked.

He shrugged. "Just lookin' around."

"See anything interesting?"

"I saw we better get out of here," he replied.

He was right. We were better off than in the other crater, but still in an exposed position. If one guy got lucky with a B-40 we had all had it.

A few seconds later we were running again, this time straight for the woodline and back to Lieutenant Linh's old position. As soon as there were woods between me and the NVA gunners I slowed to a walk, chest heaving, barely able to lift my feet. The weight of the ammo and all the running, after ten months in an office, had really got to me. I staggered into Linh's little grove of trees and collapsed, panting.

Linh was still talking on his radio and firing his M-79. He moved quickly and nervously from one to the other, beads of sweat standing out on his upper lip. I figured he was probably thinking the same way I was. We had to collect our wounded, call in the perimeter and make an orderly with drawal. Almost impossible without air cover, and for air cover we needed Ken. He might be stuck out there in one of the craters. He might be anywhere.

I was still mulling this over when a big redheaded trooper

I didn't know came up through the woods. He looked to be twenty-three or twenty-four. Following him was a slender, clean cut looking kid with black hair.

"We need some guys to help haul about fifteen wounded out of a bomb crater out here," the redhead said. I hoped he wasn't talking about that first one we'd run out of. It seemed almost impossible to try to carry someone out of there.

I followed the two young soldiers through the grove of trees we were in, back toward the area we had come from. We moved parallel to the LZ. The redheaded guy, in front, called to several people, Americans and Vietnamese Rangers both, in old NVA positions to get up and come with us. They stared at him stupidly and didn't move. Either they didn't understand, or couldn't seem to put the request into action.

We came to a spot looking down across thirty meters of flat open country on the first bomb crater we had run out of. We stood on a four or five foot dirt bank above the flat land. Once out of the trees there was scarcely a blade of grass between us and the crater. It had filled up with men again, but I didn't see anybody who looked too hurt to move. "That it?" I asked. The CH—46 was still smoking.

"That's it," said the redhead, and he started down through the trees with the other kid right behind him.

I followed, but watched them and the crater instead of where I was going. Just as they broke out of the woodline and started running I tripped and fell flat on my face in the bush.

I looked up. They were running, halfway to the crater, rounds kicking up dirt at their heels. I didn't see them get hit but if they weren't it was a miracle. They weren't going to get back unless they had some covering fire.

There appeared to be about fifteen men in the crater. Some wore green Marine flying suits. A tall guy in a tiger suit, standing in the far side of the crater, lit a cigarette.

"Hey!" I called. "Where's that fire coming from?"

He pointed to my right front and said, "In the woods over there about two hundred meters. There's a machine gun."

"Okay!" I called back. "You guys let me know when you're ready to come out of there. I'll put down covering fire. Come right through here."

"Right!" he called back.

I was standing up quite exposed, just a little way back in the woods. It was the only way I could fire over their heads when they came through. My right hand was trembling as I picked four magazines out of the ammo pouch and laid them on the ground. I could punch an empty magazine out and scoop a full one off the grass quicker than dragging them out of the pouch. I hoped he had given me the right location on that machine gun. If I stood bolt upright in only a little bit of shadow and gave my position away by firing at the wrong place the MG could cut me in half.

The guys we had passed coming here were in the woods and over a slight rise, out of sight. I didn't want to leave for fear the men in the crater would make their break so I called, "Hey!" turning around and yelling into the woods. "We've gotta put down covering fire for these guys. When I open fire, fire on that woodline over there."

I heard no reply. I yelled again and turned my attention back on the crater.

The big guy was still standing there smoking his cigarette.

"Hey!" I called. "You guys about ready?"

"Just a minute," he called back. He took a deep drag on his cigarette, took the smoke all the way down, flipped the cigarette away, exhaled slowly and called back, "Okay!"

I brought my M-16 down on where the machine gun was supposed to be and bellowed, "FIRE!" squeezing the trigger. The weapon emptied in four fast bursts. I punched the magazine release and almost beat the magazine to the ground, scooping up another. By that time the herd of camouflaged troopers was halfway to the bank. I opened up again.

The ones in the lead wavered for a split second when I fired. Without taking my finger off the trigger I called, "C'MON! GODDAMNIT! I'M FIRING OVER YOUR HEADS!"

The first ones broke into the shade and scrambled up the bank, almost knocking me over. I stepped back. The magazine emptied and I punched it out, scooping up another. As the men came through they kept on going back into the bank and into cover, clearing the way for those behind. Finally there were only two left.

"Let's go!" I said.

"Sir, I'm too weak to make it. You've got to pull me up."
It was the darkheaded kid and right behind him was the redheaded guy.

"I'll try and push him," the redhead said.

Oh Christ! I thought, *if I quit firing . . . the machine gun?
Awwwww!*

I reached down, grabbed his extended arm and pulled. He
didn't budge. The redheaded guy was pushing. It was almost
a straight pull up and the kid wasn't moving. "NEED SOME
HELP OVER HERE!" I called.

My rifle was on the ground at my feet and the kid wasn't
moving. Four rounds hit all around us in regular sequence.
Machine gun rounds. I heard nothing. I wanted to leave, but
couldn't leave them like that. I heard the second burst, saw
more rounds hit and something went *splat* hard against my
right forearm.

I looked down and saw a huge blue-black hole in my arm,
with bright red blood gushing out in spurts, like the needle
spray in a shower.

"Holy shit!" I said, realizing two things at once: (a) I
couldn't pull them up now, and (b) I was dying.

I grabbed the wound, blood spraying my hand and turned
running back toward where the medics were. A branch
knocked my hat off. I yelled, "Medic! Medic!" and barrelled
back over the brim into Lieutenant Linh's sanctuary, still
yelling "Medic!"

There was an older looking GI that I didn't know in there,
and a couple of others, younger.

"Need a tourniquet, fast!" I said.

"Uh huh!" said the older guy, nodding. He tightened a rifle
sling around my upper arm. "It needs to go higher," I said.

He shook his head calmly. "This is where it goes. I know
about these things." He was sandy haired and looked very
competent. That was all the introduction I had to Doc
Taylor, one of the best medics in Special Forces. He saved
my life. He saved a lot of lives that day.

Meder appeared from somewhere and bandaged the
wound, tearing the plastic wrapper off an ace bandage with

his teeth, while with his other hand he held gauze pads over the wound.

"We're gonna put this tourniquet on real loose," Doc said, "and try to hold the bleeding with pressure. It looks like it'll be awhile before we can get you out of here."

"L-listen," I said, shaking, "I was trying to haul two guys over that bank over there when I got hit. They're both wounded."

Doc looked me straight in the face. "They still there?" he asked.

"Yeah," I said, "yeah, they're still there."

He and Meder disappeared. I sat there feeling rotten for having left them. I couldn't have helped them if I'd stayed, and I'd have died. But I still felt rotten.

There had really been no other course of action I could have taken. A man will bleed to death from a severed artery in six to eight minutes if it is left unattended, but that didn't make me feel any better. I couldn't have pulled them up anyway after I'd been hit, but that didn't make me feel any better either. You always think that when the clutch comes you'll emerge from a phone booth in a pair of blue tights with a red towel around your neck and it's all going to be okay. This was the incident that finally got it through my head. Beret or no beret, we were just guys. There are no supermen and damned few heroes; almost no live ones.

A lot of other wounded started coming in, some limping, some carried. Most were already bandaged, but there was a lot of blood splattered around, some of it dry and some of it not so dry.

Sergeant Thompson from the Delta Intelligence section walked in, all hunkered over and extraordinarily sad looking. He had no visible wounds.

"Glad to see you're okay," I said.

He sat down, still hunkered over, and said, "Haw! I got two slugs in the chest."

The medics went to work around us; cans of albumin blood expander coming out, hypos going in. Two guys brought in a Marine helicopter pilot and laid him beside me. His flight suit was blood splattered and torn and his face waxy, yellow and blank. Doc Taylor put the albumin in. In

329

the arm, I think.

Thompson dug a cigarette out of his pocket. Now I could see the blood on his shirt. "I hold the world's record for the forty yard low crawl with a sucking chest wound," he said, starting to chuckle. The chuckle ended in a wheeze and a grimace of pain.

I shook my head in disbelief. "Don't tell me," I said, "it only hurts when you laugh?"

"It hurts all the time," he replied. "It hurts bad when I laugh." He grinned again, but was careful not to let his body shake.

Meder came back in and said, "That redheaded guy you were trying to pull out was John Link. The other guy was named Merriman."

"Did you get them up?" I asked anxiously.

He nodded. "Yeah! Link's got three slugs in the back. He's unconscious. Merriman's got three in the legs."

"Oh Jesus! Are they gonna make it?"

He unbuttoned Thompson's shirt to see if his bandage was still airtight. "Merriman will," he said. "We're not so sure about Link."

I leaned back on my good arm and shook my head, leaned up again and fished a cigarette out of my pocket with my left hand.

"Lemme give you a light!"

I shook my head. "Naw! I can do it myself."

Ken Nauman strolled back into the little grove, more cheerful than usual. His radio operator chugged along behind him, scared and winded.

"You wounded too, Jim?" he said, sitting down to light a cigarette.

"Uh huh!" I replied, leaning up. "Where you been?"

He looked over his shoulder. "Checking the perimeter," he said.

I could imagine what a hellish project that must have been in this mess.

"You mind if I make a suggestion?"

He grinned. "Shoot!"

"The next time you have to use multiple lifts like this, use more than one LZ and link up on the ground."

He laughed, reached for the radio and said, "Falcon Two-two. Crusade Zero-six. Over."

Pretty soon we had another air strike.

I couldn't sleep that night. It wasn't the B-40's falling around, because none of them were coming right into our little pocket. The other wounded were quiet. But there was the pain in my right arm. It was only a dull ache. But when I tried to quiet down and get some sleep the pain was all there was. "Awwwww dammit!" I muttered, thrashing around in frustration.

After awhile Doc Taylor materialized at my side. "Sir, I better give you something for that pain. You got any morphine?"

I got the small box of morphine syrettes out of my ammo pouch and gave him one. He jammed the needle straight into my leg and squeezed the tube dry. I barely felt it.

Three hours later pain woke me up. It was dark, but there was a moon and I could see Doc working on the helicopter pilot. I didn't want to bother him so I just watched. He worked for quite a while, feverishly. Then he stopped and sat down on the ground in the dark, his arms draped over his knees. He lowered his head and slowly shook it from side to side.

I didn't want to bother him then either, but the pain was really getting bad. "Hey Doc!"

He didn't want to give me morphine again that early, so I got a shot of demerol. A few hours later he did give me enough morphine to last the night.

In the morning my right hand was swollen up like that of a three day old corpse. I lay looking at it for a while and then started to get up. The bandage broke loose and bright red blood mixed with the dried maroon stuff already on the bandage. "Hey Meder!" I said. "This mother broke loose."

He cinched up the tourniquet and started to rebandage the wound.

"Ush!" I said.

Meder looked at me like it hurt him worse, and said, "Sorry, sir."

"S'okay," I replied. "You do what you gotta and change that bandage, and I'll do what I gotta and whimper." I

331

started whistling, toneless and dirgelike, while he worked. Once I'd made up my mind it didn't hurt so bad.

"Hey Ace," I said, "am I gonna get to keep this arm? I've sort of grown attached to it."

He looked at me levelly and replied, "If we get you out today probably so, if not, probably not." He finished rebandaging the wound. "Want a shot?"

"Not if we're going to move," I replied. "As long as I'm doing something my mind is off the pain."

We needed an airstrike to cover our withdrawal, but it was too overcast. B-40's kept coming in and Charles ran probe after probe on the companies on the perimeter. We took more casualties.

Ken was on the radio the whole time, checking with the FAC on fighters, checking with the companies. About ten o'clock he looked up from the radio with a look of undisguised glee. "Hey, Jim," he said, "we got a prisoner." The project had been looking for a prisoner to give them concrete information on what was in this valley for about three weeks. "Listen," Ken said into the microphone, "if anything happens to that prisoner, you're going to have to answer to me."

A few minutes later we got another call. Preliminary interrogation of the prisoner indicated that our two companies were engaged by two companies of NVA troops and another battalion was on its way down the road. Oh joy!

It was after eleven by the time Ken could bring an air strike in on the NVA positions. He brought in 500 pounders and napalm. One napalm went right in on the spot where the machine gun had been the day before and I hoped to God the gunner fried in it.

Men started moving around and picking things up. We began to get in some sort of formation to go. Ken kept the strikes coming in. I got up and immediately became so lightheaded from loss of blood I had to sit back down again. Then I pushed my way off slowly and floated off toward the head of the column, figuring if I couldn't stand the pace I'd drop back slowly and still get there with everybody else.

The NVA prisoner came by with two Rangers escorting him. He was a young kid, somewhere between fifteen and seventeen, wearing OD shorts and a fatigue shirt about three sizes too big, and khaki NVA tennis shoes. His fatigue shirt flapped around his skinny body. He grinned and his walk was almost a skip. He was out of the fighting and had caught on that we weren't going to hurt him.

The ragged column walked over a flat washed out muddy area and then down into a creek for half a mile, jungle covered mountains towering above. We moved single file. I was stronger than I'd expected and since almost everybody else was either walking wounded or carrying dead or wounded litter patients I was about even. Helicopter crewmen had picked up my pack and rifle.

Brush was thick. It was heavy going. Ken was in the rear, bringing in air strikes to cover our exit. I felt very vague.

After about half an hour we came to a hill overlooking a small LZ we had used before. A few Vietnamese troops had topped to rest. I collapsed against a tree next to Lieutenant Linh and pointed to the small clearing below. "Is that the one?" I asked.

"Yes," he said. I bummed some water from him and said, "You're a pretty good officer, *Chung 'Uy*. You did a good job on this patrol." It was no snow job. I really meant it.

He looked kind of embarrassed and said, "No, I am number ten officer."

I smiled and said, "No! You're pretty good."

We waited a few more minutes and he said, "You go now."

I got up and, stumbling over rocks, grasping at trees, followed a couple of his troopers down the hill to the LZ. It was a steep hill and I had to stop twice before we reached bottom. Down there I found Humphus and some others waiting by a bomb crater, ready to jump if necessary

Doc Taylor came up with some Rangers carrying wounded hanging in ponchos slung from poles. I asked him how Link and Merriman were.

He looked tired. "John Link died this morning, just as we left out," he said. "Merriman's going to make it okay."

I felt more depressed. Not guilty. Just bad. No, that's bullshit. I felt guilty.

Ken came in with his radio and the rear guard. "FAC says this isn't the LZ," he said. "Says it's about two hundred meters on further."

"Oh God!" I moaned.

"C'mon. It's not far." He went back to call another air strike on our backtrail.

We pushed ourselves up to crash into the brush again. In the intervals between air strikes B-40's started falling behind us again. None came near our part of the column. But they indicated Charles was still trying.

Three more times we stopped at small clearings. Each time the FAC told us it was further on. The troops grew more and more beat. I staggered, head thrown back watching the translucent leaves above. All the trees and rocks stood out in startling clarity, but I felt as though I myself might fade and disappear.

I tried to walk carefully so the bandage wouldn't break loose again. There was a little seepage around the edges, but not much.

Two Rangers staggered past carrying a corpse wrapped in my poncho liner, great dried blood patches superimposed on the varishaded green camouflage pattern of my uniform. I remembered giving it away the night before. The corpse's right hand was two-thirds blown away, extended upward in rigor mortis. The bloody stump waved in my face as they went by. I regarded it with interest.

At times I could see no one in front and no one behind and watched the ground for signs, hoping I wouldn't take a wrong turn. This was neither the time nor place to get lost in the woods. We walked five kilometers that way.

Light was fading when we finally came to a large open field big enough to take a dozen choppers. Men from the Project were already getting the LZ set up when we came in. Most of them didn't think we'd get out that night, and said so. If they were right, a lot of wounded would die. And I'd lose my arm.

Rangers started setting up a perimeter. I stood with my mouth open, then finally gathered enough strength to sit down.

The FAC appeared, and some fighter cover, then gunships. Chuck Allen's Command and Control helicopter came. I could visualize Chuck in the door, 250 pounds of muscle, graying crew cut and iron jaw, sitting behind his newly installed M-60 machine gun. Larrabee would be seated crosslegged in the door with his scope sighted CAR-15, both he and Chuck hooked in by radio to all the friendlies in the air and on the ground. When I saw Chuck I knew we were going to make it.

Two troopers brought John Link's body up and put it down about eight feet from where I sat. A grim looking dark-haired trooper I didn't know came up, knelt beside him and patted the pole his body was slung from. "Well, John old buddy," he said, "Goddamn!"

He got up, shook his head and walked off, head bowed.

Merriman lay on the ground, his carrying pole off to the side, over there a few feet ahead of where Link's body was. I pushed myself to my feet and walked over. He was smoking a cigarette. "Hey, listen," I said. "I feel rotten about leaving you guys like that."

He shook his head. "Forget it, sir. You had to. I saw what happened."

That made me feel a little better, but not much. I squatted down. "How long before you got out?"

He looked pained. "Fifteen minutes," he said.

"My God! That long?"

He nodded. "Yessir, but we had already taken the rounds while you were there. We just lay quiet and he didn't fire anymore."

I smiled at him. "You gonna be all right?"

He nodded, relaxed. Just glad to be alive. "Yeah! It'll be awhile, but I'll be all right."

"Good."

It was starting to get dark when the gunships set up an orbit and two Dustoffs came in for the dead and wounded. Doc Taylor stood in the fading light, supervising loading, the propblast whipping his sandy hair. I squeezed in beside the left door gunner. Merriman and Thompson were on the same ship. The passenger space was a mound of men, alive and dead, packed in on each other, blood, bandages, litter poles.

Ken Nauman came up grinning and gave me the thumbs up sign.

"Hey, Ken," I called. "When you bringing the battalion back in here?"

"Oh, next week I guess." He waved us into the air.

At dusk the mountains are beautiful, but it was cold in the chopper and wind from the open doors whipped our clothes. I held my aching arm and wondered if Ken could hold all night.

About ten minutes after we lifted off, a ragged armada of army and marine helicopters came by, seemingly flung across the fading blue-gray sky. They flew hell for leather toward our LZ. Chuck must have scraped and begged all over I Corps for them, but they were going to get everybody out that night.

Oh God! They were beautiful.

33

Sitting in the waiting room at the 22d Surgical Hospital three hours later I was worried about my arm, but I couldn't really say anything much about it. It looked like I would probably lose it, but what could I say? People who had come in with us were dying all around me. Arms had a low priority. The medical people were taking the most badly wounded first, regardless of whether they were Viets or Americans, and for that I was grateful, but I was still worried about my arm. The hand that extended from Doc Taylor's pressure bandage had swollen up like a purple rubber glove blown up like a balloon. It didn't look like anything you'd want to carry around on the end of your arm.

We had over thirty percent casualties, and I didn't know how many were killed and how many were wounded. But of all the badly wounded who had held out, the ones hanging on by main strength who had clung to life while their buddies dragged them on one pole litters the five miles back to that LZ, almost half had died in the choppers. I believe they held on until help arrived and then surrendered, knowing that they were saved.

Finally, after I had been sitting there for God knows how long, a couple of medics in green surgical suits came up and put me on an examining table and started cutting my shirt off the arm. I was beginning to feel right at home on one of those things. They filled out the usual cards and finally I was wheeled into an operating room, which was a little rubber quonset hut kept inflated by its own air conditioning.

A rangy looking fellow in a green cap and gown came in and introduced himself in a New England accent. "I'm going to give you a nerve block in that arm and operate on it," he said in a slightly tired tone.

Lying back on the table feeling dirty, I nodaed. The room was filled with medicinal smells and shining instruments. The heavy glow of the operating light beat down on me. I was tired. But I was interested in the surgical procedures they were going to do on the arm. I'd never seen major surgery before.

"Am I going to be awake during the operation?"

"Yeah," he replied.

I would like to describe the insertion of the nerve block in detail, but all I can remember is a quick sharp pain under my right collarbone and some more chitchat with the New England doctor. I was very impressed with him. He seemed unusually calm and competent. He was one of the good people. An unusual percentage of the good people are physicians.

"Think I'll get to keep the arm?" I asked, somewhat anxiously. I had decided to stay in the army and without an arm I'd never get out from behind a desk. I'd be damn lucky to get to stay in an airborne unit. Try to convince some klutz you can pull your reserve with a hook.

He nodded. "Yes. You'll lose some motion, but I'm pretty sure you'll get to keep the arm."

That was a relief. One hurdle out of the way. Now with just a little more luck . "You don't suppose there's any chance I could stay in Nam, you know, do it all here, you know?"

He looked at me closly for a moment. Then he shook his head. "No, there's no possibility of that. You're going home."

Oh no, my mind thought as my feeling sank. No, I'm home now. What I'll be doing is going back to the nightmare world of lines to stand in and forms with numbers in little blocks to fill out. That world with all its picayune irritations. No, better by far the total involvement in some monster crusade like Vietnam than being eight-to-fived to death in some foul little job in some foul little office somewhere. Better by far to wind up, as I'd once predicted, dead in a rice paddy, face down with my guts in my hand, than that.

He and his assistant, a young man that I took to be a medic, an operating room specialist, started to arrange some green surgical cloth over the arm. It was still wrapped up in Doc Taylor's bandage.

"How's about if I watch?" I asked.

He shook his head. "Huh uh!"

I was slightly irritated at how fast he fobbed off my request. Did he think I was going to faint at the sight of my own blood? I'd seen plenty of it before, and I'd probably see it again. "Oh, c'mon, Doc," I said, my irritation plain in my voice, "I'm a big boy, I've seen surgery before. I just want to see what this one is like."

He shook his head again quite clearly, but not exasperated, as a man might be expected to be who gets constantly hassled while he is preparing to do major surgery. "It's not the same when it's yours. I was going to watch some mortar fragments taken out of my leg a couple of weeks back. Couldn't take it. Had to look away."

Well, that did it. I couldn't say I could stand it when he couldn't, certainly not just before he was going to start carving on my arm. Nothing to do but just lie there while he did it.

Dum-dum-de-dum. Damn lights were very bright. I couldn't feel the arm at all. Somehow I had the feeling it was still elevated, pointing up toward the sky. I guess not though, because the doctor was doing something and I was the only patient he had in there.

Seems like I heard some whomp—whomp—whomp noises outside before I drifted off to sleep on the table. Maybe incoming mortars, I couldn't tell for sure. It was all very vague.

Two months and another operation later I was in Fitzsimons General Hospital, waiting for the three or four other operations that would give me an opposing thumb. My right arm was missing two nerves and an artery, and in any war before Vietnam I'd have lost it all, probably died again just as I'd have probably died of getting my left nut shot off. Both times I'd been shot messing around with helicopters, and saved by helicopters. A mixed blessing, the helicopter.

There were other injuries too. I still think about John Link a lot. I have been over that incident more than a thousand times in my mind, and I still can't think of any way I could have saved him, but I would feel better if I'd been cooler about it. I don't exactly blame myself, but it's a sort of regret that won't go away.

It seems to me there should be a point in every book in which the meaning is clearly and simply stated, but the fact is that I have no certain idea of what the meaning of this book is, nor what it says about me, or my comrades, or the war. A person who was so disposed might note those occasions on which I threw myself full bore into the face of the enemy's guns and conclude that the lead character of this book was a truly heroic person. Another, less charitable, might cite those examples of occasions when my knees turned to jelly and my guts to ice and conclude that I was a chicken, masquerading in a green beret.

Similarly, one who was of a jingoistic nature might feel that we were all true patriots, battling bravely against insurmountable odds. Another reader, suborned by the odious propaganda of the New Left, would conclude that we were nothing but a rancid bunch of bloodthirsty Huns, who got exactly what they deserved.

For myself I feel the effort was worthwhile. I am not sorry I did it, nor would I hesitate to do it again. Most of my friends feel the same way. In any case I have decided to designate myself, however arbitrarily, as the Good Guy in my own book.

But in some respects I am not entirely displeased with the outcome. It is difficult to imagine two human institutions which deserve each other more than the Vietnamese and Communism.

My only true sorrow is for the Montagnards. Their lives, before we came, were short, frequently nasty, but seldom brutish, and aside from my missionary friends, they were the happiest people I have ever met. They did not want to have their way of life destroyed, but it has been, no less by Coca-Cola and pointy-toed shoes than by the doctrines of Marx and Engels. With the Americans gone, the Viets, any Viets, have license to ravage them to infinity. To the Montagnards' eternal credit they are not giving up without a fight, and for all I know, like the Kurds of Iraq, or the Seminole of Florida, they may keep it up forever.

I've given a lot of thought to my Vietnam experience and what it meant. The best explanation I've been able to come up with is in the books of Carlos Castaneda. I believe now that I was happy at Buon Beng, not, as I supposed, because I was in combat, but because I was unwittingly practicing the warrior disciplines outlined in the Castaneda books.

I was using Death as an advisor, because that was what was going on. I had lost self-importance in the face of the momentous events around me. I had no personal history in Vietnam. I accepted responsibility for my own acts because I was the guy in charge. These were the factors working on a spiritual level, but I had been thrown into them accidentally, and thought my happiness was a result of my physical situation.

So I spent the two subsequent tours trying to reproduce those feelings by reproducing the physical situation, not realizing that that time would never come again. I would have to learn to reproduce the attitude in any situation. In the Castaneda books the old Indian sorcerer, Don Juan Matus, says that it is not so difficult to let the spirit of man flow free and clear, but only a warrior can sustain it. That is the challenge of my life, to sustain the warrior spirit, right here in the eight to five world.

But that is now. I felt far differently about it then.

About a week after I got to Fitzsimons I wandered out on the sun porch. It was precisely at four-thirty in the afternoon. The sun porch on the surgical ward is four stories up. I wandered out on the porch in the hot June afternoon, leaned against the railing, and looked down at the well-kept green lawn and the storm fence and the Colorado mountains in the distance.

I felt silly in my crumpled blue pajamas and the hospital bathrobe with the caduceus flanked by the letters U and S on the pocket. I felt especially silly in the floppy canvas slippers they give you in the hospital, that seem designed as much to limit mobility as to keep your feet clean. I missed my jungle fatigues and my cargo strap belt, my knife and my rifle. I felt insecure without them. I felt especially insecure looking at my right arm, the fingers suspended in an outrigger brace.

This gadget, made of aluminum, straps on to your

341

forearm and extends out over the hand, with four little slings, hanging from rubber bands over each of the fingers, to keep the hand from curling into a permanent fist. I couldn't close my fingers laterally, and, in fact, would never be able to do so again, and the grip was weak, but, by God, there was one. I pulled against the rubber bands, *badoing, badoing.* Some hand. It looked like a hand of bananas, hanging from its little science fiction brace. What would my code name be if I ever got back to Nam, FUNNY FINGERS? I'd never be able to salute right with my fingers pointing in all directions like that.

While I was mulling all that over, three MP's in white caps marched out to the flagpole in front of the hospital and stood at parade rest while Retreat blared from some loudspeakers somewhere. Not too loudly though. This was a hospital after all.

Then the MP's came to attention and two of them marched forward and loosened the rope from the flagpole. The other, the sergeant, saluted. The notes of *To The Colors* came from the loudspeaker and I, too, put my hand to my forehead, the fingers bobbing at the end of the outrigger brace.

I must have been eleven the first time I stood at attention and saluted at Retreat, and I must have done it about a thousand times in the years since. This was the first time I had been looking down on the flag when it came down. It didn't seem right somehow. I was like some kind of angel looking down from a cloud or something, at something that was past me, that I couldn't reach anymore. A feeling of almost overwhelming sadness, almost grief, came over me and I stole a glance out of the corner of my eye at my ridiculous hand in its ridiculous brace, the fingers that wouldn't be "extended and joined," as it says in the book, because they couldn't, bobbing in their little cradles.

I stood and saluted the flag as it came down for the evening, crying like a baby because I couldn't do it right.

THE END